BIRTHPLACE OF DREAMS

THE FIRST HOME OF THE BRONTËS

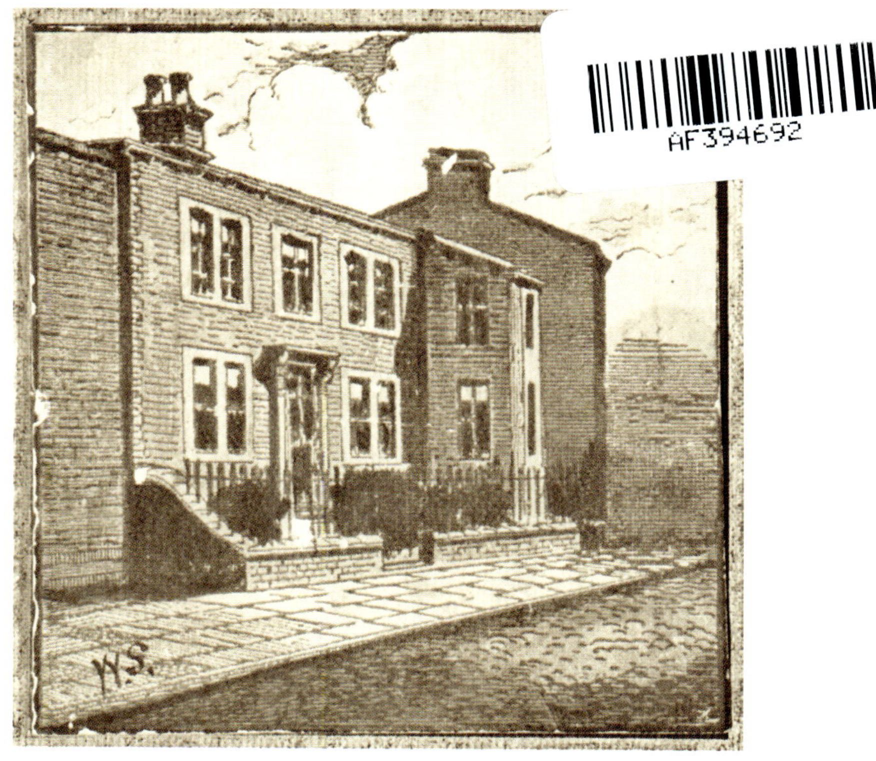

MARK DAVIS & STEVEN STANWORTH

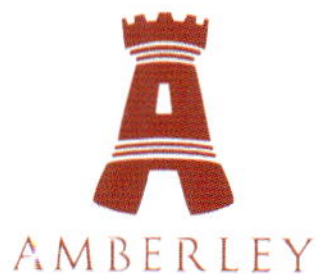

AMBERLEY

Acknowledgements

'bless them that curse you'
Helen Burns, *Jane Eyre*

Thanks to respected author Nick Holland for his much-appreciated foreword; my good friend and artist John Ellis for contributing his inspirational worldwide admired artwork to the book; Ann Dinsdale for her very best wishes; Emma Clayton, from the *Telegraph & Argus* for her excellent published articles; Cath Boyden for her unwavering loyalty and friendship; Andrea Seddon for her steadfast support and help; Richard C. Cobb for always being a loyal, selfless friend; Charlie and Mark from the Old Post Office, Haworth, for their decade-long friendship and support; St James' churchwarden and social butterfly Jayne Dibb for her valuable information and knowledge covering the history relating to her time living at the birthplace; Alan and Barbara Lovette for recalling their memories of the butcher's shop; Steven Stanworth's wife, Cathy, for her long-term support and expert proofreading; The Birthplace Committee, whose actions wholly reinforced the determination to complete the book; Sarah Dixon for allowing me to use my contemporary images of Kipping House; Becky Wilson, Fiona, Shirley, Clare and all the volunteers at St James' Church, Thornton, who every Saturday show my old dad Gordon so much kindness and care; and lastly, but no means least, my long-suffering girlfriend Caroline Rhodes, for her continual love, support and valuable assistance while writing this book.

Dedicated with much love to
Mark's dear departed mum, Jennifer Sigrid Davis
Aka Genaveve Sigrid Dilly
(1944–2024)

Images, book design and words by Mark Davis – the original inspiration from Steven Stanworth, who wrote pages 81–93.

First published 2025

Amberley Publishing, The Hill, Stroud
Gloucestershire GL5 4EP

www.amberley-books.com

Copyright © Mark Davis and Steven Stanworth, 2025

The right of Mark Davis and Steven Stanworth to be identified as the Authors of this work has been asserted in accordance with the Copyrights, Designs and Patents Act 1988.

British Library Cataloguing in Publication Data.
A catalogue record for this book is available from the British Library.

ISBN 978 1 3981 2925 2 (print)
ISBN 978 1 3981 2926 9 (ebook)

Typesetting by SJmagic DESIGN SERVICES, India.
Printed in Great Britain.

Appointed GPSR EU Representative: Easy Access System Europe Oü, 16879218
Address: Mustamäe tee 50, 10621, Tallinn, Estonia
Contact Details: gpsr.requests@easproject.com,
+358 40 500 3575

Contents

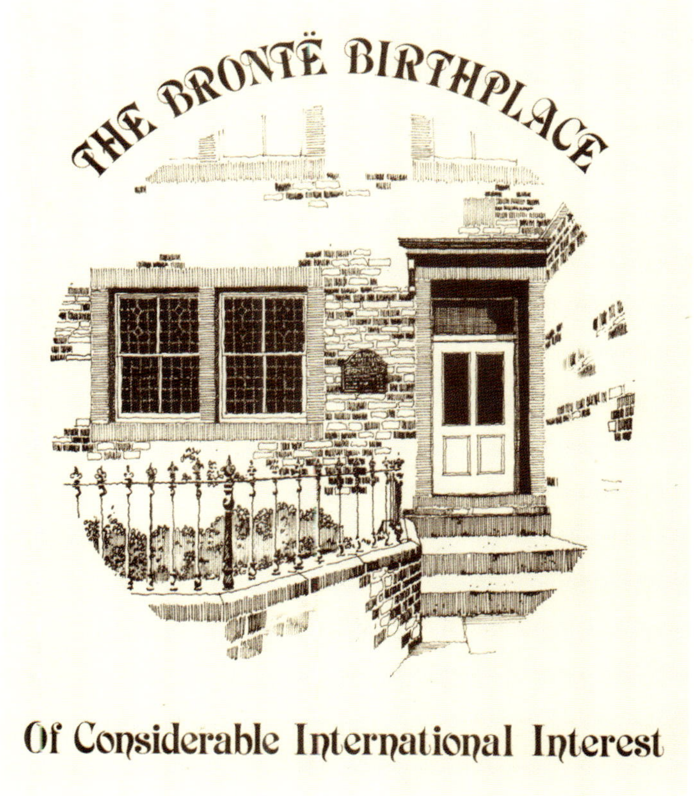

The cover of a sales brochure, *c.* 1995.

Foreword by Nick Holland

As a Brontë biographer, I am privileged to have visited many of the places they knew, from Haworth to Brussels. For the complete Brontë story, however, it is essential to include the very place where it all began: the Brontë birthplace, at Thornton near Bradford.

This fantastic new book from Mark Davis and Steven Stanworth explores the impact Thornton had on the Brontës and how the Brontës shaped it. Mark and Steven have done much to promote the Brontë cause in recent years. Mark is an award-winning photographer and author, and Steven works tirelessly to preserve Thornton's Brontë Bell Chapel. In my opinion, without the determined efforts of Steven, the recent campaign to buy, refurbish and reopen the Brontë birthplace would not have succeeded.

The world has changed greatly since the days of the Brontës, yet we still feel close to them when we walk the steep streets of Haworth or the cobbled well-worn paths of Thornton. When we follow in the Brontë footsteps we get a glimpse of the world as they saw it, and realise they were more like us than we imagined. They faced the same challenges we face today: they wanted to be happy, they wanted to love and in turn be loved, they wanted to do something useful and leave their mark on the world. In this latter hope they exceeded all expectations.

Little could the Brontës have guessed that we would be discussing their books and lives nearly two hundred years after their passing. One reason for the continued success of the Brontë novels is that they remain compelling, they remain relevant, and their life story continues to fascinate us. How we consume novels may change, but as long as this world keeps spinning on its axis people will continue to be inspired by the works of Charlotte, Emily and Anne Brontë.

This image-driven book allows the reader to get closer to the sisters, to their troubled brother, their tragic mother and their determined father; it helps us learn more about the places they knew and loved and the places which inspired their work. It is time to follow in the Brontë footsteps to the birthplace of dreams.

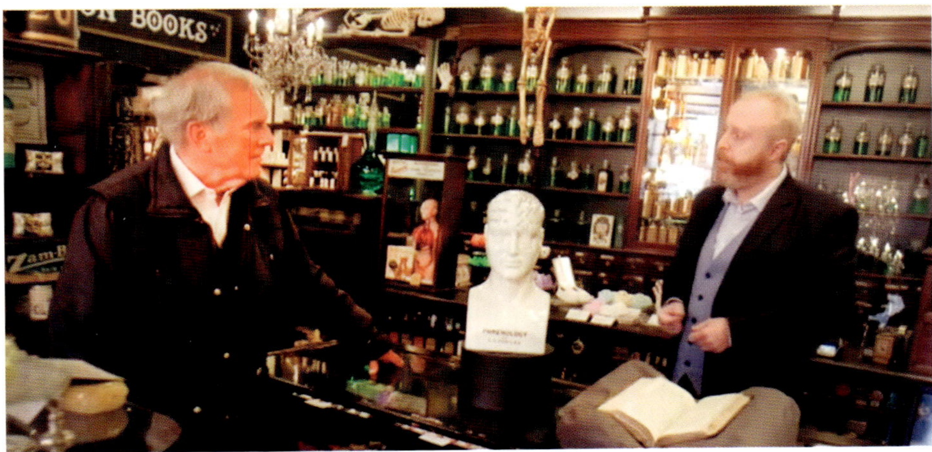

Nick Holland is the author of *In Search of Anne Brontë, Emily Brontë: A Life in 20 Poems, Aunt Branwell and the Brontë Legacy* and *Crave the Rose: Anne Brontë at 200.*

Introduction

When visiting Dewsbury Minster, where the then thirty-two-year-old Patrick Brontë was curate in 1809, to gather images for this book, I casually asked one of the two older ladies who were guarding the religious edifice in the entrance way if it was ok to go inside and photograph. Raising her head momentarily, she looked at me enquiringly and asked why I would want to do that. With my enthusiasm overload for the project, I explained, 'It's for a new book I am compiling on the Brontë family.' Her lacklustre, bored response was not the one I anticipated. She looked down as she replied, 'Oh no, not yet another Brontë book.' As I tried to explain this one was different, with even less interest her final words as she let me into the church were 'they all are'.

Quite an interesting conversation really, and I remember, when leaving, wondering how many other people had been there in relation to Patrick with a similar goal as mine. I also contemplated if the lady I had just spoken to was, like most, under the common misconception that the famous Brontë sisters not only wrote their masterpieces in Haworth but were also born there. It really is surprising just how many people think Haworth is the one-stop shop in terms of the famous literary family.

Any negative thoughts were banished from my mind even before I got into my car, parked just 10 metres away, because this book is actually different. Although like some publications we follow Patrick's journey from humble beginnings in Ireland all the way to Yorkshire, we, however, do not head immediately to the parsonage in Haworth, the world-renowned literary shrine that attracts tens of thousands of visitors per year from nationalities worldwide.

This little book, filled to capacity, is unique in that its focus rests on the very place that saw Charlotte, Emily and Anne Brontë first breath in Yorkshire air as their divine literary spark struck the world, in front of the fire in the front parlour of the parsonage on Market Street, Thornton. And let us not forget their brother Branwell; he, like his sisters, was born there too, and had big dreams, but unlike his siblings, his were mostly unfulfilled.

Although the Brontë family only spent five years in Thornton, they were incredibly important years. Patrick in later life would refer to his years in the village as being 'his happiest time'. Given the tragedy that followed just a year after the family left the village in 1820, it is a statement no one could ever dispute. The genteel social life enjoyed at Thornton was in stark contrast to the previous life at Hartshead Moor, which was dominated then by the revolutionary Luddite movement. The family met the young Elizabeth Firth and her father within days of arriving in Thornton, after which a warm friendship blossomed. Elizabeth was to become godmother to Elizabeth and Anne and invite the Brontë family to dinner regularly at Kipping House, her comfortable family residence that she shared with her father, close by on Lower Kipping Lane.

Such was the relationship between the Brontë and Firth family that Patrick, looking for a new wife and stepmother for his six motherless children after the tragic premature death of his wife Maria, felt comfortable enough to ask Elizabeth for her hand in marriage, which she refused. In 1815, when the families had first met, Elizabeth, seventeen years Patrick's junior, was mourning the death of her mother the previous year and like her father was a committed churchgoer. We know much more about the inter-family relationship between the Brontës and

Firths than we would normally expect because Elizabeth kept a basic diary. The entries were almost bullet points; however, they show a consistent mutual support structure in place throughout the time the Brontës were in Thornton. When Elizabeth died in 1837, it was the money she had left Anne that financed her last tragic trip to Scarborough.

It is interesting to see how the family's lives in Thornton overlapped with Haworth, certainly for the first few years in any event. Through the pages therein we of course take in Haworth, the sisters' education, achievements and sadly their premature, in today's terms, deaths. Towards the end of the book, we return to Thornton to explore the birthplace's history and evolution up to the present day in 2025.

This book is no academic work by any stretch of the imagination; however, we are quite proud to offer our work as a small contribution to the living, breathing Brontë legacy that will continue to evolve long after we are all but dust.

We hope the reader enjoys their journey through the pages of this book as much as we have done bringing the birthplace of dreams, which is Nos 72–74 Market Street, out of the shadows in written form. It is the very house where three apparently ordinary girls were born, three girls who dared to reach for excellence beyond their wildest dreams and surpass them all. Three girls who would take on a male-dominated, nineteenth-century literary world and whose names 200 years after they were born would continue to inspire young and old alike.

Haworth may justifiably lay claim to the Brontë sisters' literary success, their works having been written there; however, there is no changing the fact that their first spark of life quite rightly belongs to Thornton.

The Brontë sisters' published works:

Poems by Currer, Ellis & Acton Bell, 1846
Jane Eyre by Currer Bell, 1847
Wuthering Heights by Ellis Bell, 1847
Agnes Grey by Acton Bell, 1847
The Tenant of Wildfell Hall by Acton Bell, 1848
Shirley by Currer Bell, 1849
Villette by Currer Bell, 1853
The Professor by Currer Bell, 1857

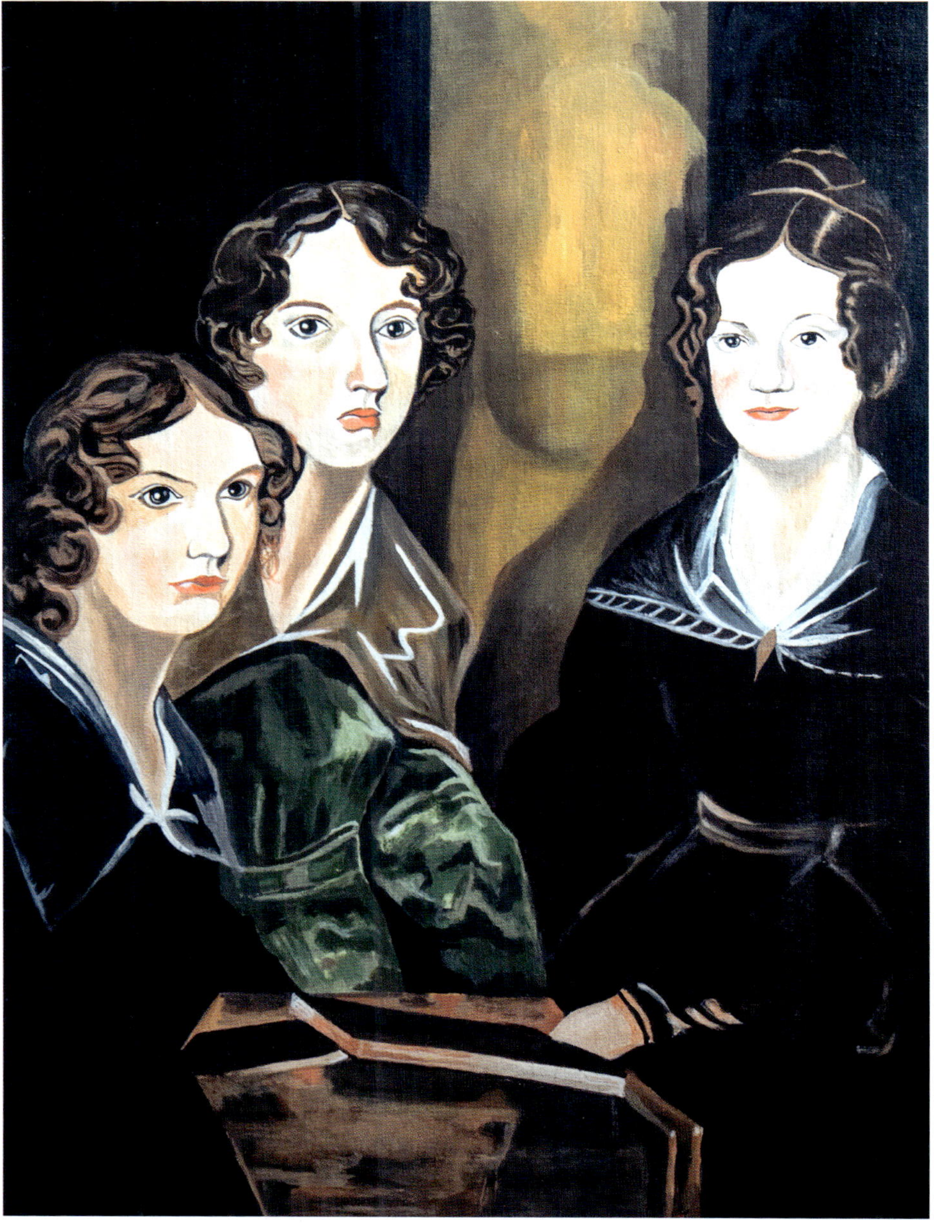

The 'Pillar portrait' was painted by Branwell in the 1830s. From left to right is Anne (Acton Bell), Emily (Ellis Bell), and Charlotte (Currer Bell); Branwell is the painted-out figure in the pillar of light, just visible right off centre. This repaint copy of the original is the work of Bradford artist John Ellis.

1

From Humble Beginnings

Today in 2025, very little remains of the humble two-bedroom thatched cottage at Fairy Glen, Emdale, in Drumballyroney, where Patrick Brontë first entered this world as Patrick Brunty on St Patrick's Day in 1777. Given his birth date, it will come as no surprise that he was duly named after the primary patron saint of Ireland.

Partick was the first born of the ten children to be blessed to his parents, Hugh and Alice. Although his father was Protestant and his mother Catholic, young Patrick was brought up in his father's faith. Hugh, who was orphaned at a young age, was a native of southern Ireland but had made the move north of the border at the age of fifteen, where he later married Alice McClory (believed to be at Magherally church). Patrick in later life described the wedding as 'an early but suitable marriage'. With little money, the couple, by sheer hard work, brought up the large family in a respectable manner despite being of the industrious poor class.

Patrick and his siblings helped their mother and father on the small farm, picking potatoes and labouring generally. It is said of an evening Hugh would regale his children with tales and was known in the area for his storytelling prowess.

By his own admission Patrick had an early interest in books and although he used to like visiting the local blacksmiths, he also had some training in weaving, yet he was to follow neither profession.

Critical to his intellectual development was Revd Andrew Harshaw, who saw his potential when the Presbyterian minister overheard him reading aloud from Milton's *Paradise Lost*. Revd Harshaw mentored Patrick to such an extent that he was able to open his own school at the church in Glascar, which he ran for five years when he was only sixteen. Although little more than a child himself, he was teaching students not much younger than himself. This was not unusual in rural Northern Ireland at that time. Unfortunately, he was sacked when he was twenty-one for being caught in a romantic situation with one of his female students. Despite the small scandal in his life, it was during this period that Revd Thomas Tighe, Vicar of Drumballyroney, took a keen interest in Patrick's progress.

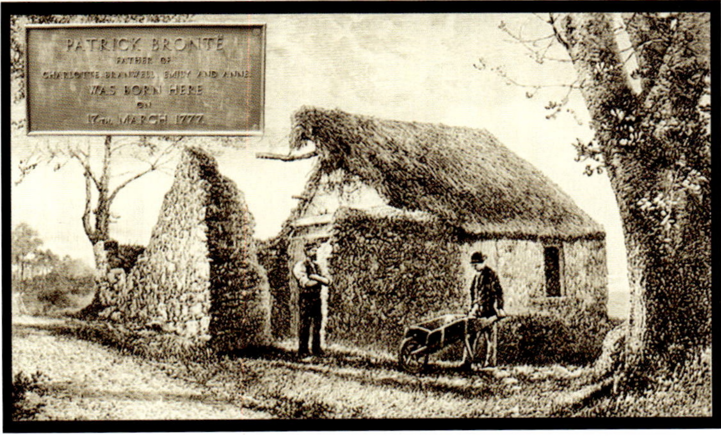

Patrick Brontë's birthplace, Drumballyroney.

In 1802, the friendship and patronage of Thomas Tighe would change the whole course of Patrick's life. It was in that year that Tighe, a former student of St John's College himself at Cambridge, who graduated in 1775, was to recommend and enable twenty-two-year-old Patrick to leave his native Ireland with just £7 to his name and enter the prestigious college in July of that year. He was officially enrolled on 1 October 1802, as a sizar. This must have been a very proud moment for his father, Hugh, for just like him, Patrick in his mid-teens had been proactive in taking positive moves for self-betterment, and unbeknown to them both, they would go down in history for fathering children who would be famous long after their deaths.

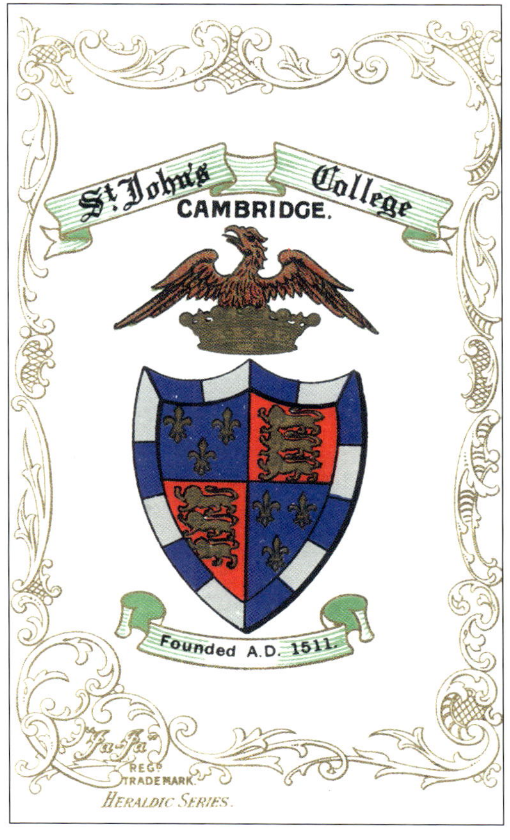

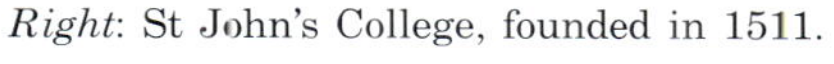

Right: St John's College, founded in 1511.

Below: St John's College, Cambridge, c. 1905.

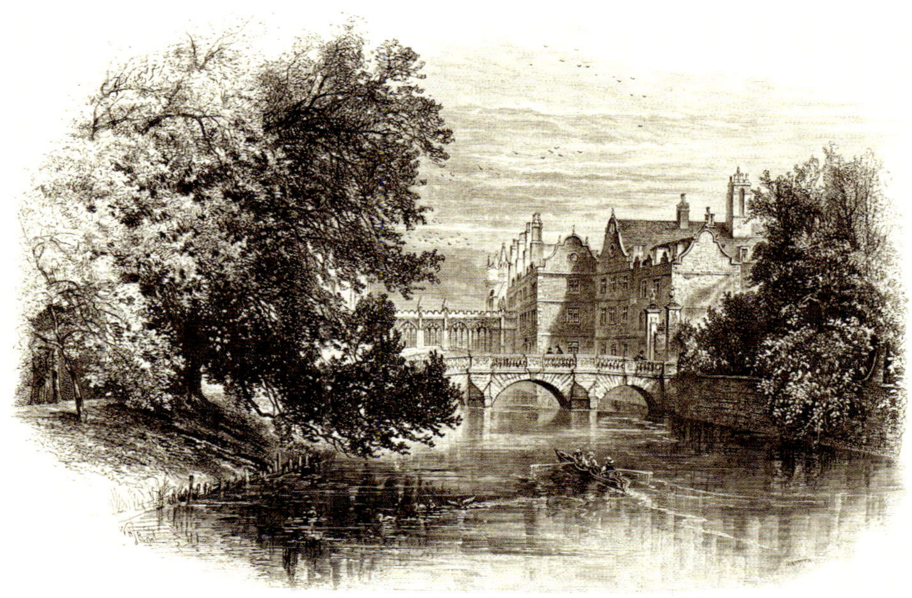

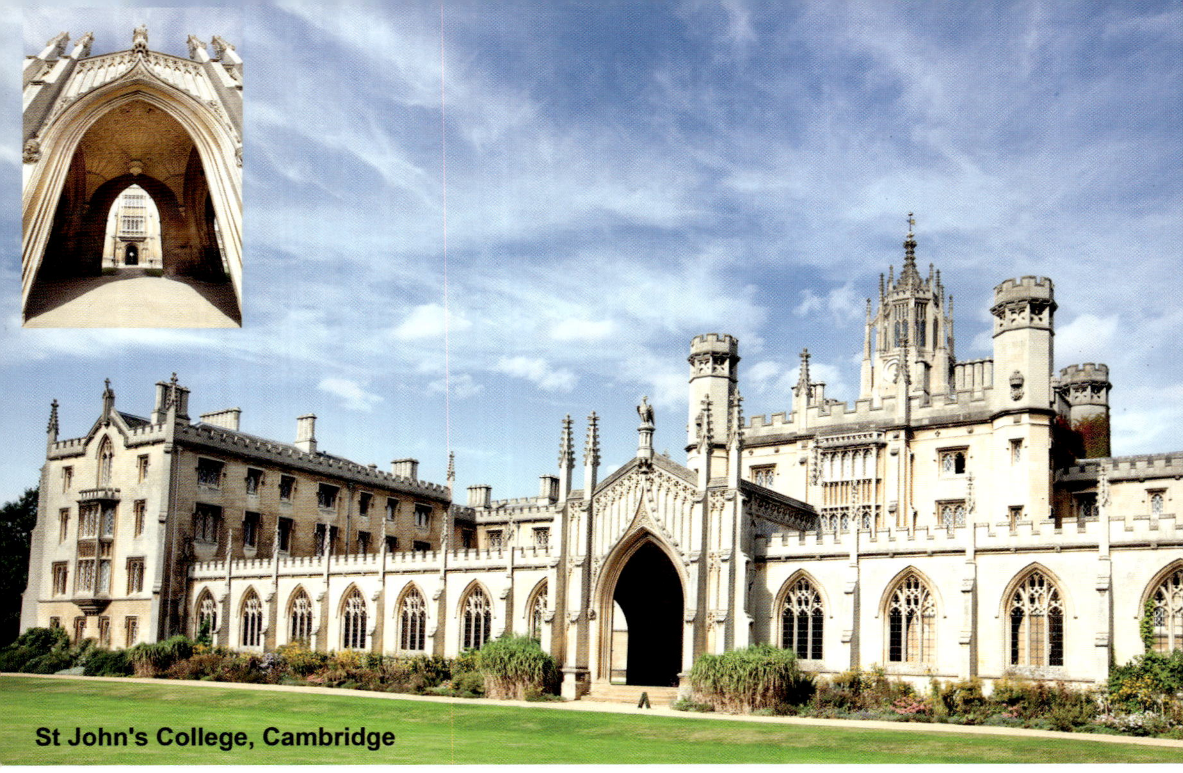

St John's College, Cambridge

St John's College, Cambridge, in the present day.

Patrick was, without doubt, ambitious, determined and extremely intelligent and he wasted no time in acquiring the education that would enable him to leave his humble roots far behind him. On 1 October, the Admissions Register at Cambridge recorded:

'1235 Patrick Branty Ireland Sizar Tutors: Wood & Smith'

Within two days the register was amended to Patrick Brontë at his request. It is said that he did so in reference to Horatio Nelson's Italian Dukedom in the province of Catania, Sicily, Nelson thus becoming the Duke of Brontë. The tall, well-formed scholar who was described as a having a good presence was making his mark on the world.

Enrolled as a sizar, Patrick received financial assistance from the college in the form of reduced fees and free accommodation; in return he would have been expected to carry out certain duties or engage in some form of domestic service. He was further sponsored, and one such patron was the influential William Willberforce, the anti-slavery campaigner. St John's was renowned for its evangelical connections and was the perfect setting for Patrick's fast-developing ambitions.

With the threat and fear of a French invasion of England in the early years of Patrick's time at Cambridge, volunteers were recruited across the country for the local militia and by 1803 nearly half a million men had enrolled. At St John's College a volunteer corps was formed, and Patrick was one of the thirty-five members. The group of volunteers was led by eighteen-year-old John Henry Temple, better known as Lord Palmerston, who would later, in 1855, be the elected prime minister.

Patrick was a diligent student and worked hard, winning prizes every year before he graduated with a Bachelor of Arts on 23 April 1806.

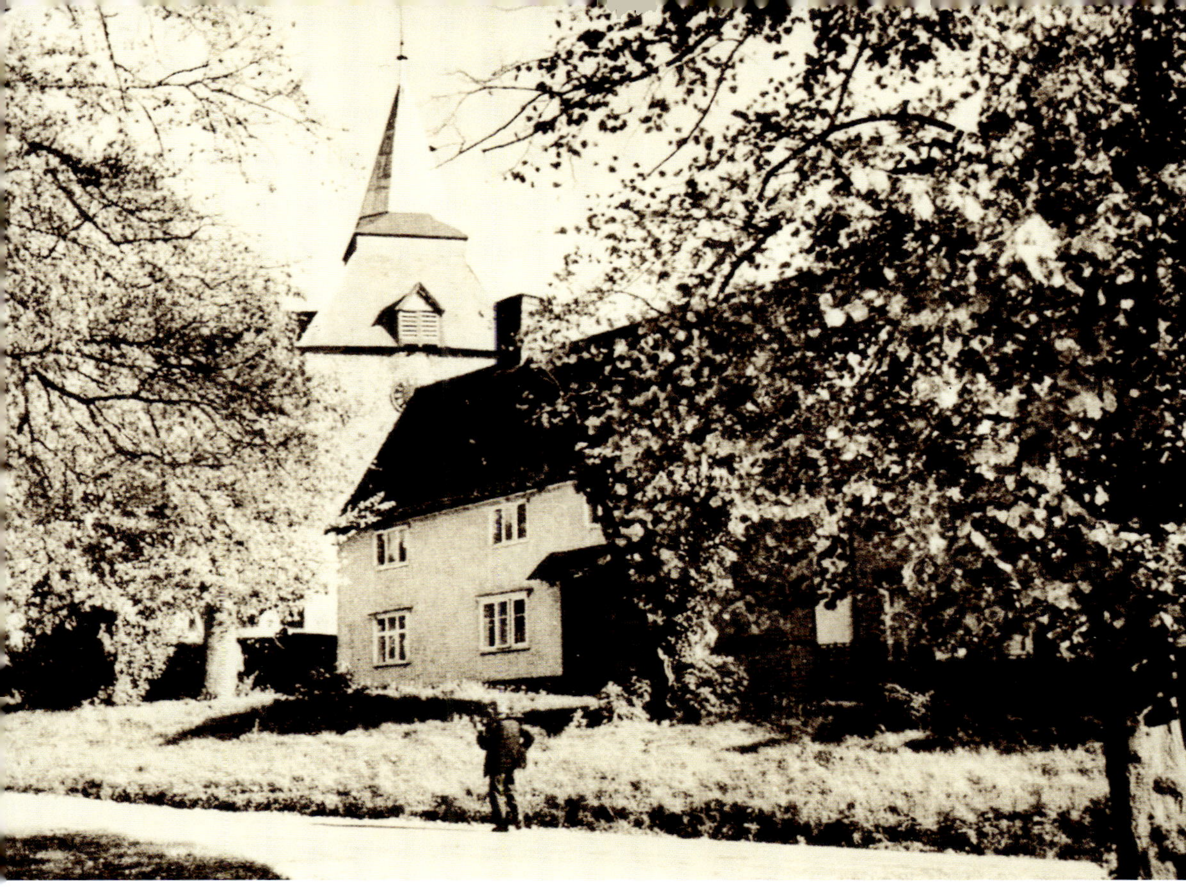

St Mary Magdalene Church, Wethersfield, Essex.

After graduation, he was to visit Ireland one last time in 1806, where he preached in Drumballyroney. Alice Brontë, Patrick's younger sister, recalled the event many years later, remembering how the church was packed with family and friends as 'he preached a gran' sermon'.

Returning from Ireland, he took up his first position after graduation as the curate with the vicar being Joseph Jowett, Regius Professor of Law at Cambridge, at Weathersfield, as it was known. Over the years the 'A' has been dropped in favour of Wethersfield, as it is known today.

The village in Essex, situated only around 35 miles from Cambridge, had a population of around 1,300 residents, of which the majority were farming folk and he was to remain there for two years and three months on a salary of £60 per annum.

While at St Mary Magdalene he was ordained a deacon of the Church of England in 1806, and then as a priest in 1807 by the Bishop of Salisbury at St James' Palace.

A pivotal moment occurred when he fell in love with the niece of his landlady. His love interest was eighteen-year-old Mary Burder, who shared a common interest in books and walking with him. The relationship was ultimately to end abruptly, possibly as a result of her family's resistance, or the fact that she was an ardent Nonconformist and he was Anglican, making the situation all but impossible.

The ambitious curate officiated over his last burial service at St Mary's on 22 December 1808, which he registered on New Year's Day 1809.

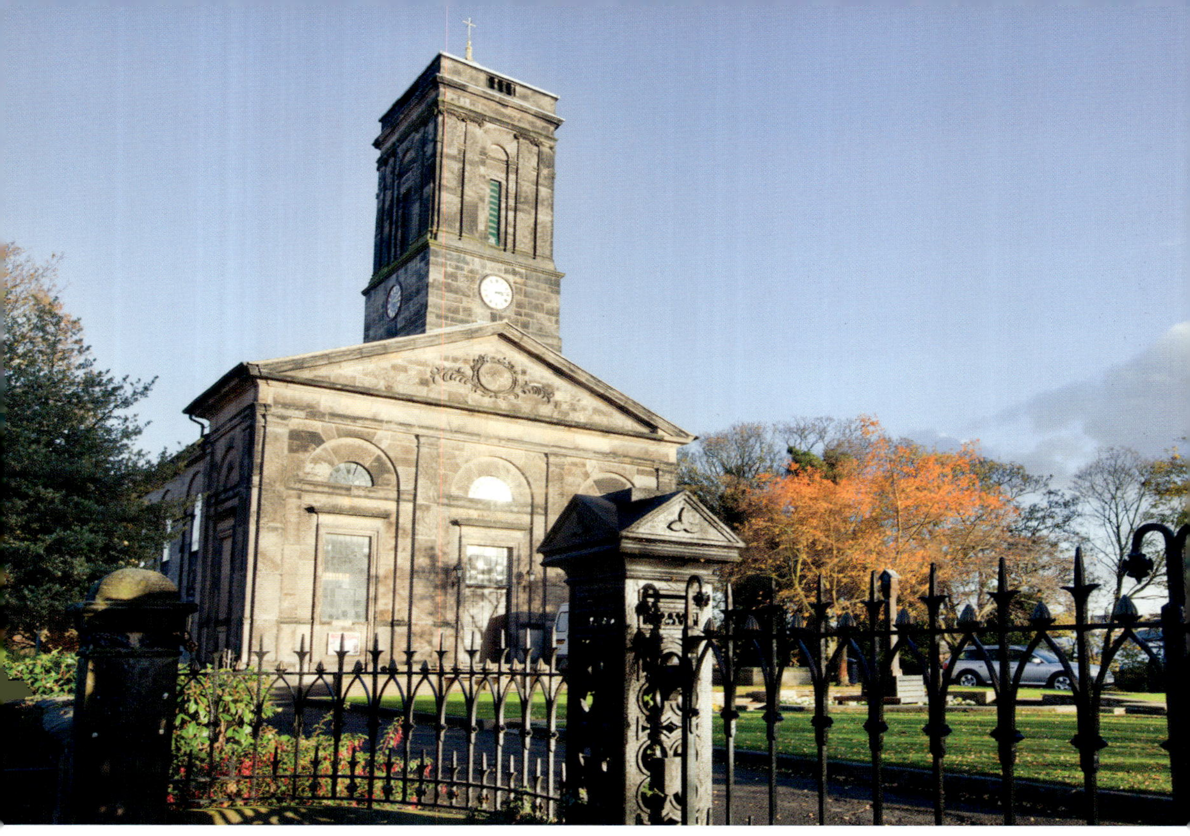

All Saints Church, Wellington.

Late in September 1808, possibly early October, Patrick, keen to find a position away from Essex, travelled to Glenfield on the outskirts of Leicester. Revd Robert Cox offered him a curacy at St Peter's. Robert knew the cleric from Cambridge and was aware of the Mary Burder situation but offered him the job regardless. This, however, was not to be, and he turned down the position. He informed his friend John Nunn (his former college roommate at Cambridge), who was by now the curate of St Chad's, Shrewsbury. John was probably instrumental in Patrick gaining employment as a curate near to him at All Saints Church, Wellington, under Revd John Eyton, who had been the vicar there since 1802.

When Patrick arrived at Wellington in early January 1809, the church was relatively new, having been completed only nineteen years earlier in 1790. This, however, was not the first church on the site and it was at the least the third incarnation over a thousand-year lineage. The church was constructed in a classical style with rectangular windows, a stone grey façade and appeared elegant with its clock and bell tower.

Revd John Eyton was the third son of local squire Thomas Eyton and like Patrick he was a graduate of St John's, Cambridge, although they were not contemporaries. While at Wellington Patrick was to forge friendships with the five-years-younger William Morgan (his fellow curate at Wellington) and John Fennell, the master of the local day school. Both these men would be lifelong friends and we will meet them again in the following pages.

Patrick conducted his last wedding at All Saints' on 18 November 1809, after spending less than a year at Wellington.

2

God's Own Country

It was a cold winter's day on 5 December 1809, when the now thirty-two-year-old Patrick, clutching a leather-bound volume titled *Sermons or Homilies appointed to be read in churches* (a parting gift from William Morgan), journeyed to the industrial town of Dewsbury in the West Riding of Yorkshire. The rapidly expanding town was situated close to the River Calder, which was ideally suited for the wool trade. He was, and probably unknowingly, embarking on a Yorkshire adventure that would keep him busy in 'God's Own Country' right up until his death in 1861.

He took up the position as the curate for Revd John Buckworth at All Saints Church as it was then – today it is more commonly known as Dewsbury Minster. Initially he lodged at the vicarage. Later he found alternative accommodation at Ancient Well House (his landlord Elliot Carrot). It was, in time, reported that Patrick was considered to be clever and good hearted but also hot tempered and a little odd, for want of a better word.

It is said that one of the first things he bought was a shillelagh (a traditional Irish walking stick and club) that he took everywhere with him, earning the nickname 'old staff' by his parishioners.

In 1810, he was to publish two pieces of his work entitled *Winter Evening Thoughts* and *Cottage Poems*, taking the honour of being the first Brontë to have literature in print. More was to follow: *The Rural Minstrel: A Miscellany of Descriptive Poems* in 1813, *The Cottage in the Wood* in 1816, *The Maid of Killarney* in 1818, and *The Signs of the Times* in 1835.

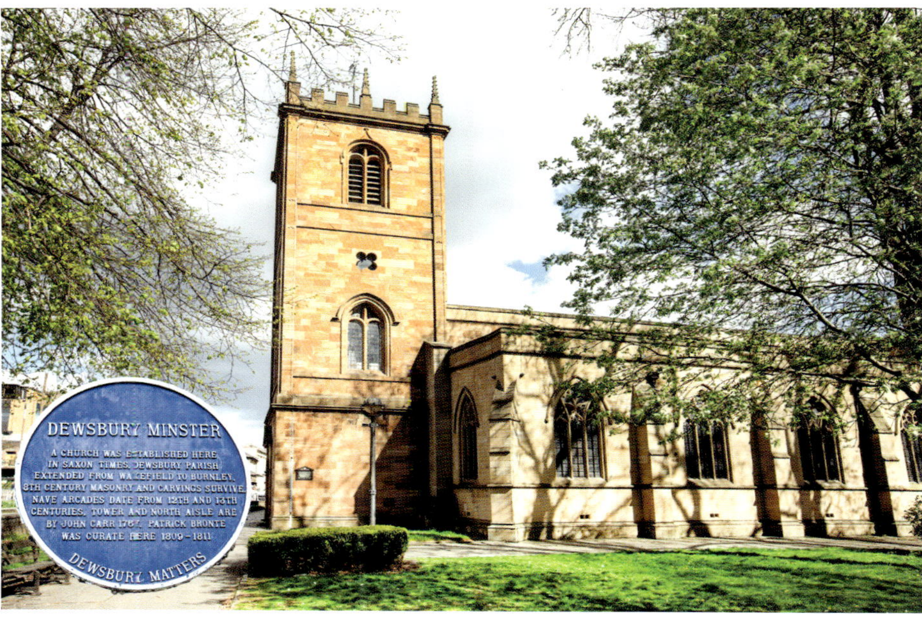

Dewsbury Minster.

Although only at Dewsbury for little over a year, he made quite an impression, rescuing a drowning child and on another occasion defending grave injustice with the assistance of the Secretary of War, Lord Palmerston, who Patrick knew from Cambridge.

Due to the continuing ill health of John Buckworth, much of the church work fell upon Patrick's shoulders. In the sixteenth months he spent at Dewsbury he was to perform nearly 130 marriages, hundreds of baptisms and a minimum of twenty funerals a month, although that rose to around fifty in the latter months. Upon leaving Dewsbury he was presented with a volume of his latest sermons by Revd Buckworth in which he had written inside 'Revd P Brontë, 1811. A testimony of sincere esteem from the author.'

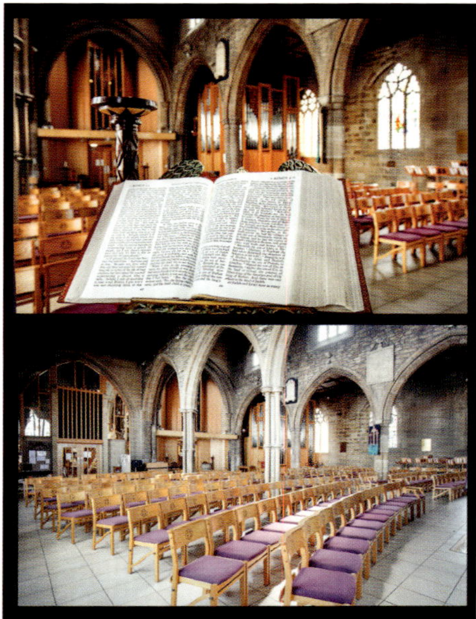

Left: Modern-day images of the Dewsbury church internally.

Below: The church here is depicted in the early nineteenth century.

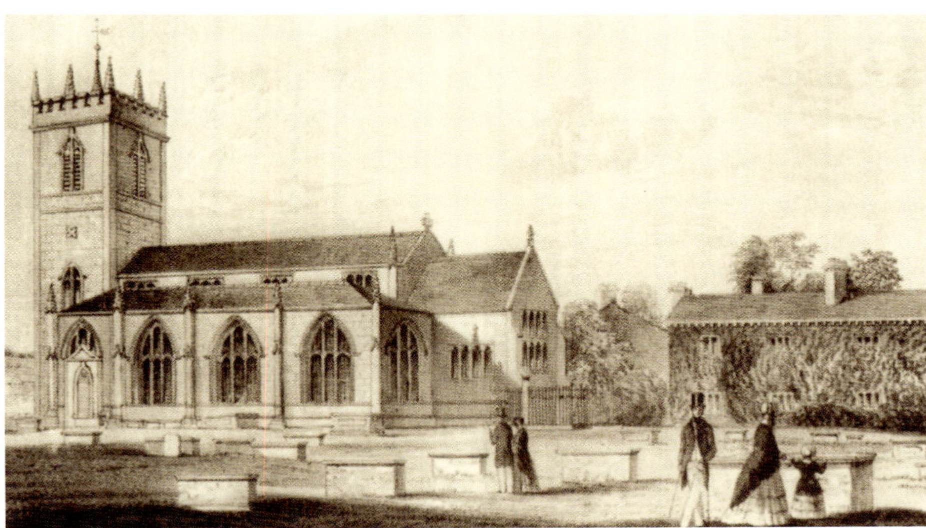

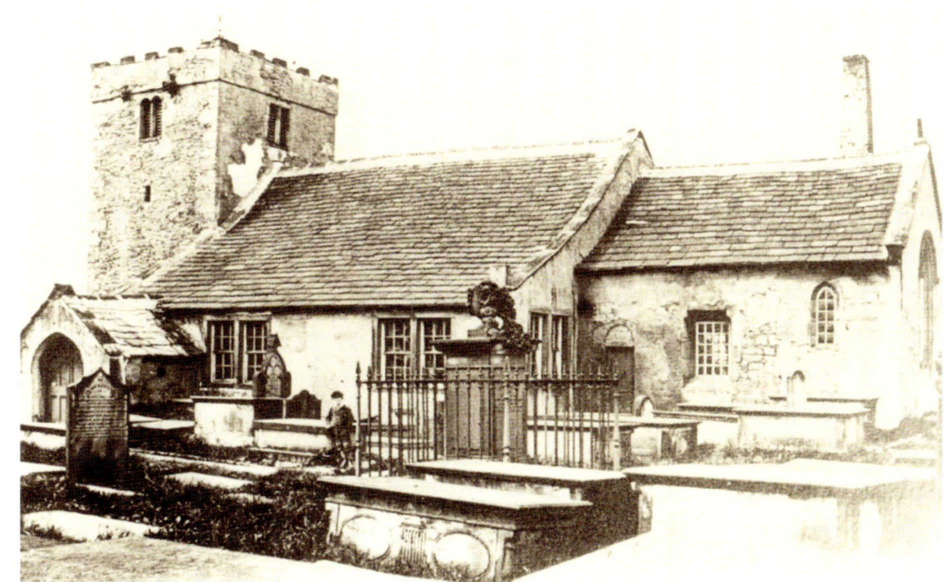

St Peter's, Hartshead cum Clifton.

Hartshead, 1810–15

His apprenticeship was finally over when Patrick was appointed the minister of St Peter's, Hartshead cum Clifton, on 19 July 1810. However, it would be some months before he made the relatively short 4-mile journey away from Dewsbury All Saints in late March of the following year, when the position was made official.

Hartshead at the time was a hamlet isolated high on the moor in between Huddersfield and Dewsbury but still classed as being within the parish of Dewsbury. More local were the villages of Hightown, Roberttown and Cleckheaton, the latter less than 3 miles away. This was to be Patrick's longest stay in one job since graduating and his last appointment as a bachelor. His life was to change forever in so many ways.

The image above shows the Norman church prior to major improvements carried out in the late nineteenth century. Charlotte Brontë later based her book *Shirley* on the area, with Hartshead church being the model for Nunneley.

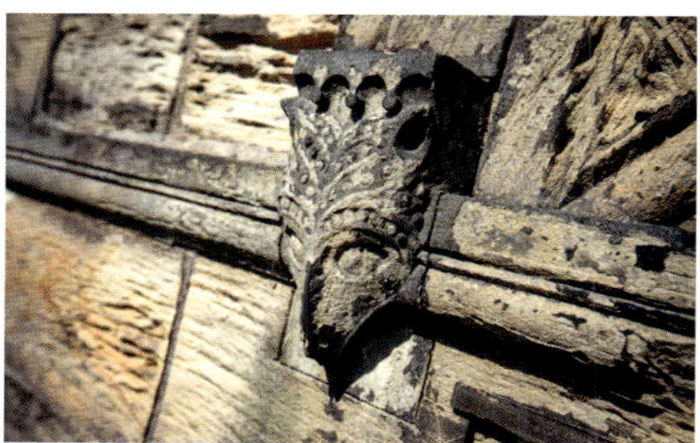

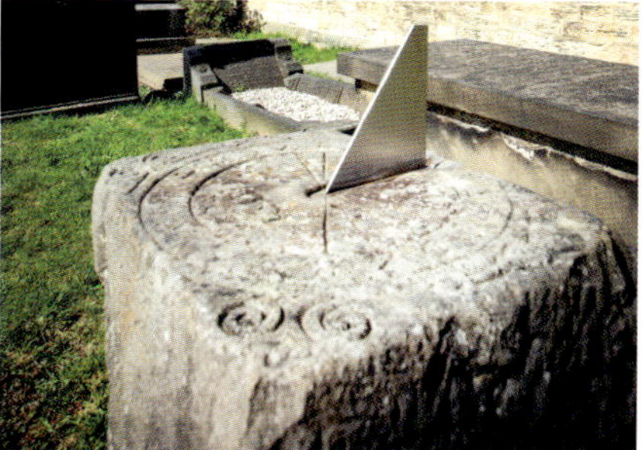

Above left and above right: Ornate stonework and the sundial.

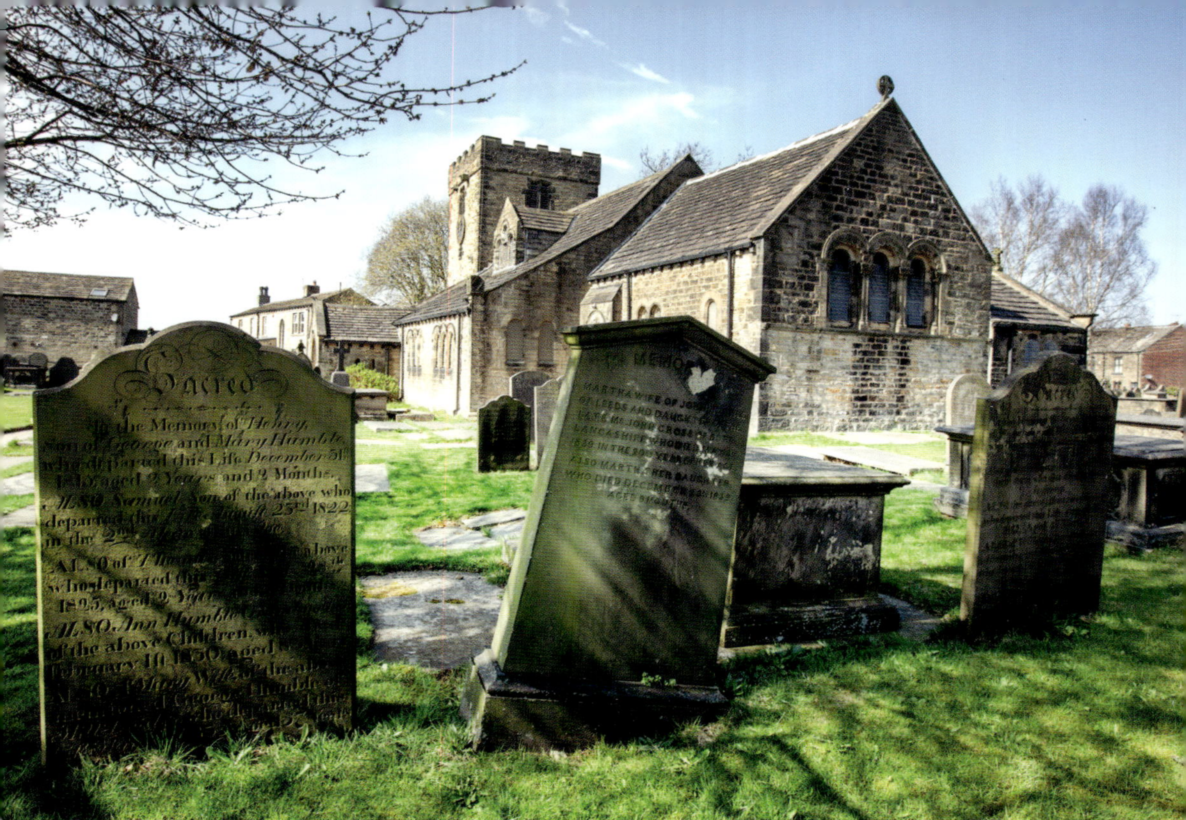

St Peter's, looking splendid in May 2025.

Within two years of Patrick's appointment at Hartshead trouble was brewing. It was at a time when the Industrial Revolution was gathering momentum and mechanised machinery was putting people who made hand-produced textiles out of work. No work in those days meant certain starvation. With textile workers growing restless, secret groups were formed, first in Nottingham and then Yorkshire and the Spen valley. They were called 'Luddites' after a Leicestershire stocking knitter called Ned Ludd, who in 1782 had smashed the machinery he had been working on. The aim of the Luddites was to destroy the modern technology by attacking the mills and sabotaging the newly installed machinery in the hope it would save their livelihoods. They were seen as dangerous industrial terrorists by the government, who garrisoned around 1,000 soldiers in the area to suppress the revolutionaries.

In February 1812, the Luddites ambushed delivery wagons on Hartshead moor that were en route to William Cartwright's mill at Rawfolds in nearby Cleckheaton. On this occasion they successfully escaped after wrecking the machinery. They were not so lucky when they tried again on 11 April 1812 when between 150 and 300 Luddites set off over the moor, their route passing both the church and Lousy Thorn Farm. This time they were intent on storming Cartwright's mill. They arrived in the early hours of the 20th, broke down the gates and attempted to batter the door down. Unfortunately the element of surprise was lost as the mill owner had been tipped off and he was lying in wait for them along with five soldiers, with more on call. Following a fierce battle many of the Luddites were injured but managed to get away; however, two of the revolutionaries, Samuel Hartley and John Booth, who were mortally wounded, were left behind and promptly captured.

Taken initially to the Yew Tree public house, but due to Luddite sympathisers gathering outside they were removed to the Star Inn at Roberttown for interrogation aimed at betraying their fellow rioters. Legend has it that John Booth, calling Revd Hammond Booth close, whispered to him 'Can you keep a secret?' When the reverend, a friend of the mill owner, responded in the affirmative, Booth, with his last breath of life, replied 'so can I'. It was said by Patrick's eventual successor at Hartshead, Thomas Atkinson, that later some of the Luddites executed at York were allowed to be buried secretly in the middle of the night in the graveyard at St Peter's. This account was told many years on by a Mrs Hurst, the former servant of Revd Atkinson, who heard from his very lips. However, given the executed were allowed public funerals with no need for secrecy it is likely the tale relates to Hartley and Booth.

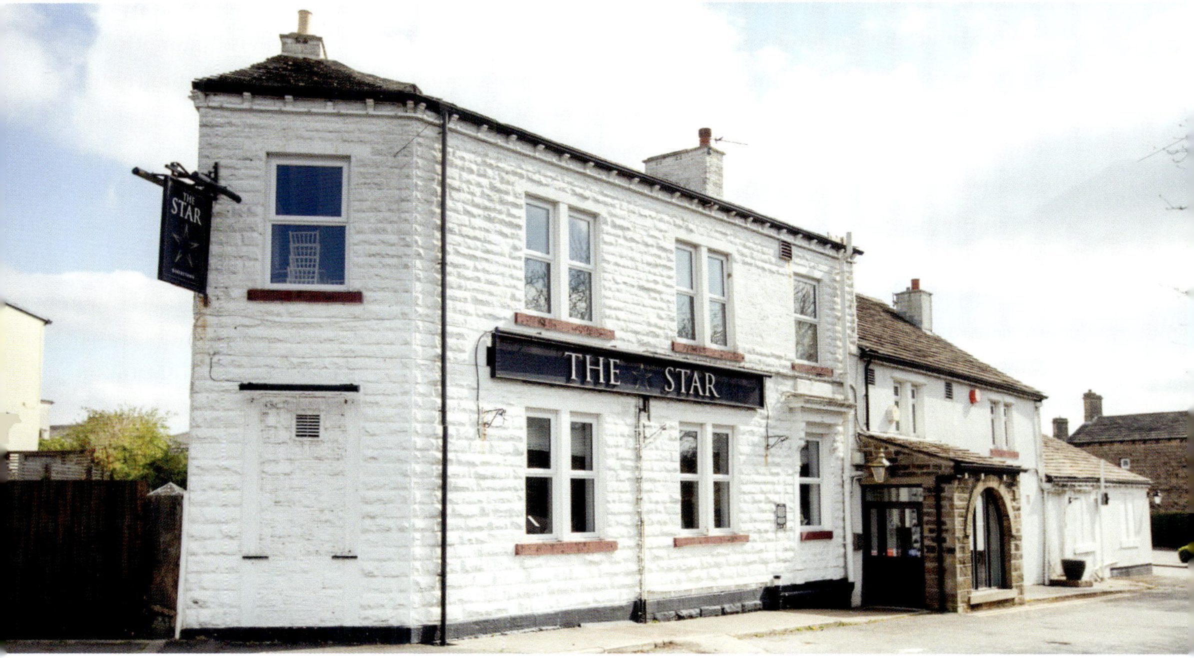

Above: The Star, Roberttown.

Right and far right: SVCS's statue of a Luddite is the only one in the country and can be found at Sparrow Park, Liversedge.

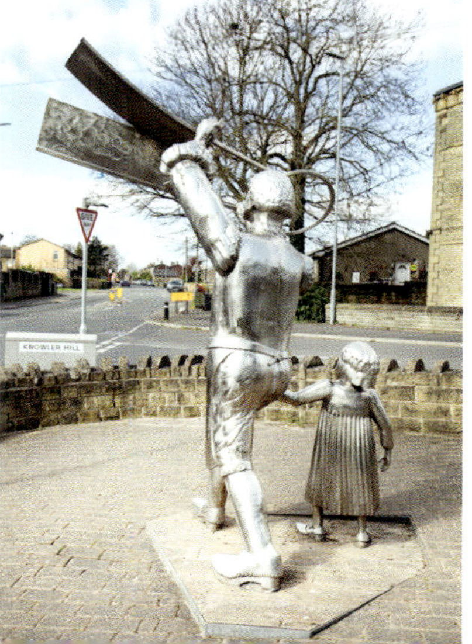

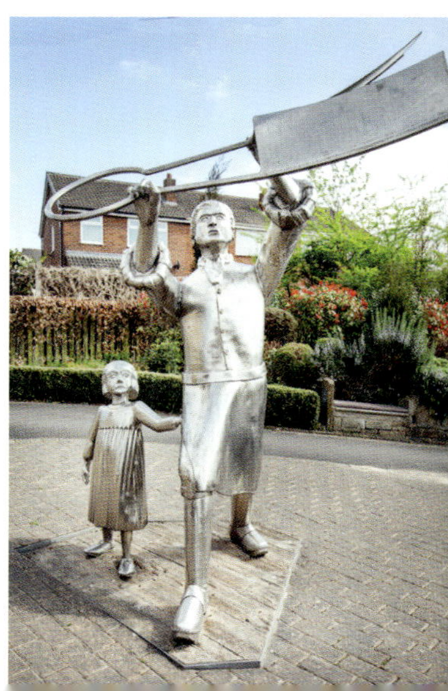

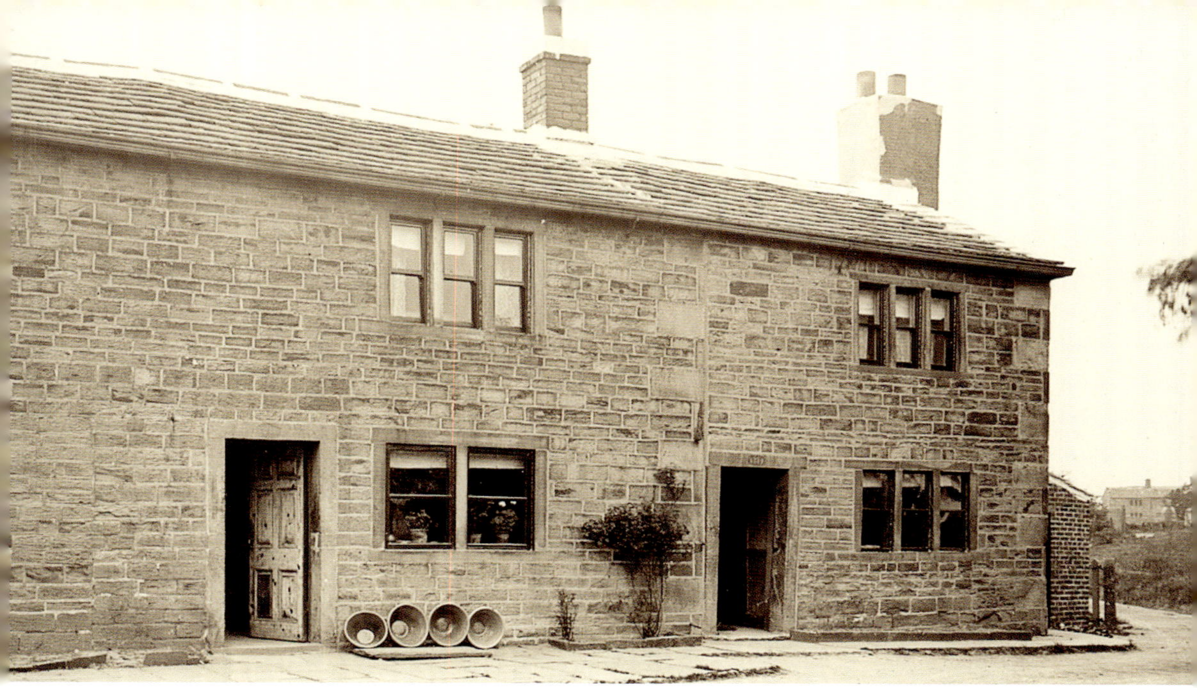

Lousy Farm. This image is dated to very early in the 1900s. The farm was eventually listed in 2006. (The Brontë Society)

Patrick initially lodged at Lousy Thorn farm with Mr and Mrs Bedford while at Hartshead as there wasn't an official parsonage in existence. Although it was not the prettiest of places to live, it had the benefit of its close proximity to the church.

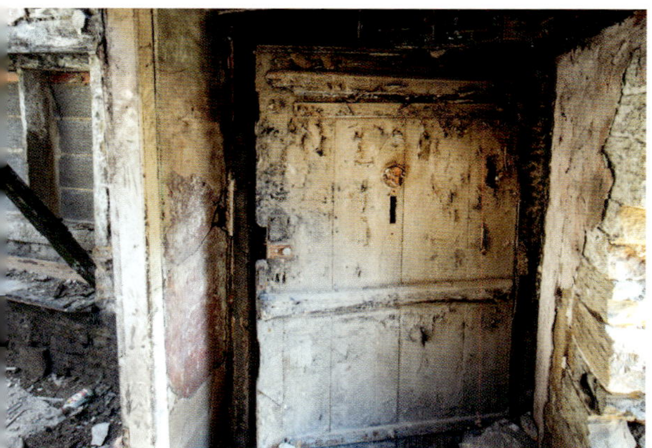

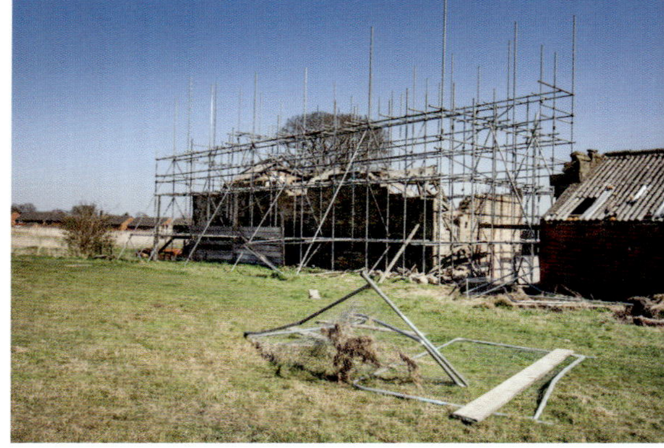

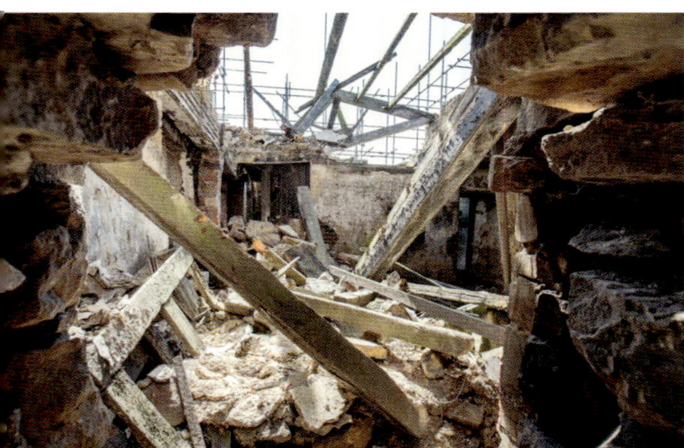

Above left, above right and left: In 2025 and now called Thornbush Farm, the dwelling is in ruins with an uncertain future.

Woodhouse Grove School

In January 1812 the newly formed school was opened by Wesleyan Methodists to educate the sons of both ministers and preachers. Patrick's old friend John Fennell from Wellington was appointed as the headmaster. With their friendship renewed on Yorkshire soil, John invited Patrick to visit the school in July of that year to examine the students in classics. Fennell was keen to impress the board of governors as to the quality of education, and because of Patrick's unfavourable findings Mr Burgess, the current classics master, was dismissed. Patrick took up the post of examiner and was to attend the school regularly.

The headmaster's wife, Jane, who married John in 1790, was the school's acting matron and housekeeper, and in time as the school grew so did the workload. Keeping it in the family, Jane was to ask her niece twenty-nine-year-old Maria Branwell from Penzance, and from strong Wesleyan stock, to join her as housekeeper. Maria had been living with her unmarried sisters Elizabeth and Charlotte at the family home some 400 miles away from Bradford following the deaths of her successful grocer and tea merchant father Thomas (Jane's brother) in 1808 and her mother in 1809.

The scene was set for the budding romance that was about to flourish. With Patrick's regular visits to the school, where he would often walk the 24-mile round trip in a day, it wasn't long before they were both smitten and their courtship soon evolved. Wedding plans were firmly made by early December. There is no question that this was not a love match for it is evidenced by their letters in which Maria refers to the Anglican minister as her 'Saucy Pat'. In addition, Patrick's close friend from Wellington, William Morgan, was simultaneously courting John and Jane Fennell's only daughter, Jane.

Although a relatively short romance had ensued, it is widely believed that thirty-five-year-old Patrick chose the grounds of the magnificent romantic ruins of Kirkstall Abbey to take the knee and make his proposal of marriage to Maria; history has shown she showed no hesitation in accepting.

Woodhouse Grove School, Rawdon.

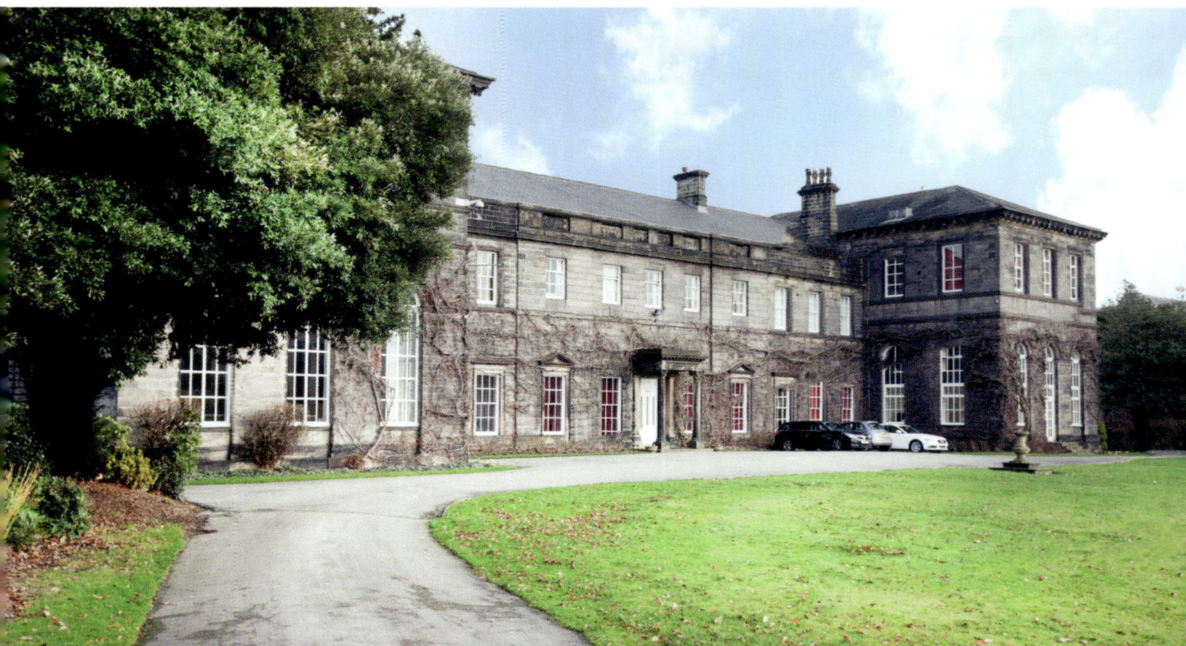

St Oswald's Church, Guiseley

If you google historic events on 29 December, top of the list is the murder of the Archbishop of Canterbury Thomas à Becket in 1155 by four knights. This is closely followed by the marriage of Patrick Brontë to Maria Branwell at St Oswald's. Many will say quite rightly so, for their marriage was to change literary history forever, but that is for later. For now let us enjoy the moment.

The entry in the register of St Oswald's Church reads:

29 December 1812 The Revd Patrick Brontë of the Parish of Birstall and Minister of Hartshead-cum-Clifton and Maria Branwell of this parish, Spinster, by William Morgan, Offcg. Minister.

His good friend William Morgan performed the ceremony. What makes this day even more unique is this was a double event in which Patrick officiated over William and Jane Fennell's wedding, with each bride in turn serving as bridesmaid. Both brides were given away by John Fennell, Jane's father, and Maria's uncle. In Penzance at the same time, Maria's sister Charlotte married her cousin Joseph Branwell in what was now a triple event, although a little disjointed by the 400-mile distance between locations.

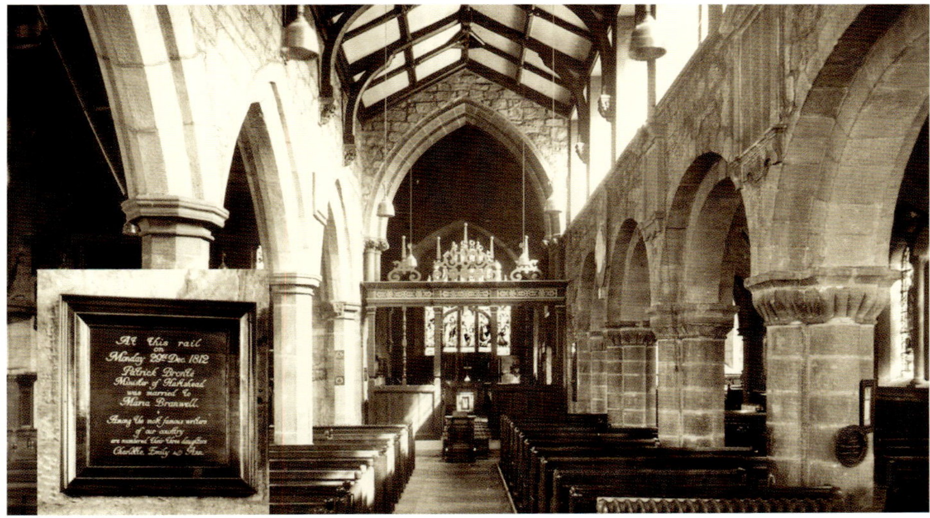

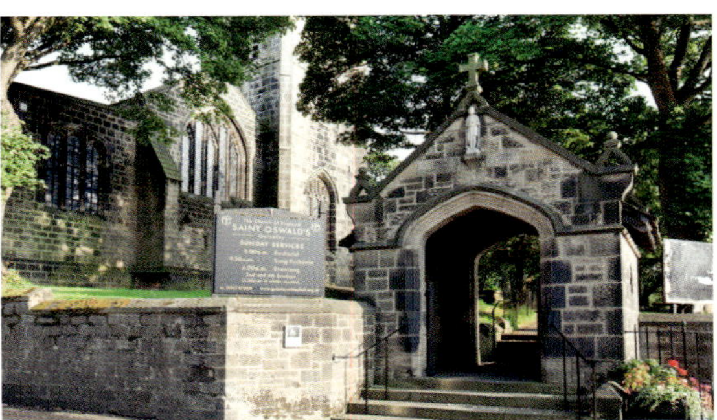

Above: St Oswald's Church, Guiseley. A plaque in the church bears witness to the historic Brontë wedding.

Left: St Oswald's Church is still much loved in the community.

Clough House, Hightown

Although love was aplenty, unfortunately funds were thin on the ground after the wedding and the newlyweds found themselves initially living together at the dreary but convenient Lousy Thorn Farm. 'Quite a Lousy start' one could imagine them jokingly saying as they embarked on their new life together. This arrangement, however, was short-lived and they moved to Clough House, a mile away in Hightown. The spacious stone-built property situated on the hill above Hartshead boasted three living rooms and five bedrooms and must have seemed like a palace in comparison to the former lodgings. It wasn't long before Maria was pregnant with their first daughter, also named Maria, who was baptised on 23 April 1814 at Hartshead, just twelve days after Napoleon Bonaparte's abdication as Emperor of France. A joyous month without doubt. There was little rest for Maria as she was to fall pregnant again within two months of baby Maria's baptism. Elizabeth was born on 8 February 1815 and named after her maternal aunt as was customary back in those days.

At the time of Elizabeth's birth, Patrick was contacted by Revd Thomas Atkinson, who had served as the Perpetual Curate at Thornton in Bradford since his ordination in 1804. Thomas suggested they exchange livings as it appears he had an ambition to win the hand of Frances Walker of Lascelles Hall, near Huddersfield, and felt being in closer proximity to her would give him extra advantage.

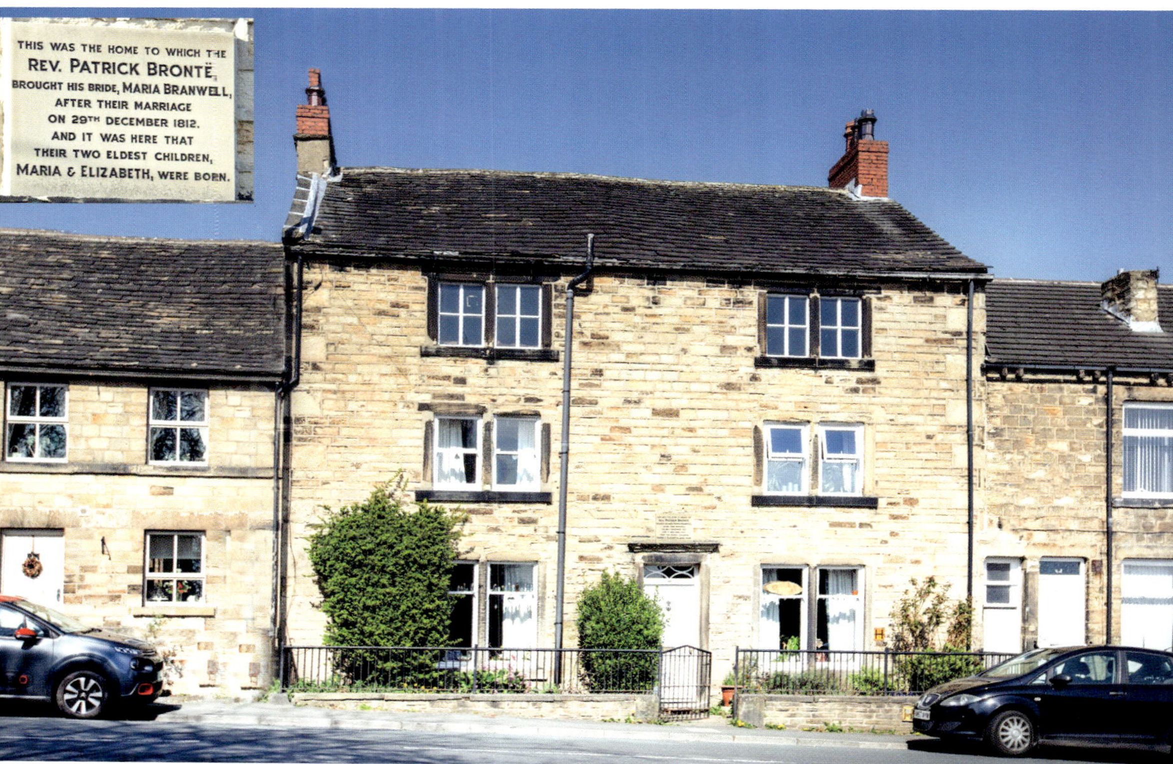

Clough House, to this day, remains a family home, having stood the test of time. A memorial stone above the door references the Brontë occupancy.

3

Our Happiest Place

There was good reason for Patrick to accept the would-be Romeo Thomas Atkinson's proposal to exchange livings. For one, the move to Thornton would give him £140 income per year, which was very useful to help provide for his family, and secondly the incumbency would provide an official parsonage house. In addition, the Bradford parish was much larger with an ever-growing population.

Arrangements were made, and so it came to pass that Revd John Crosse, Vicar of Bradford, nominated him to the perpetual curacy of Thornton in the middle of March 1815. Two months would pass before Patrick took his final funeral and two baptisms at Hartshead on 18 May. Thomas Atkinson took his last service in Thornton on 30 April.

John Crosse MA was the Vicar of Bradford for thirty-two years. Although he went blind in his later years, he continued to work right up until a fortnight before his death. At the point he nominated Patrick, he had just over a year left to live – he died on 17 June 1816, aged seventy-seven. There is a tablet erected to his memory at Bradford Cathedral. Patrick would have known the cathedral as St Peter's in his life as the church only achieved cathedral status in 1919.

On 19 May the family packed up their worldly possessions and made the journey to their new life and home some 13 miles away in Bradford. This must have been a monumental moment for Patrick, for this was the first time in his clerical ministry that he had a proper home, an official church residence for him and his family to thrive and grow in.

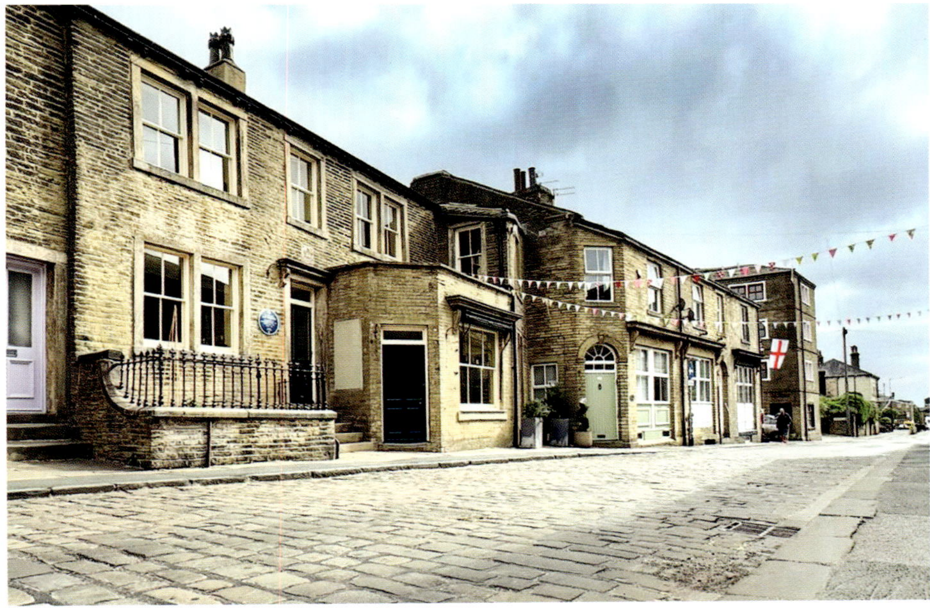

The Brontë parsonage, Thornton. The blue plaque details the births of Charlotte, Branwell, Emily and Anne Brontë.

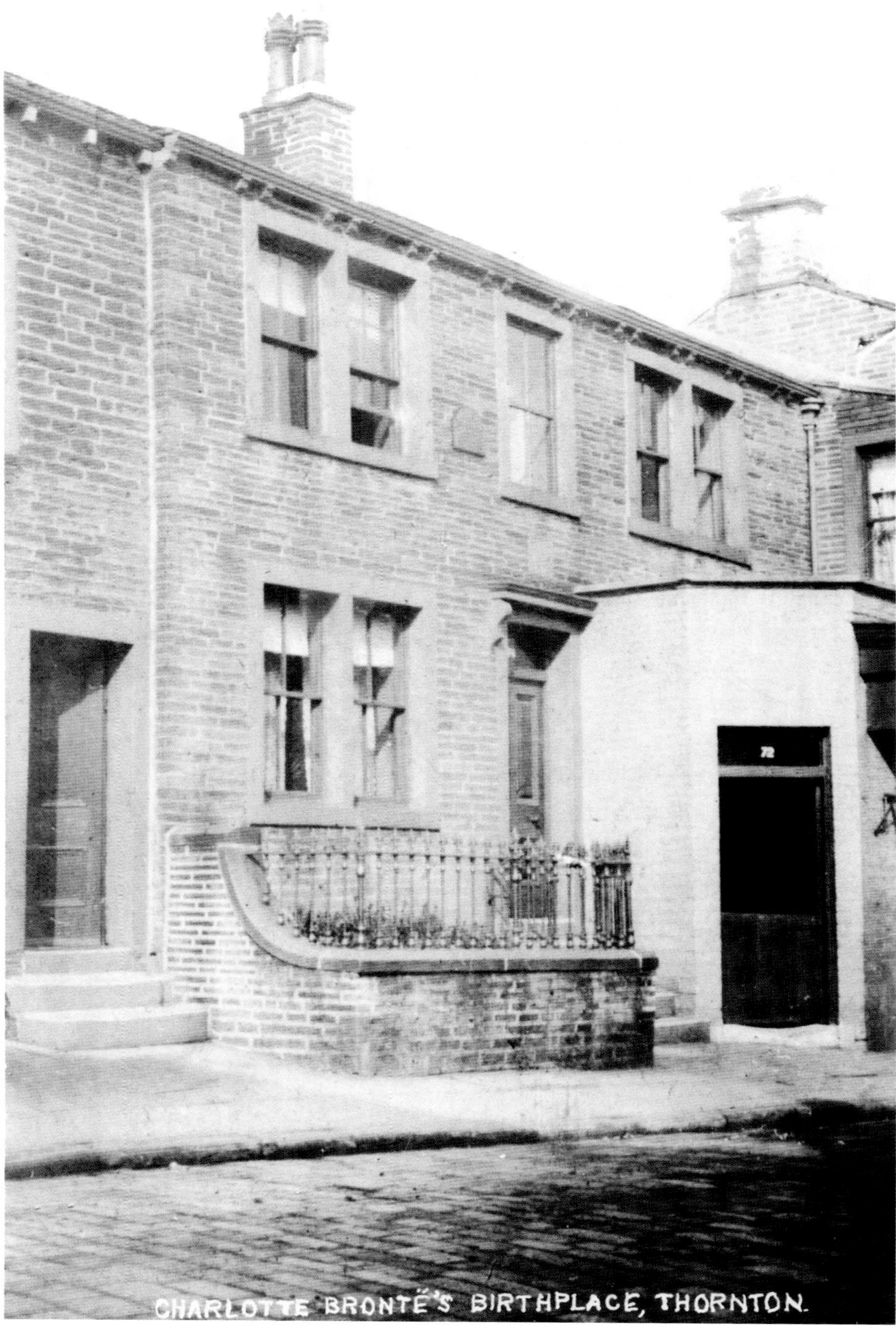

This Edwardian postcard shows the house with the extension which was added long after the Brontës' departure.

Thornton Parsonage, located at Nos 72–74 Market Street, was a comparatively recent construction in 1815, having been built in 1802. The date is scribed into the stonework above the front door along with the letters J. A. S., which relate to John and Sarah Ashworth, who owned many properties in the village. The late Georgian property is one of a row and mid-terrace; however, this house is larger than its immediate neighbour, being double fronted. The downstairs consists of two good-sized main rooms, one either side of the front door, with the kitchen placed at the rear of the house. Upstairs there are two bedrooms and a dressing room. This description relates to when the Brontë family lived there. In later years it was extended.

A document from 1817, copied below, describes the advantages of a permanent church position:

The Chapel is endowed with a parsonage, situated in the village of Thornton, consisting of six rooms, three on the ground floor, and three bedchambers, having a stand for a Cow and a Horse at one end, and a cottage at the other – All built of stone and lime, purchased partly by contribution, and partly by the governors of Queen Annes's Bounty &c – There is a road round the West End into a garden at the back of the House which is enclosed by a stone wall, the greater part of the eastern side of which is built at the expense of the owner of the adjoining field, and the remainder of the building.

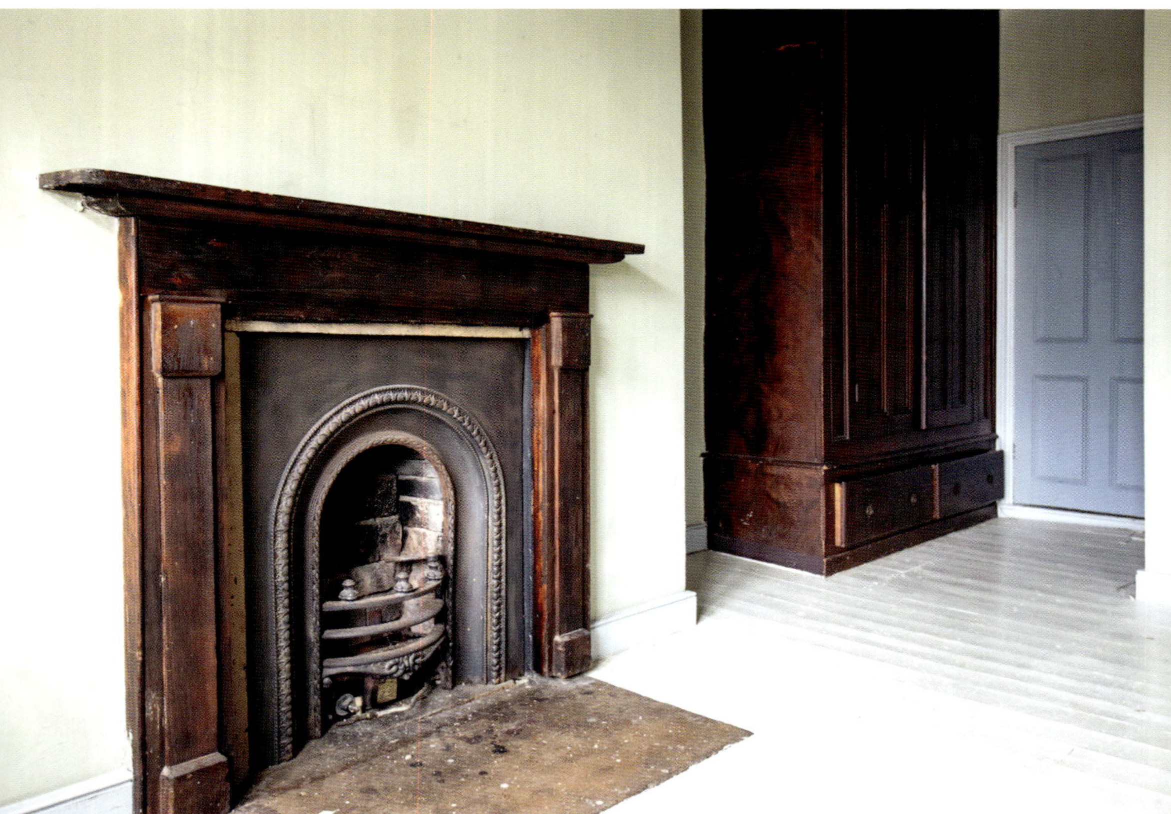

The main bedroom to the left of the front of the house, showing Patrick's original wardrobe.

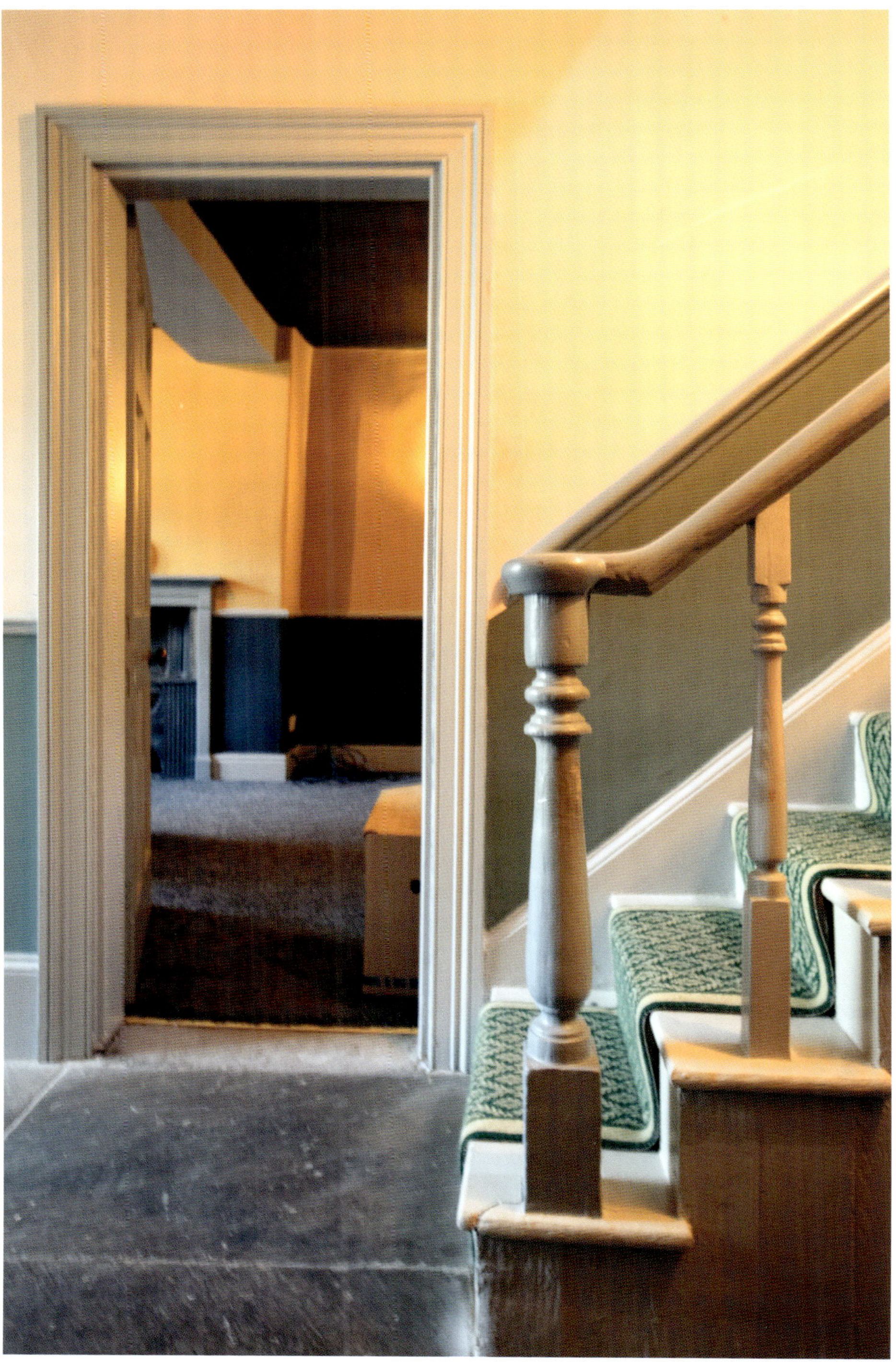

Looking from the parlour where the children were born, taking in the main staircase.

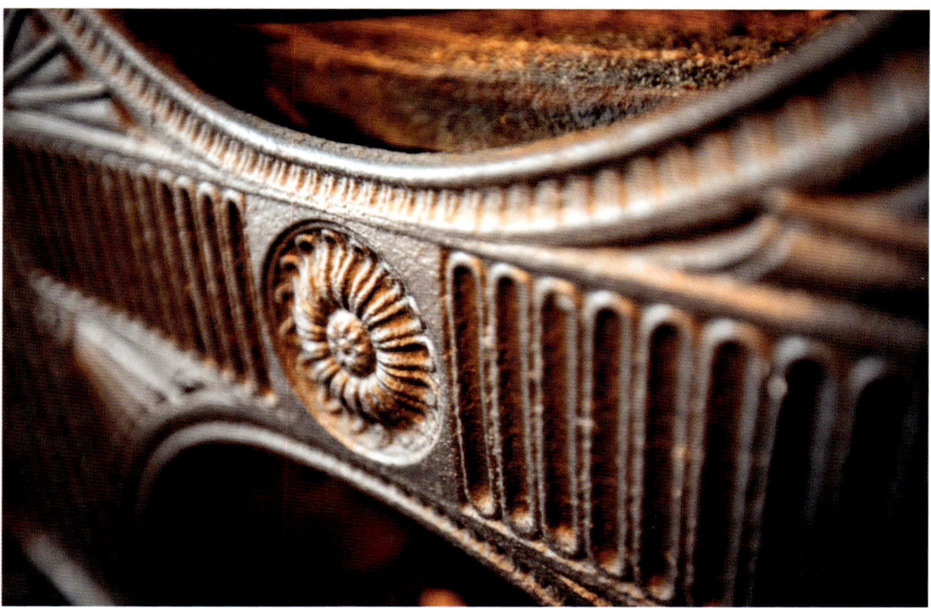

Above and below: In a world of change where properties of historic value have been demolished or converted to meet modern-day requirements, it is refreshing to find the old parsonage not only remains, but in addition many of the original features including these fire grates are still in place.

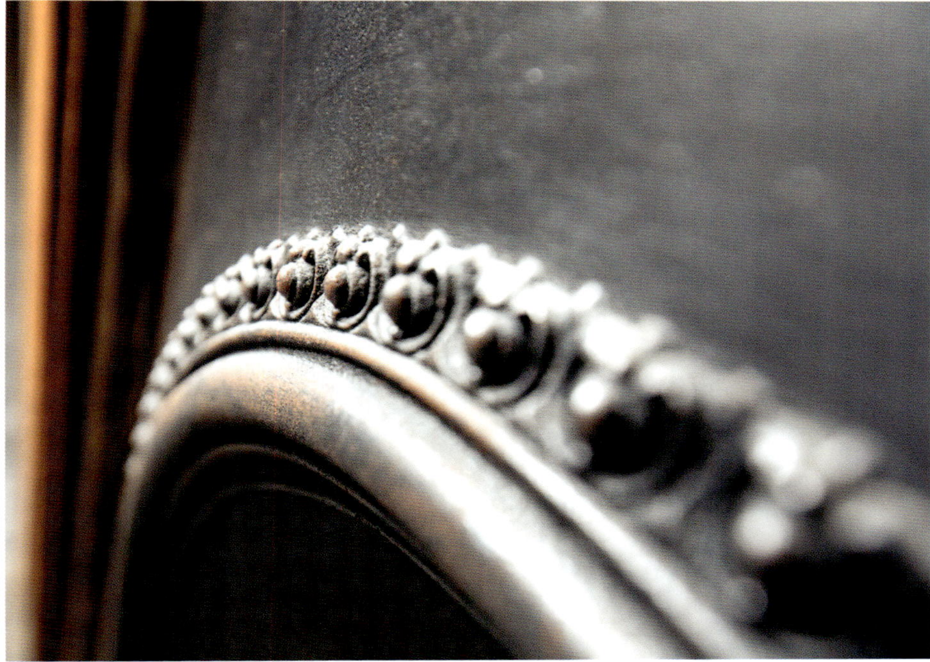

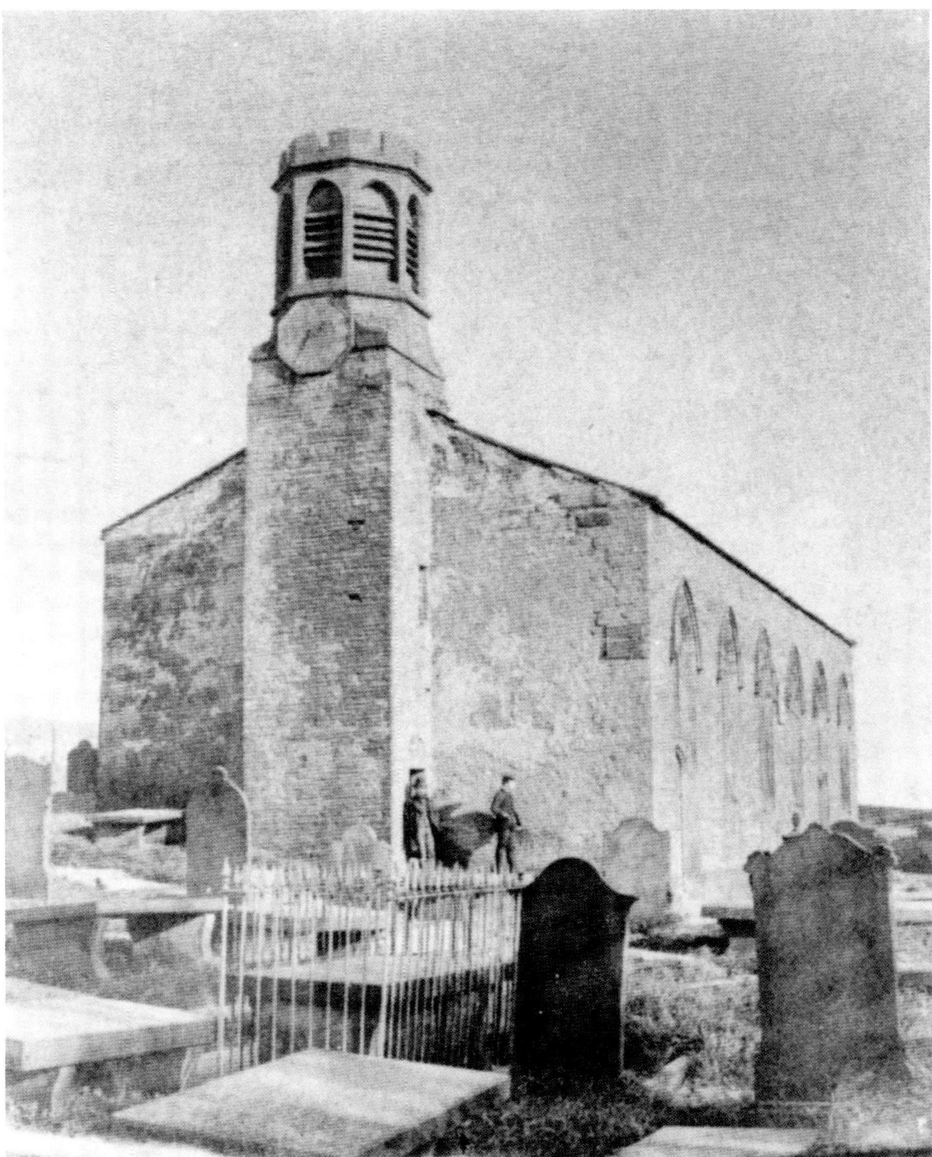

The church in Thornton was known as the Bell Chapel and dedicated to St James. At the time the Brontës arrived the old religious edifice was tired and in dire need of repairs. Originally known as St Leonard's, it had been rebuilt in 1612 and rededicated to St James. Although functional in the design, the building lacked any architectural beauty and would have appeared to be a downgrade compared to St Peter's at Hartshead. It was during Patrick's time at Thornton that the chapel was renovated and the cupola added, as seen in the image above.

The chapel's plain exterior unfortunately was not hiding a hidden gem to behold. Internally it was a gloomy space lacking natural light and was damp. Despite the presence of windows, a significant amount of light was obstructed by the two galleries. The situation was further exacerbated by the aisles having been

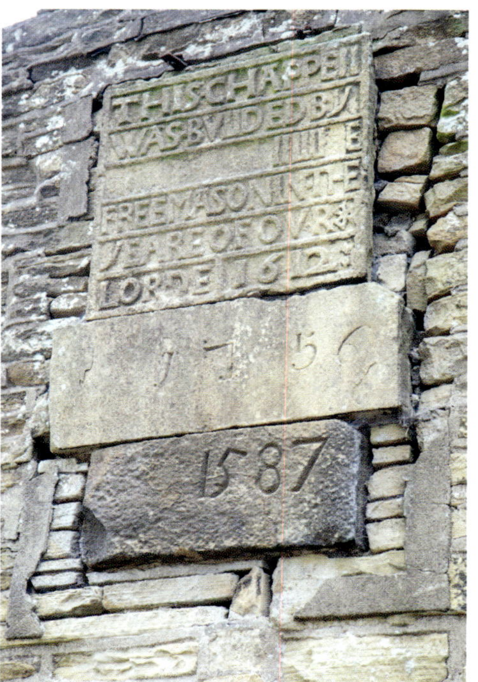

paved with gravestones, which, during periods of significant dampness, became slippery and posed a potential hazard for parishioners traversing them. It was said that a fetid musty smell floated through the damp mouldering interior. And to cap it all the roof needed serious attention because of its dangerous state.

In addition, although he was living rent free, Patrick found his new family home at the parsonage to be very badly constructed, which would require a considerable amount of money to maintain every year. It would appear at this stage that the move to Thornton wasn't as fortuitous as he had first imagined.

Left: Ancient stone markings at the Bell Chapel charting significant dates.

Below: The list of perpetual curates can be found at St James' Church across the road from the Bell Chapel ruins.

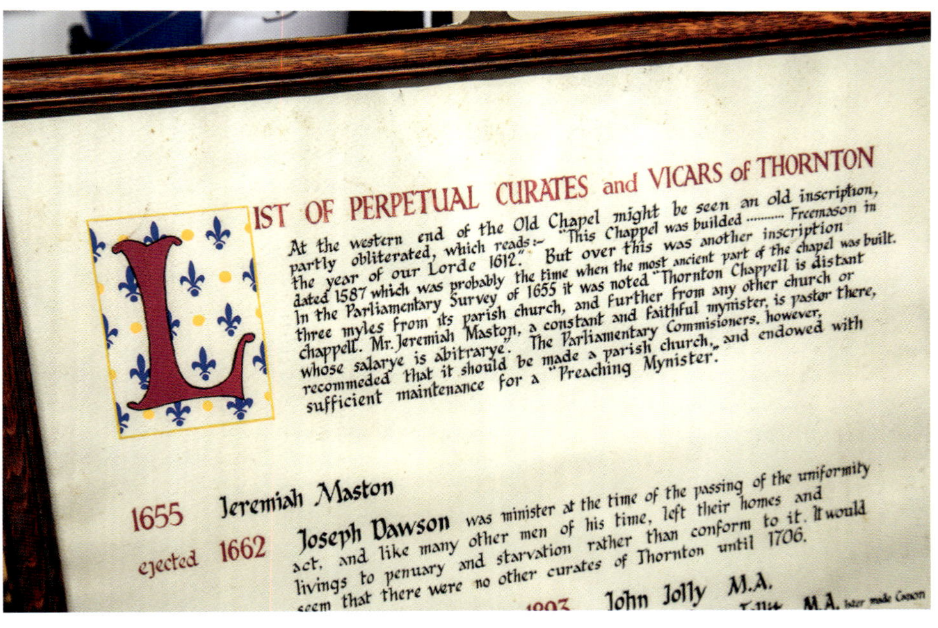

LIST OF PERPETUAL CURATES and VICARS of THORNTON

At the western end of the Old Chapel might be seen an old inscription, partly obliterated, which reads:- "This Chappel was builded .... Freemason in the year of our Lorde 1612." But over this was another inscription dated 1587 which was probably the time when the most ancient part of the chapel was built. In the Parliamentary Survey of 1655 it was noted "Thornton Chappell is distant three myles from its parish church, and further from any other church or chappell. Mr. Jeremiah Maston, a constant and faithful mynister, is pastor there, whose salarye is abitrarye". The Parliamentary Commisioners, however, recommeded that it should be made a parish church, and endowed with sufficient maintenance for a "Preaching Mynister".

1655   Jeremiah Maston

ejected 1662   Joseph Dawson was minister at the time of the passing of the uniformity act, and like many other men of his time, left their homes and livings to penuary and starvation rather than conform to it. It would seem that there were no other curates of Thornton until 1706.

1003   John Jolly M.A.

At the time the Brontë's residence at Thornton, situated 4 miles west of Bradford centre, was regarded as a small hamlet. The main thoroughfare through the village was Market Street where the parsonage is situated. It would be six years after their departure in 1826 that the new Thornton Road would bypass Market Street. As a result, the street still preserves much of its original charm, having avoided the demolition and road changes that have altered many other old villages.

The nineteenth century was to see an unprecedented growth in both population and industry in West Yorkshire, as the map below shows. For example, in 1811 there were only five mills and a population of 16,000 in Bradford, whereas ten years later in 1821 there were 20 mills and 26,000 inhabitants. Thornton itself was to see a considerable rise in its fortunes as the century progressed, due mostly to the Industrial Revolution and the production of sandstone from local quarries. Low Mill, Thornton's first textile mill, opened in 1826 and was later converted to steam power by Denholme-born Simeon Townend. In Thornton there were many hand weavers working from home in 1815. Benjamin Kaye, of nearby Allerton Hall, which we will hear about later, organised a group of the weavers, taking their work by packhorse once a week to be sold in Manchester at the market.

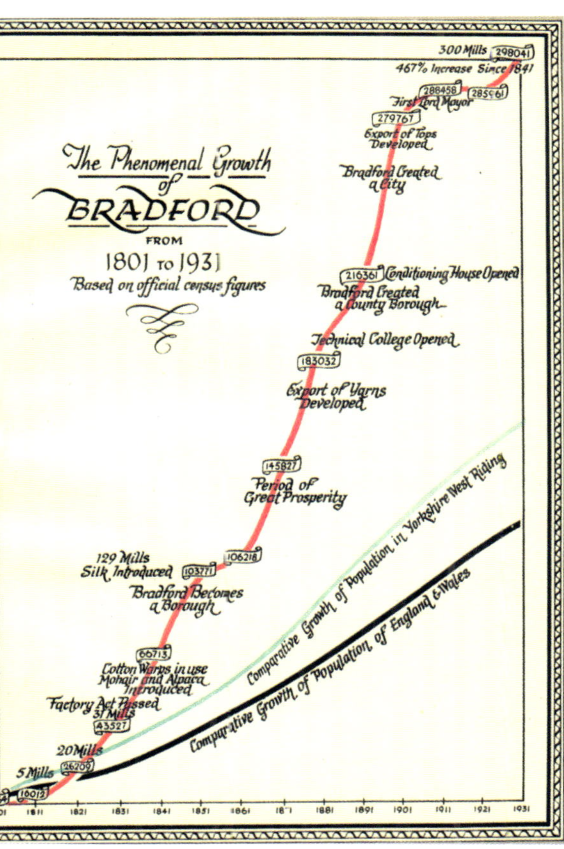

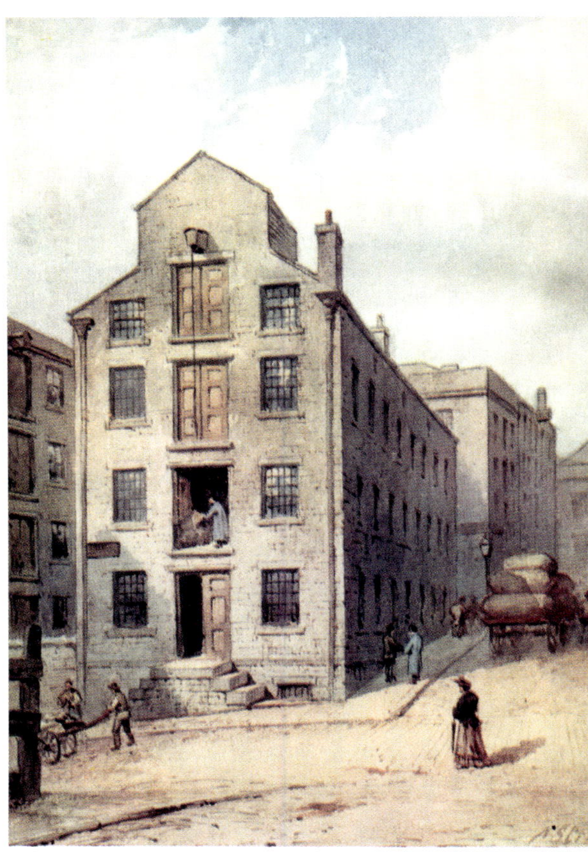

Above left: Growth in the Bradford district from 1801–1931.

Above right: An early nineteenth-century mill at Cheapside, Bradford.

Kipping Independent Chapel

The parishioners at Thornton were a divided group, but the majority were Nonconformists who attended the Kipping Independent Chapel situated on Market Street, just a stone's throw away from the parsonage's front door. Although the population was greater than at Hartshead, Patrick conducted approximately the same number of funerals – about fifty per year – at the Bell Chapel, while the number of baptisms he performed was about half of what he previously managed. In 1815, Revd John Calvert was minister at Kipping, succeeded in 1816 by Revd Robinson Pool, who reportedly had a good relationship with Patrick.

Unlike the Bell Chapel, which is little more than a skeletal ruin now, Kipping Chapel has weathered the ensuing years and still stands firm on Market Street after last being enlarged over 200 years ago in 1823.

You only have to look at the records relating to Undercliffe cemetery situated just outside the centre of Bradford, which opened in 1854, to see that it was a Nonconformist town – there is a huge burial area set aside for the Nonconformists. In 1851 the Bradford Census of Religious Worship states that 68 per cent of the worshipers were Nonconformists.

Interestingly, at Undercliffe, the average age of tradesmen and the labouring class including their families buried in the cemetery is just seventeen years old, whilst the professionals, middle and upper classes is thirty. These low average ages relate directly to the excessive child mortality in the nineteenth century. Families often had eight children, expecting only half to reach adulthood.

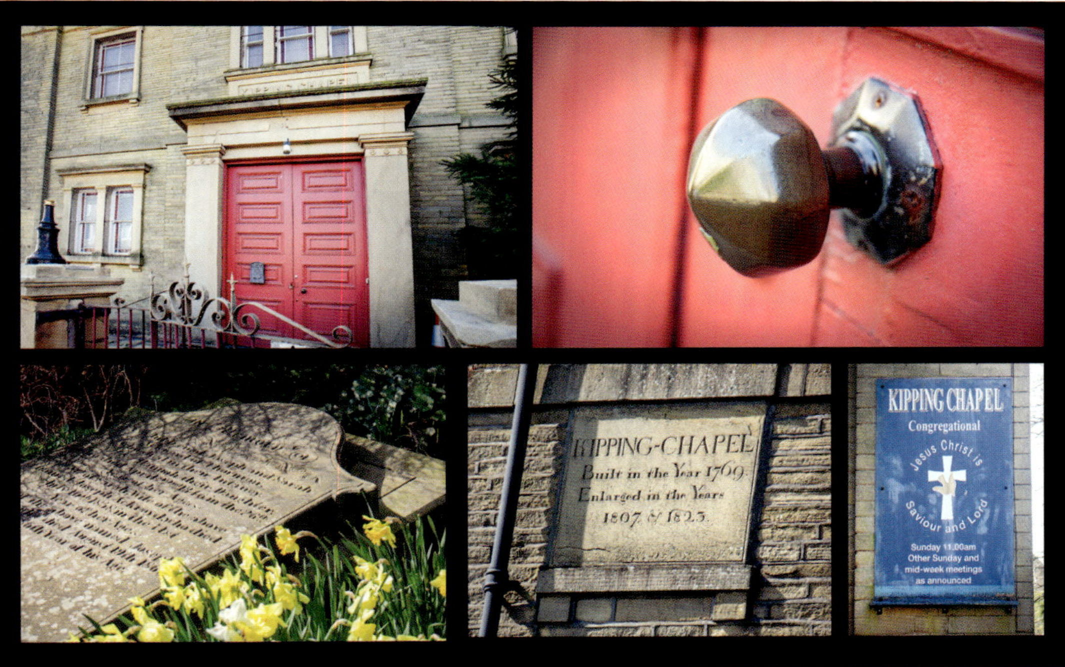

Various images from spring 2025 of Kipping Independent Chapel.

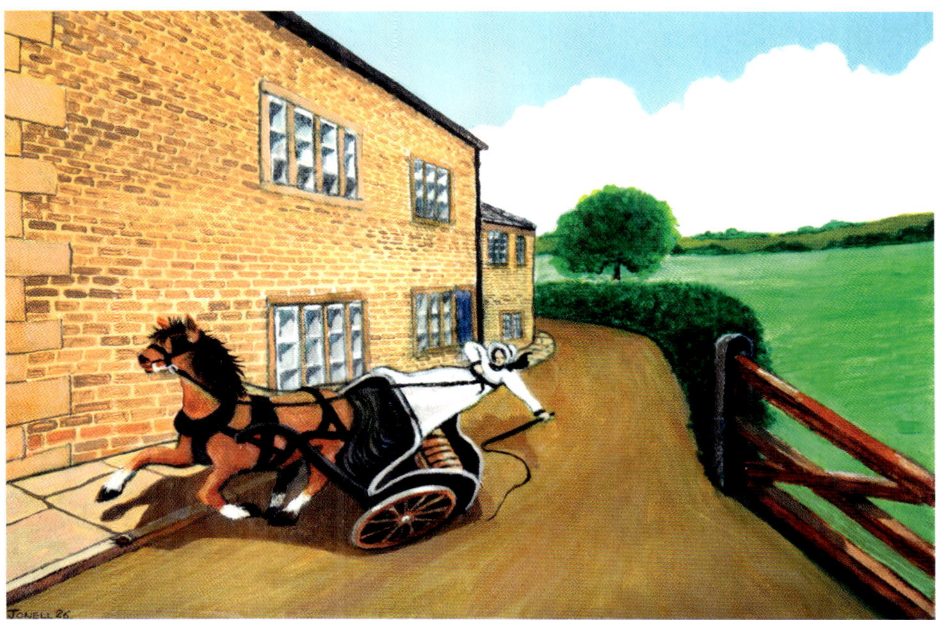

The artwork above, depicting the tragic accident on Kipping Lane that killed Elizabeth Firth's mother, is painted by Bradford artist John Ellis.

Within a relatively short space of time after arriving in Thornton, the Brontë family were to forge new friendships and begin to enjoy quite a refined and engaging social life. One new acquaintance that proved pivotal was eighteen-year-old Elizabeth Firth of nearby Kipping House, a handsome seventeenth-century property on Lower Kipping Lane. Elizabeth was soon to be regarded as a genuine close family friend. She had searched out the family at the first opportunity, calling on them on 7 June after returning home from visiting her cousin; however, it would be two days later, 9 June, before she finally met the family 1.2 miles away at Allerton Hall, the relatively new home to her friends Benjamin Kaye (a master clothier) and his wife, Mercy. Allerton Hall was built in 1777 by Elizabeth's uncle Joshua, who had passed away in London in 1814 – his memorial can be found on p. 52. Joshua, who was Elizabeth's father's brother, was a wealthy influential man, who had a bank from which he issued his own notes, known as Firth notes.

From the age of fifteen back in 1812, Elizabeth had kept diaries detailing her day-to-day social life, which now provides a valuable resource of information despite the entries being in effect bullet points rather than expanded accounts. Her first entry relating to the Brontës was on 19 May, where she wrote, 'Mr Bronte's came to reside at Thornton', referring to the family as a whole.

Within days of meeting the new incumbent she was taking tea with Mrs Brontë, inviting the family to dinner and enjoying walks with Mr Brontë to the top of Allerton and Swill Hill on 26 June. She first heard him preach on 11 June.

Elizabeth, although small in stature at just 5 feet 3 inches and only 7 stone, was quite a character. She had more recently taken on the role of keeping house for her doctor father, John Scholefield Firth. Her mother, also called Elizabeth (née Holt), had died in an accident the year before. In her diary on 2 July 1814, she had written an understandably more detailed entry than usual relating to her tragic loss as follows: 'My ever to be lamented Mother was thrown out of the gig and killed on the spot by a blood vessel breaking in the head; aged 56. The accident happened in the lane by the kitchen windows.'

Elizabeth senior was interred on 6 July 1814 at the old Bell Chapel in the vault under the Firth family pew.

The Firths were a well-respected family in the area at large and had a good circle of friends. Elizabeth's cousin was Frances Walker of Lascelles Hall, the woman Patrick's predecessor Thomas Atkinson had been keen to leave Thornton to be closer to, in hope that he might lead her down the aisle.

The more you read about Miss Firth the more you realise the Brontë family were blessed to have her in their lives.

There is a memorial tablet mounted high on the wall in St James' Church dedicated to Elizabeth, who sadly, like all the Brontë girls, was to die young, in her case at the age of forty in 1837. The tablet also memorialises her stepmother Ann. Elizabeth was in fact buried at Huddersfield. The memorial was originally in the Bell Chapel.

Around the same time that the Firth-Brontë family friendship began to develop, Elizabeth Branwell, Maria's sister, had arrived in Thornton to help the family settle into their new surroundings. She was to stay for over a year, only returning to Cornwall on 28 July 1816.

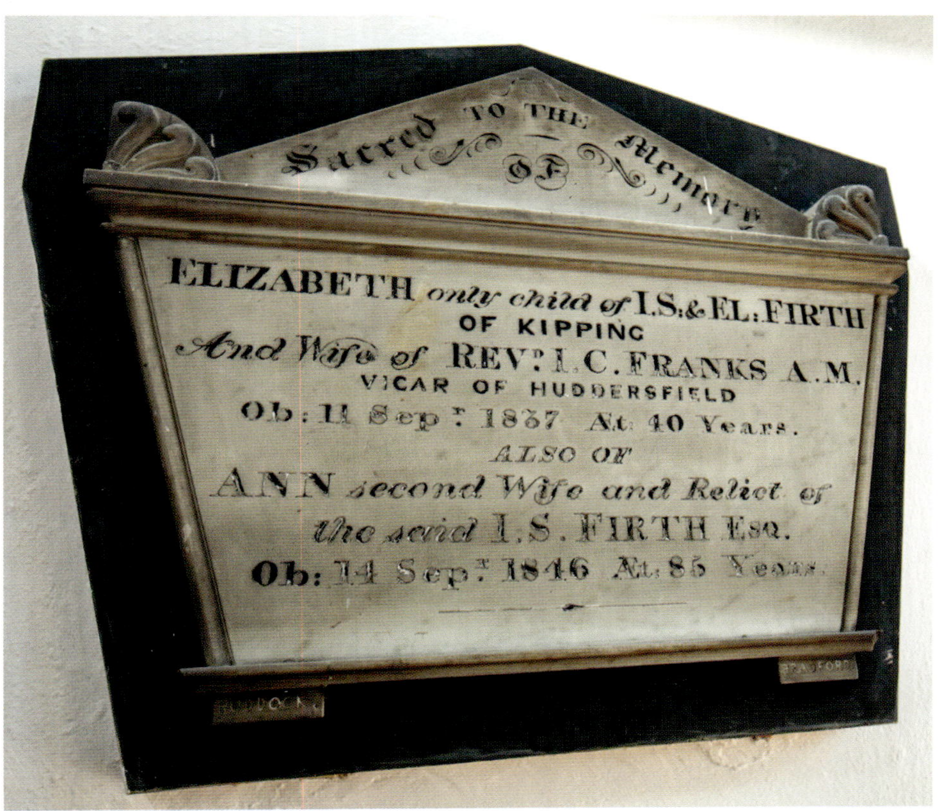

Elizabeth Firth's memorial at St James' Church.

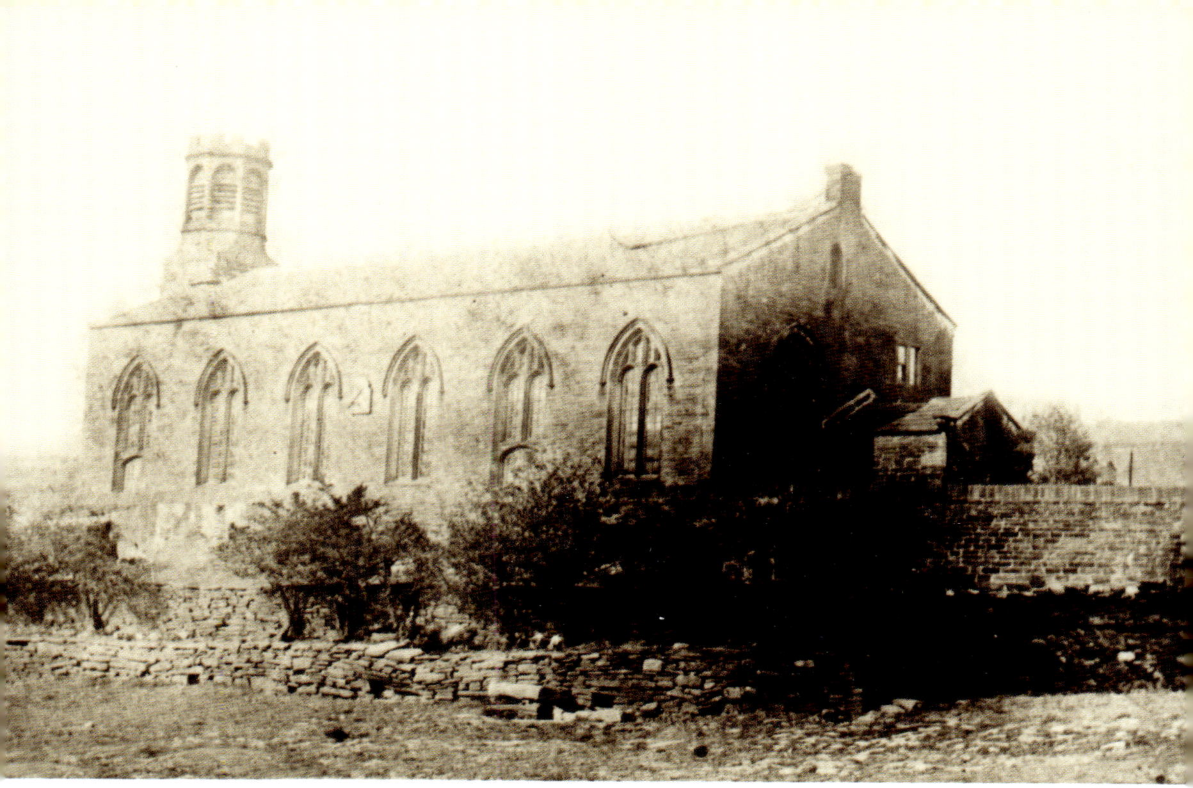

Above: From this angle you can clearly see Patrick's vestry at the rear of the Bell Chapel. The vestry was an addition from 1793.

Right: The font at which all the children apart from Maria were baptised can be found at St James' Church, opposite the old Bell Chapel.

Three months after arriving in Thornton on 26 August 1815, Patrick and Maria's youngest daughter, Elizabeth, was baptised at the old Bell Chapel. She was by then nearly seven months old. Her baptism was performed by Maria's uncle, Revd John Fennell, the former Methodist headmaster of Woodhouse Grove where Patrick met Maria. John had recently been ordained to the priesthood of the Church of England. Their new friends Elizabeth Firth and her father were asked to be the infant's godparents.

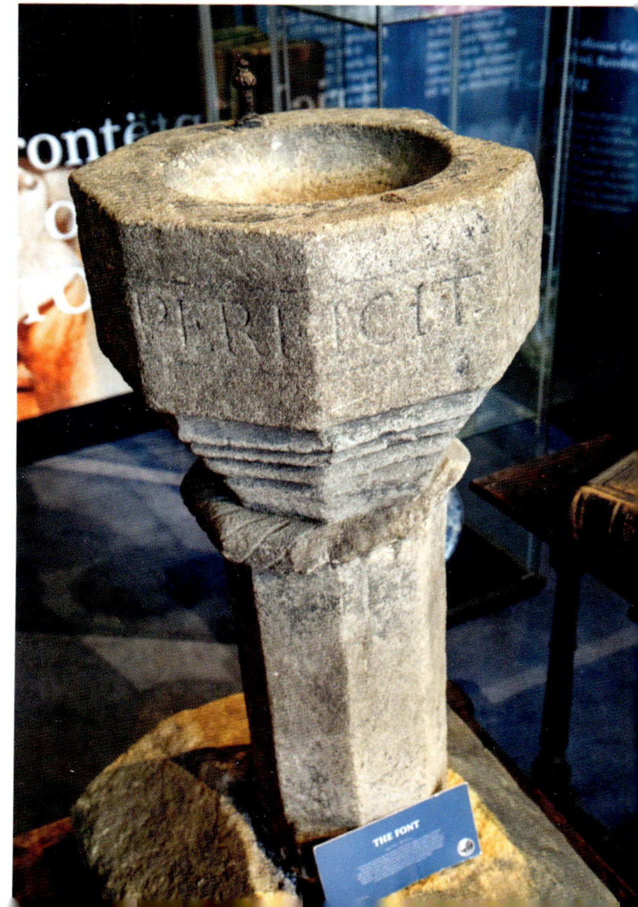

Charlotte Brontë

'I am no bird; and no net ensnares me; I am a free human being, with an independent will.'

Jane Eyre

On 21 April 1816, Mr and Mrs Brontë were blessed with the arrival of their third child, a daughter. Charlotte was born in front of the fire in the parlour at the parsonage in Thornton at the very place you see in the image above. The newly born literary genius was named after Maria's youngest sister. It was a time of great joy and Elizabeth Firth presented the new baby with a little cap she had made for her.

Charlotte's birth would in the fullness of time change the world of literature forever – if only they had known!

Charlotte Brontë was duly baptised on 29 June 1816 at the old Bell Chapel like her sister Elizabeth previously. This time Patrick's old friend William Morgan performed the baptism. Revd Morgan was by now the minister of the newly built Christ Church near North Parade in Bradford. Frances Walker and her now fiancé, Revd Thomas Atkinson, were asked to be godparents. To mark the event the whole Brontë family was invited to Kipping House on 12 July for a celebration meal.

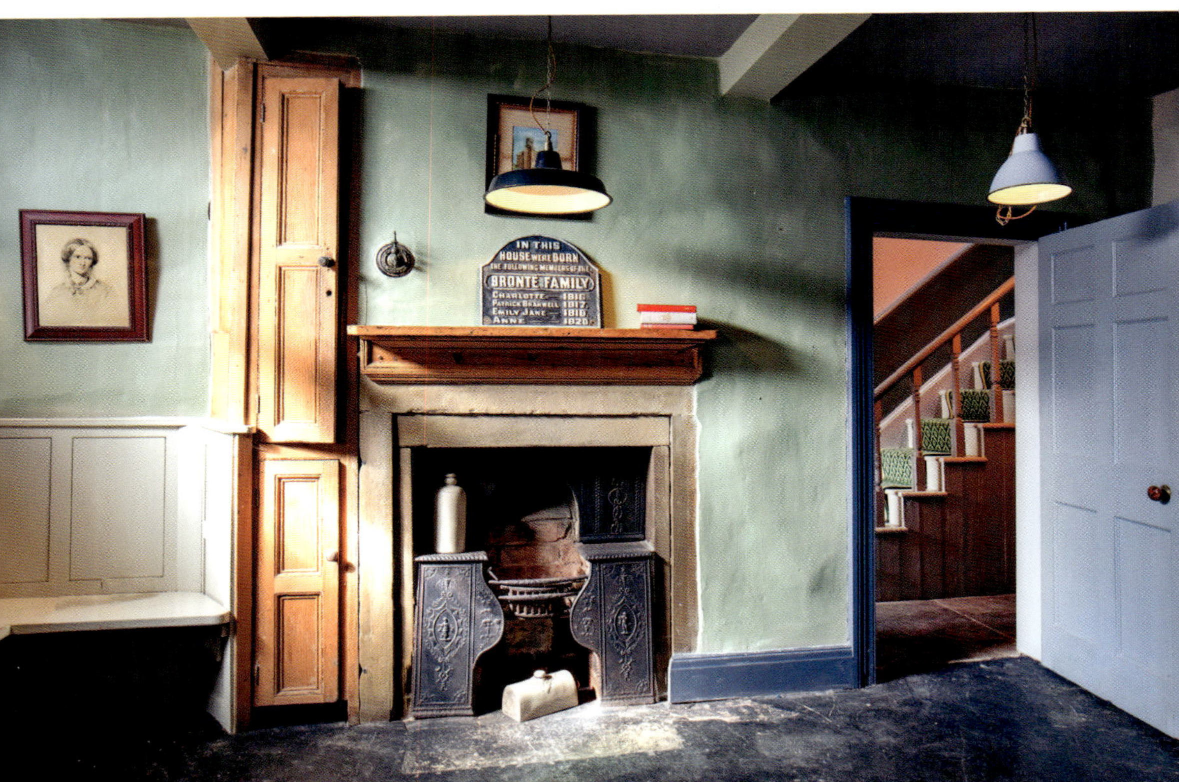

The front parlour at the Thornton Birthplace, where Charlotte was born.

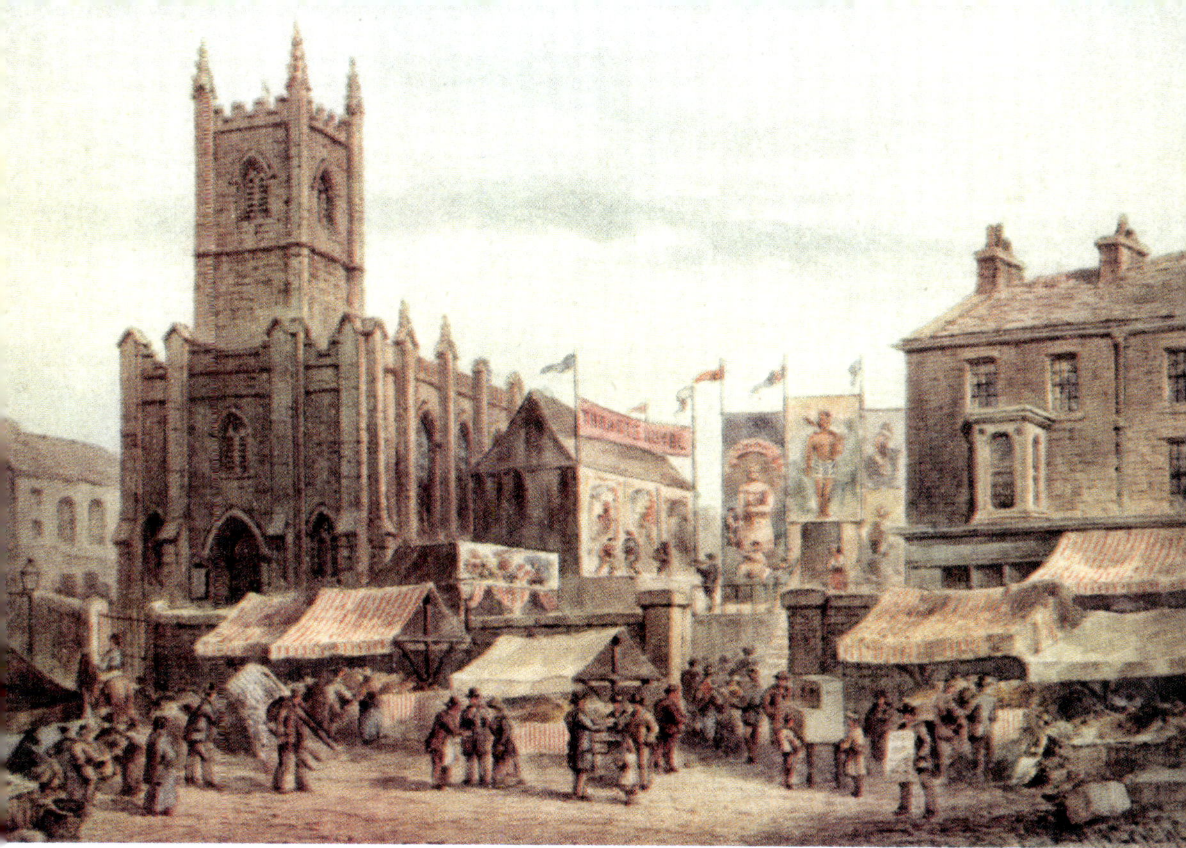

Above: The impressive Christ Church, which was designed by the architect J. Taylor of Leeds. It was built at a cost of £5,400 and completed in 1815.

Below: Charlotte's baptism record.

Nancy De Garrs

In the summer of 1816, after her sister Elizabeth's departure back to Cornwall, Maria, with three young children to look after and with the added day-to-day running of the parsonage, was in dire need of some help. Assistance came in the form of Nancy De Garrs, who Patrick found when he applied to the Bradford School of Industry, which was a charitable institution specifically set up to train the daughters of impoverished parents.

Nancy, who was aged thirteen at the time she joined the family, was one of twelve children of Richard De Garrs, a shoemaker from Westgate in the centre of Bradford. Richard's father was French but because Bradford folk struggled to pronounce his surname the 'De' was dropped in favour of just Garrs, hence why Nancy is often referred to as Nancy Garrs.

She was to become devoted to the children and remain a loyal lifelong friend after leaving the family's employment.

Such was the impression that she made on the family that her twelve-year-old sister Sarah was also taken on. The young siblings remained in the employ of the Brontës until 1824.

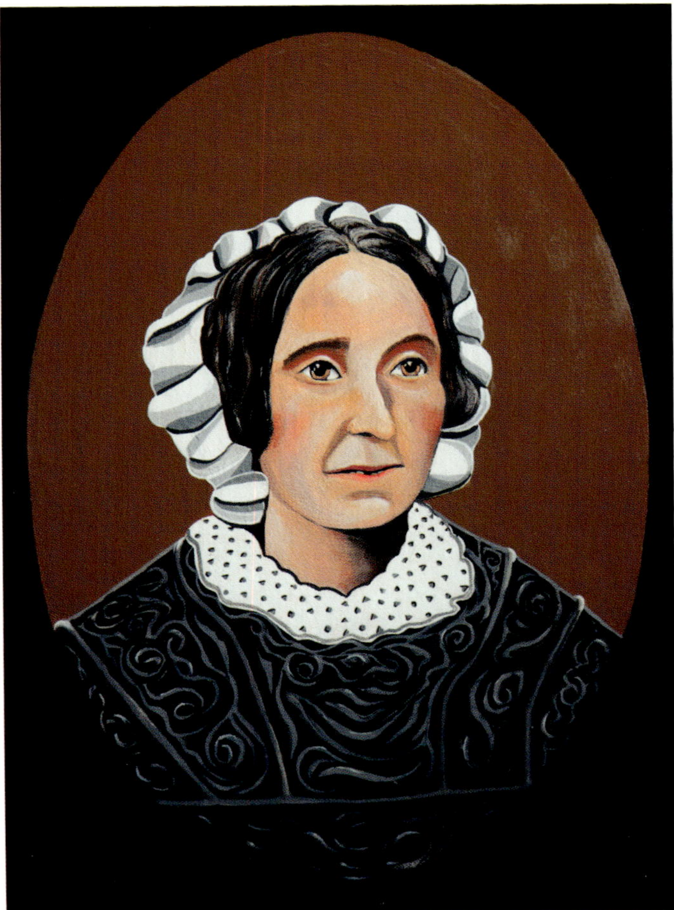

Left: Nancy Garrs in later life, painted by Bradford artist John Ellis.

Opposite: Nancy's grave at the historic Undercliffe cemetery, overlooking the city of Bradford.

Patrick later in life in August 1857 wrote the following letter regarding their time with the family.

I leave to state to all whom it may concern that Nancy and Sarah Garrs, during the time they were in service, were kind to my children, honest, and not wasteful, but sufficiently careful in regard to food and all other things entrusted to their care. P. Brontë, A.B., Incumbent of Haworth.

Sadly, much later in life Nancy found herself destitute and was to enter the Bradford workhouse where she was to be an inmate right up until her death in 1886, which was reported on 27 March in the *Bradford Daily Telegraph*.

This morning Mrs Nancy Malone, better known as Nancy Wainwright, died at the Bradford Workhouse at twenty minutes to one o'clock. The old lady, who was in her eighty-third year, enjoyed a considerable amount of notoriety amongst admirers of the Brontë family from the fact that in her younger days she acted as nurse for Charlotte and her talented sisters, with whom for the whole of their lifetime she continued on terms of intimacy ... Admirers of the Brontës, not only local but from distant parts of the country, visited her at the workhouse, and she had repeated offers of a home outside of the workhouse gates, but she declined to avail herself of them ... Notwithstanding her great age she enjoyed fairly good health up to a fortnight ago, but from that period has failed rapidly. Her condition during the past few days was seen to be hopeless, and she expired peaceably and quietly at the hour named.

She was interred at Undercliffe cemetery where she was to lay in an unmarked family grave for over 130 years before action was taken more recently to install a headstone with a poem by Charlotte carved into the stone. It seems fitting that given Nancy cared for Charlotte in the cradle that now the famous author's words are with her in the grave.

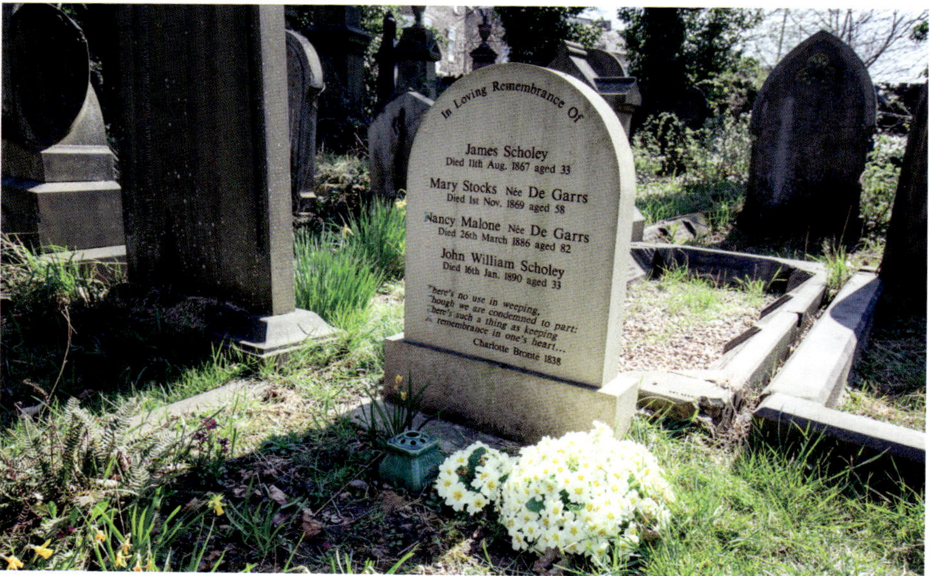

Patrick Branwell Brontë

I sit, this evening, far away, From all I used to know,

And nought reminds my soul today of happy long ago.

Branwell Brontë

Just fourteen months after Charlotte was born in the parlour at the parsonage Maria gave birth to their only son in the same room. He entered the world early in the morning of 26 June 1817 – just less than a week after the Prince Regent had opened John Rennie's Waterloo Bridge in London.

After having produced three daughters in quick succession, the event of finally having a son must have been an extra joyous occasion for both Patrick and Maria. More commonly known to us all as 'Branwell', he was named Patrick Branwell Brontë following a tradition that he was named after his father but given his mother's maiden surname as his middle name.

Branwell was duly baptised at the old Bell Chapel on Wednesday 23 July by John Fennell, who by now was the curate at Christ Church. Elizabeth Firth's father, John, and her stepmother, Ann, were asked to be the godparents.

With Branwell occupying the privileged position of being the only boy in the family, great achievements were anticipated from him.

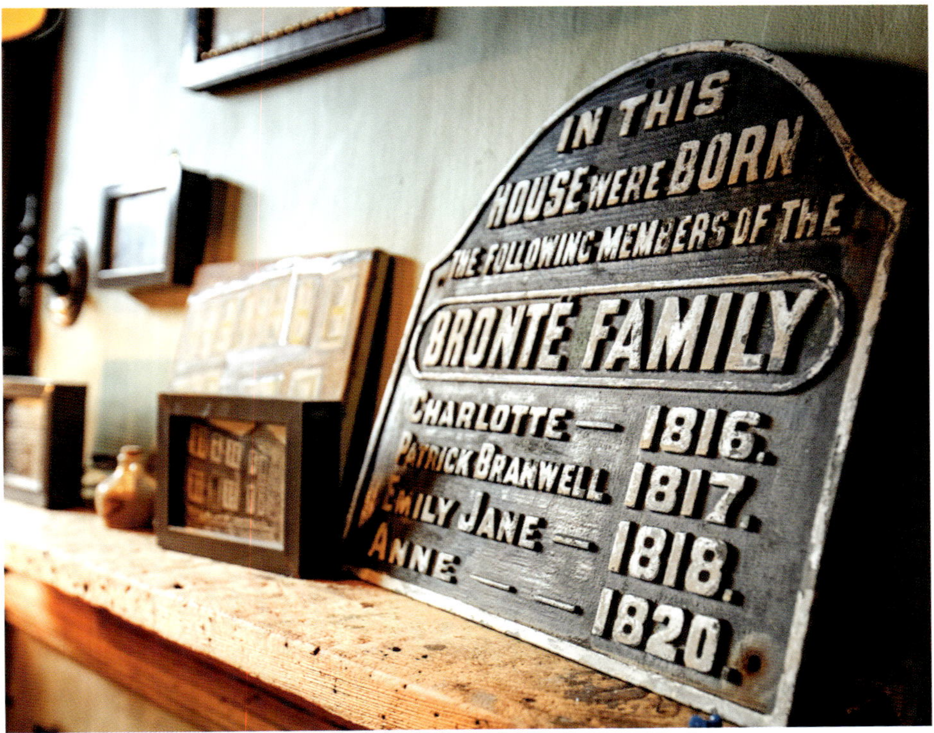

The original plaque commemorating the birth years of Charlotte, Branwell, Emily and Anne at the Thornton Birthplace.

Kipping House

It is clear by now that during the Brontë family's time in Thornton that nearby Kipping House and more especially the Firth family who lived there played an important part of their social lives. The Firths were without doubt in the upper echelons of Thornton society, which must have appeared genteel to Patrick in comparison to the harder circumstances faced at Hartshead. Having emerged from humble beginnings, he had gathered a good circle of influential friends in Yorkshire.

The wealthy recently widowed but quickly remarried John Firth was a staunch supporter of the Anglican Church, who, along with his teenage daughter Elizabeth, made the Brontë family very welcome at their comfortable and elegant home at Kipping House. We can see just in terms of the Brontë christenings so far in Thornton that either the Firths or their extended family were asked to be godparents, such was the warmth of the friendships that had quickly emerged.

Patrick must have felt truly blessed in Thornton despite his initial appraisal of the parsonage and chapel, for here he had a young thriving family, good friends and the Napoleonic Wars, during which France tried to dominate Europe, were finally over after victory at the Battle of Waterloo on 18 June 1815, just less than a year before Charlotte was born. And finally, Patrick had a son.

Kipping House still survives to this day as a family home.

Let us leave the Firths for now and join the Brontës at the parsonage where preparations for the next literary genius to join the family are afoot.

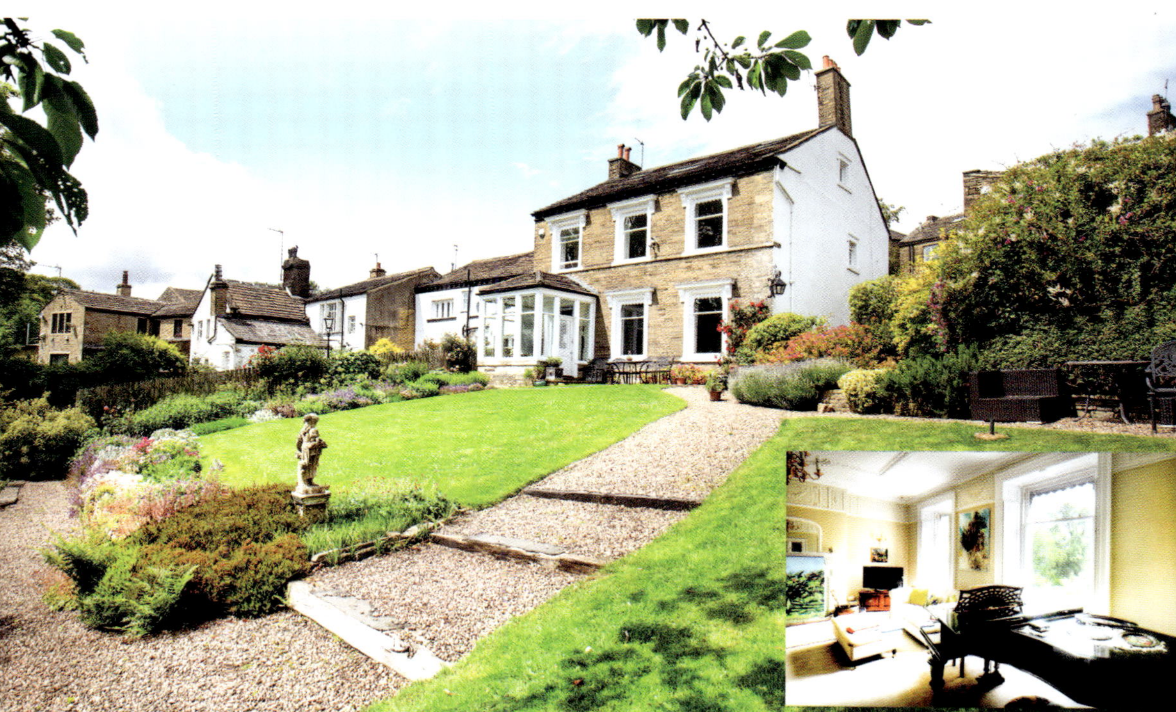

Kipping House (Many thanks to Sarah Dixon for allowing my photographs of her splendid home to be used)

Emily Jane Brontë

'He's more myself than I am. Whatever our souls are made of, his and mine are the same.

Emily Brontë, Wuthering Heights

With Branwell barely walking Patrick and Maria were to welcome the birth of their fourth daughter, the inimitable Emily Jane, who was born just thirteen months after Branwell on Thursday 30 July 1818. The location, as with all the births in Thornton, was in the front parlour of the parsonage.

On 20 August, she was baptised at the old Bell Chapel by Patrick's old friend Revd William Morgan of Christ Church. William's wife, Jane, was a god parent along with her parents John and Jane Fennell, who, as we know, were Maria's aunt and uncle.

Emily was the only daughter of the family to have been given a middle name and given that two of her godparents were called Jane, it's fair to presume her middle name was given in Maria's aunt and cousin's honour.

In the same year Emily was born the Duke of Wellington withdrew the last of his troops from France at the end of November, thus ending the allied occupation.

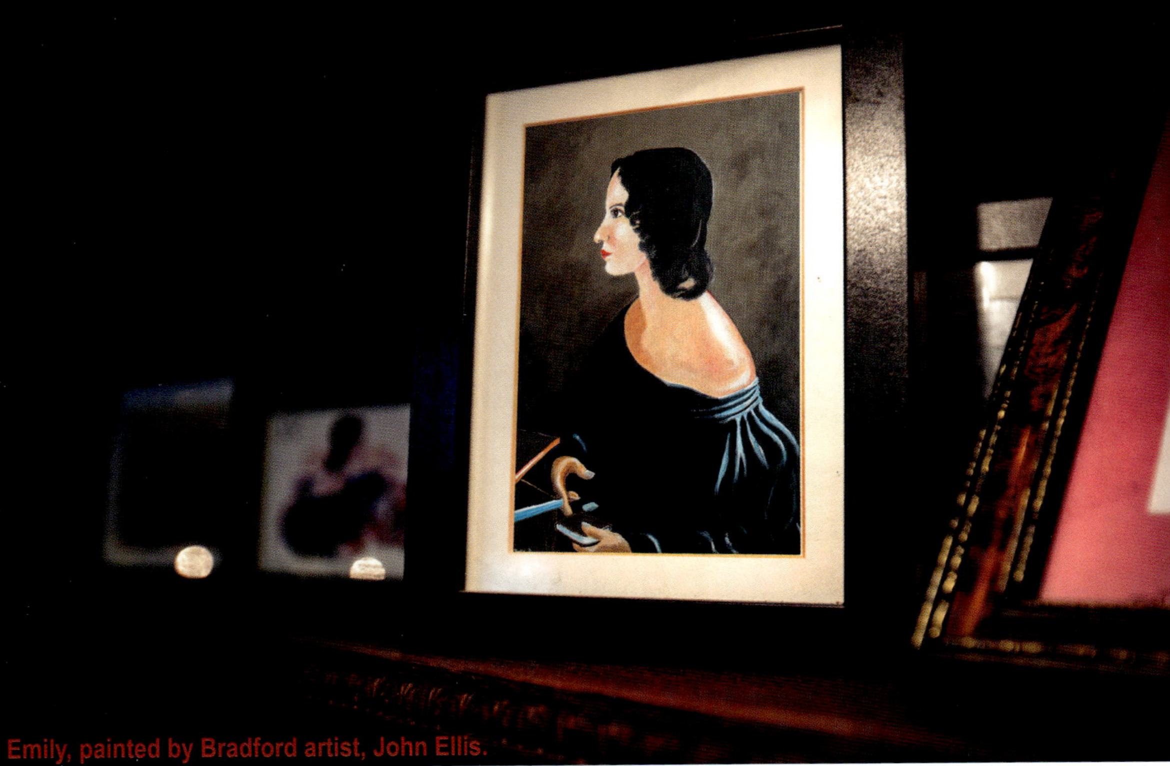

Emily Jane, painted by Bradford artist John Ellis.

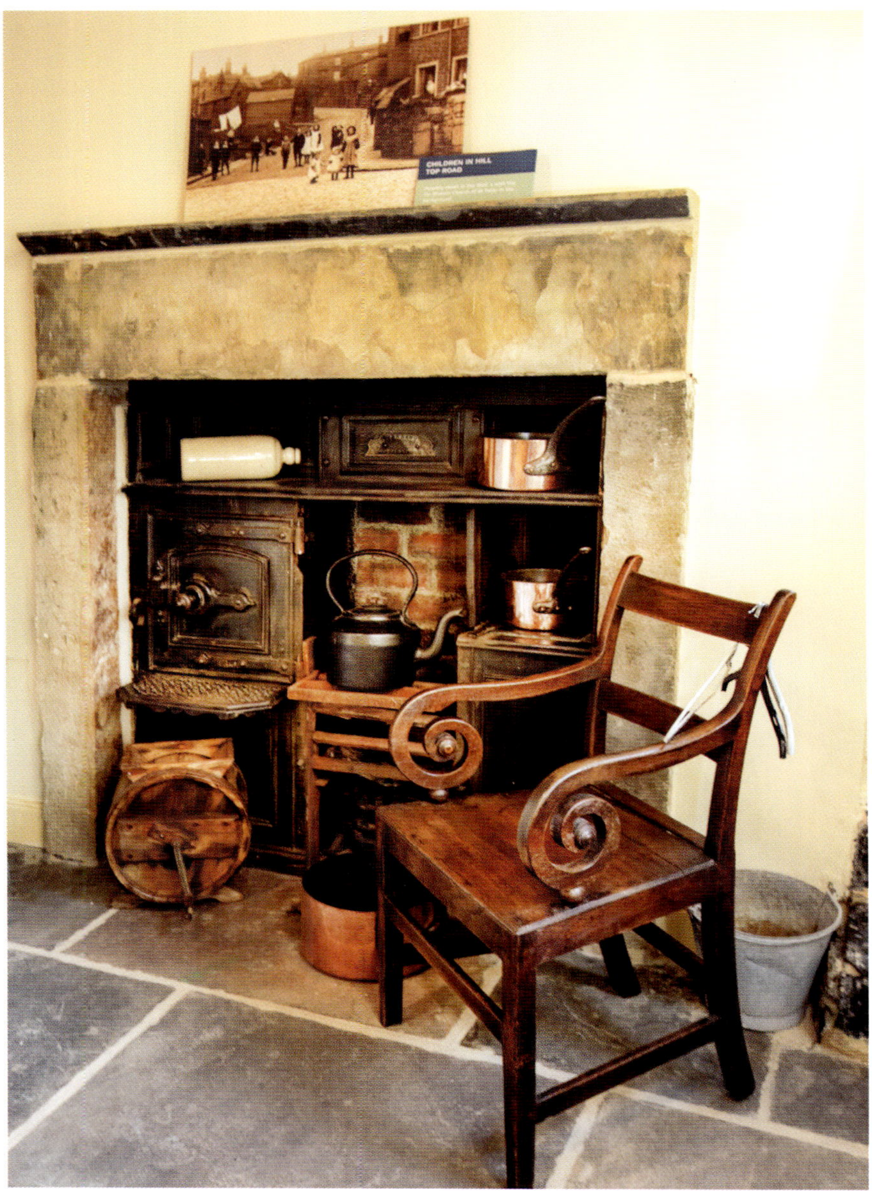

The restored range at the Birthplace. The range was sourced from an old public house in Huddersfield.

Patrick and Maria had been incredibly busy producing five children in just over four years. The raising and management of so many young children at the parsonage must have been chaotic and overwhelming. With that in mind changes were made; Nancy De Garrs, who would have been fifteen years old in 1818, and had up until now been the sole carer of the children, was given a promotion to cook and housekeeper. Her younger sister Sarah took on the role of nursemaid.

Thornton Hall

The ancient Thornton Hall nestles mostly hidden away by trees and foliage behind the old Bell Chapel. In the sixteenth century it was owned by Sir Richard Tempest, one of Henry VIII's knights, and by 1620 the owner was William Illingworth, a miller. In the nineteenth century after the Brontës had long gone it was in the ownership of John Foster, of Black Dyke mills, a textile manufacturer who extensively renovated the property including installing a carved fire surround for the hall. Going back to 1822, it is noted that the hall was divided with the church clerk and sexton living in one section.

When the Brontës left Thornton, Charlotte would have been just four years old. And although it is said that she and her siblings used to play in the extensive grounds, it is difficult to believe the claims from 2011 when it was listed for sale that she used Thornton Hall as the model for 'Thornfield' in her novel *Jane Eyre*. This is especially so when North Lees Hall in Hathersage and Norton Conyers near Ripon are better considered contenders.

Thornton Hall, nevertheless, is without doubt a property of historical interest; Patrick would have passed it accessing the now bricked-up walled gate to arrive at the old Bell Chapel every day he attended the church. And it boasts not one but three secret passageways under the property, one of which leads to the rear of the Bell Chapel.

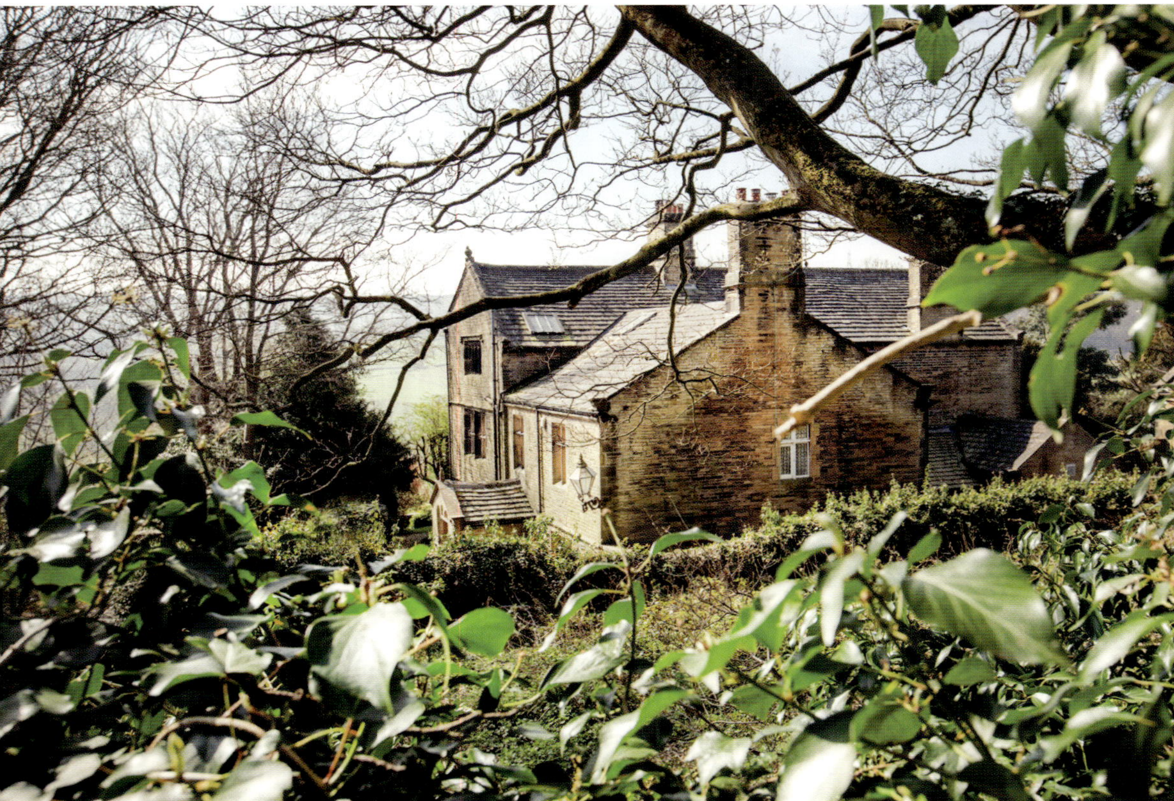

Historic Thornton Hall.

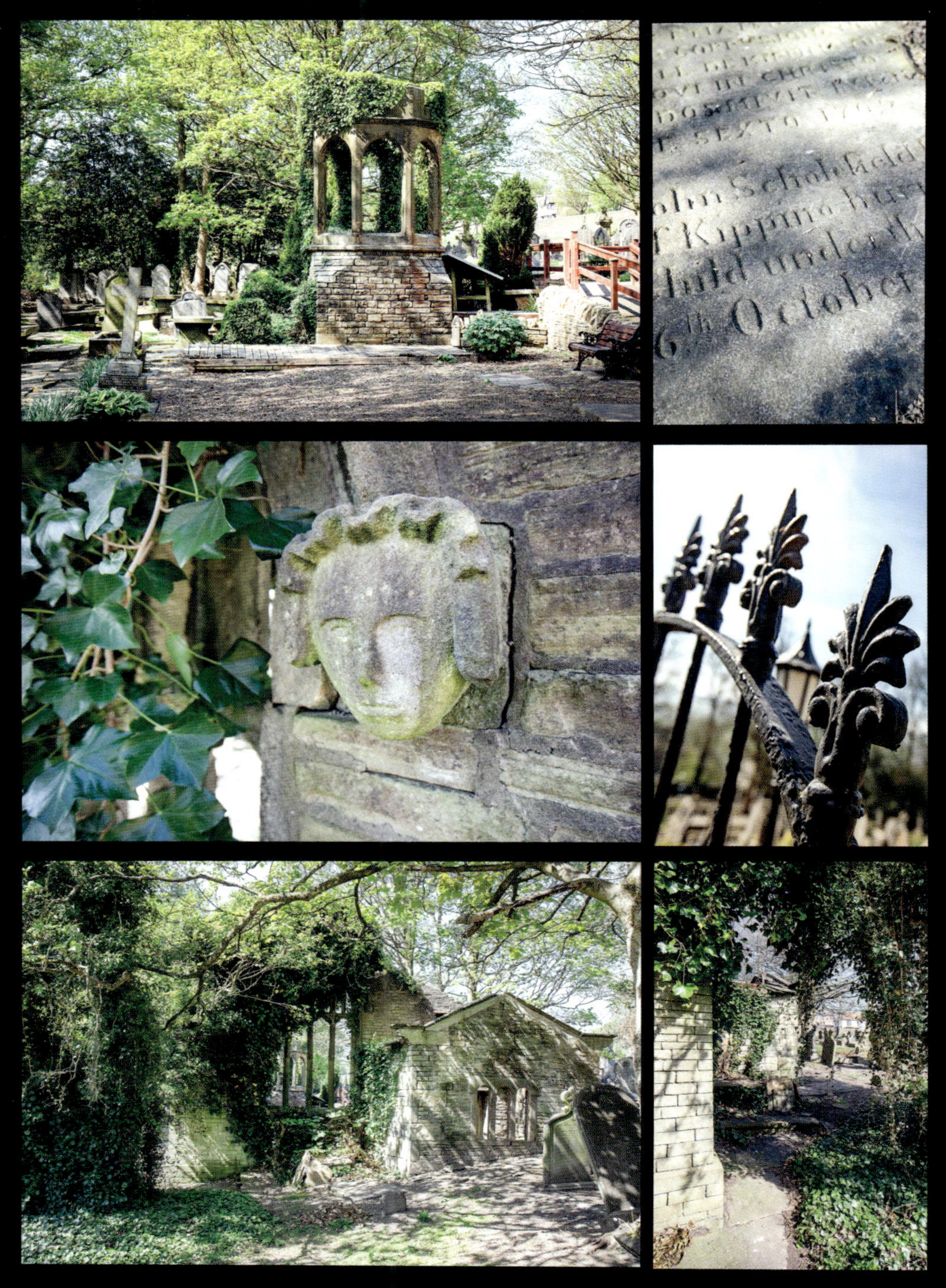

The old Bell Chapel ruins photographed in spring 2025.

Renovation and Restoration

In the autumn of 1818, Patrick finally initiated the long-overdue renovation of the old Bell Chapel. The gallery at the east end had become dangerously unsafe and had been closed. For many years this area had been used by the choir and instrumentalists, who provided the church music as the chapel was without an organ. The church records at the time show that there were two treble violins, one tenor violin and a violoncello, plus about half a dozen manuscript music books. Plans to make the building less austere included installing a cupola (a bell tower) and to rebuild the south wall incorporating six new large windows. In addition, the roof was completely restored and the interior refurbished. Elizabeth Firth assisted with the refurbishments of the books.

On completion of the work a painted headboard memorialised the transformation with the words, 'This chapel was repaired and Beautified AD1818. Rev P. Brontë BA Minister.'

Fifty years after Patrick's departure the chapel fell into disrepair after the new and more spacious St James' Church, situated opposite, was opened in 1872 to accommodate the growing population. Abandoned to the elements, nature reclaimed the former place of worship and over time all that was to remain was one wall and the original cupola, which was later rebuilt at ground level as a lasting monument. The ruins today remain, holding their ground as a testament to the little chapel's historical importance from a time best remembered by the occupants of the cemetery of that era.

In 2000 an action group of volunteers was created to preserve the ruins; the team meet weekly to carry out routine maintenance of the cemetery in addition to other tasks.

Below is an artistic interpretation of how the chapel would have looked at the time of the Brontës. Near Robin Hoods Bay at Fylingdales stands old St Stephen's Church, which remains complete and very closely replicates the Bell Chapel internally and externally. Inside are painted box pews and a full-length gallery to the left of the centrally placed three-decker pulpit.

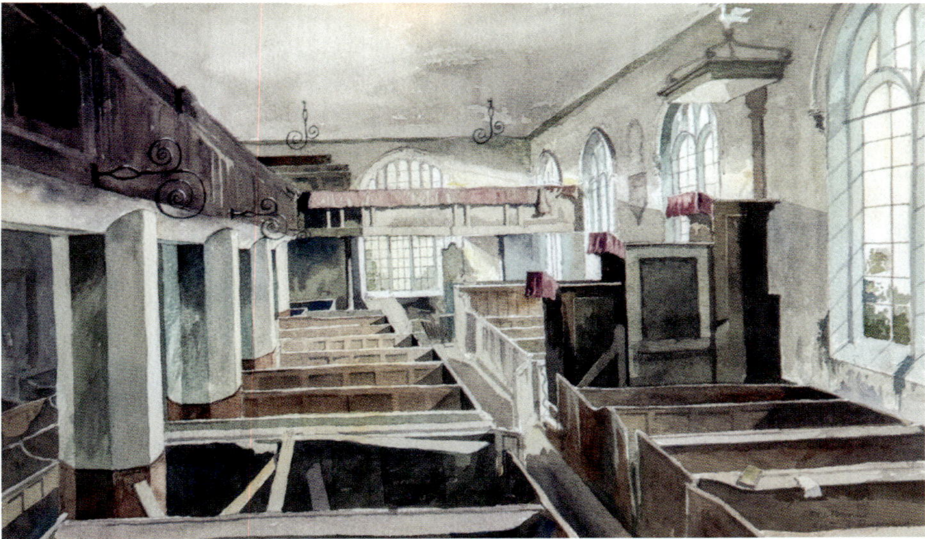

An artistic interpretation of how the chapel would have appeared during the time Patrick Brontë was the minister. (Image courtesy of Hazel Kenningham, whose son Andrew sadly passed away on the very day Queen Camilla visited Thornton in 2025)

One event that was to be remembered in Thornton long after Patrick's removal to Haworth occurred in March 1819 and gives us an insight into Patrick's pastoral care of his parishioners.

Confirmations were taking place at St Peter's parish church in Bradford (now known as the cathedral), close to Christ Church. Patrick led a party of sixty young candidates on the 4-mile walk from Thornton.

As they arrived on Kirkgate, which is one of Bradford's oldest thoroughfares, the weather deteriorated to the point of snowing and anticipating the hardship the weather would bring, Patrick quickly ordered and paid for hot meals to be ready at the conclusion of the confirmations at the Talbot Hotel. This allowed sustenance and shelter for the youngsters before commencing the journey home.

The Talbot would in time be frequented by Branwell when he lived in nearby Fountain Street working as a portrait painter.

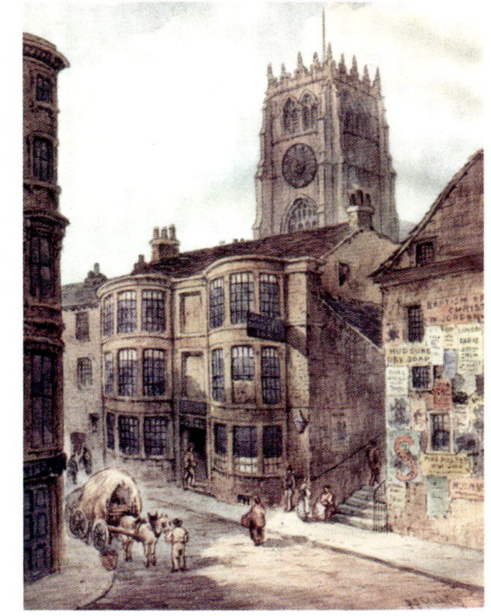

Right: A view of Bradford in the early nineteenth century taking in the parish church and step.

Below: The Talbot Hotel, drawn by Bradford, historian Thomas Thornton Empsall (1824–96).

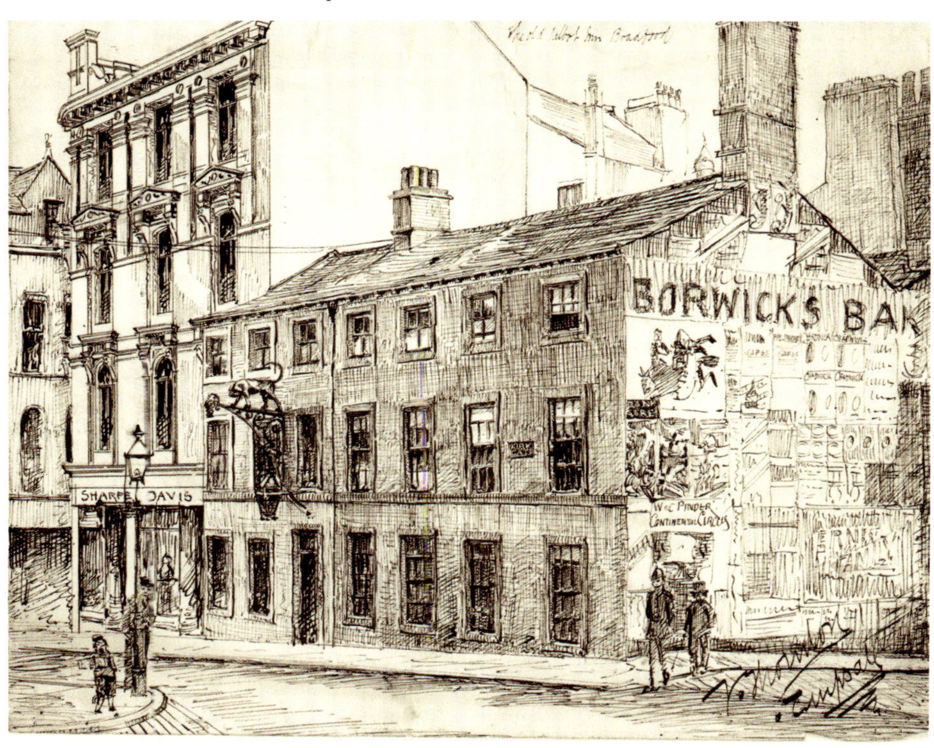

Anne Brontë

'But he who dares not grasp the thorn, should never crave the rose.'

Anne Brontë

As the dawn of the new decade emerged on Monday 17 January 1820 the family welcomed the arrival of Anne, their fifth daughter and the last of the six children to bless the family. Born just seventeen months after Emily, as always Maria had only enjoyed a short respite in between being perpetually pregnant. Giving birth to six children in six years is quite an achievement by anyone's standards. The day Anne entered the world her siblings spent the day at Kipping House with the Firth family.

On 29 January, King George III passed away at Windsor Castle following a reign of nearly sixty years commencing on 25 October 1760. He was, at the time of his death, the longest-reigning British monarch and the only sovereign the Brontë family had known at that point.

Anne's baptism took place once again at the old Bell Chapel on 25 March, with Revd Morgan officiating. Elizabeth Firth and Fanny Outhwaite were asked to be godparents. The day was later celebrated at Kipping House, with the party enjoying afternoon tea. Fanny was an old school friend of Elizabeth's at the exclusive Crofton Hall School that they jointly attended, near Wakefield. They had become best friends and thus she was a regular visitor to Kipping House and in turn became friendly with the Brontë family.

The year 1820 was to be a memorable year because it would be the last full year they would experience as a complete family.

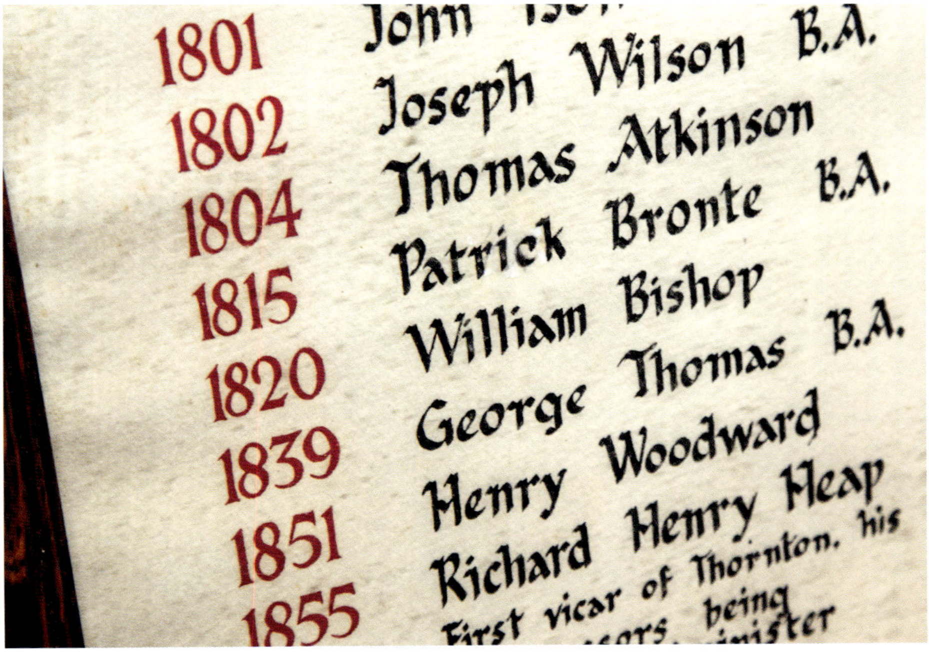

The list of ministers for Thornton, showing Patrick Brontë's tenure.

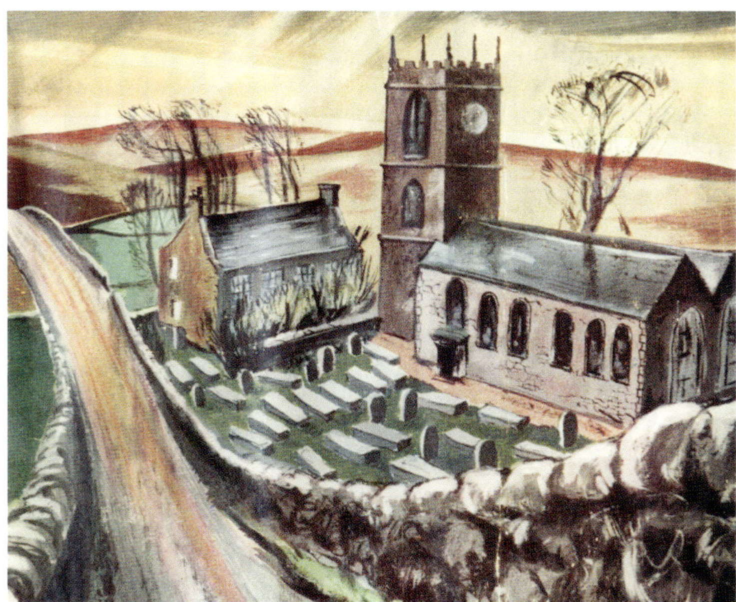

Haworth as depicted on the front cover of Ernest Raymond's book *In the Steps of the Brontës*, first published in 1948, the centenary year of Emily and Branwell's deaths.

Prior to Anne's birth back in 1819, news had arrived that Revd James Charnock, the long-term incumbent at nearby Haworth, had passed away, leaving a vacancy. The Revd Henry Heap, Vicar of Bradford, in May 1819 wrote to Patrick with a view to nominating him for the perpetual curacy, to which he was both surprised and delighted to be offered the position. The obvious benefits were a larger house with a garden which was much closer to the church. There was also a bigger stipend than his current £140 per year and an increased Anglican evangelical congregation. The nomination was supported by Michael Stocks, who was a well-respected magistrate and wrote to the Haworth Church Trustees recommending his appointment. You would imagine it would be plain sailing from this point.

However, unbeknown to Patrick at that time the Haworth Church Land Trustees, who had the responsibility for paying the curate's salary, also had the sole right to choose their own minister, awarded to them by royal charter since Elizabethan times. There was, however, a clause that if their choice of minister was debarred, they then had the right to withhold the minister's wages and distribute the funds to the poor or any other good charitable use.

The good Revd Brontë, unfortunately, was not the choice of the trustees. Patrick, however, had an ally living within his parish at Allerton Hall in Mercy Kaye, the wife of Benjamin Kaye. She was related to Stephen Taylor, who lived at the Manor House in Stanbury and was one of the trustees of Haworth church. Patrick visited Stephen at Stanbury to discuss the possibility of a resolution being found. At a meeting in Haworth with Mr Taylor and other trustees, he learned that opposition to his appointment stemmed from Revd Heap's unilateral decision to appoint him, not from any personal issue with Patrick. The trustees would not approve the nomination without their consent being given previously. Several months of wrangling could not render the situation resolved in his favour. Interestingly, when Stephen Taylor passed away years later in 1831, his burial service was conducted by Patrick on 26 December at Haworth. His wife, Mary, who died in 1855, was laid to rest just three days after Charlotte on 7 April.

Realising the impossibility of the situation, Revd Brontë informed Revd Heap that he intended to resign from the nomination. Revd Heap was not deterred and told Patrick that to withdraw would incur the displeasure of the archbishop, at the risk of his wages being withheld until the matter was determined. The situation appeared to be without any viable solution.

After his withdrawal letter the trustees offered Patrick an 'audition sermon' at Haworth, to which he politely declined and in essence said, 'you are more than welcome to call at the chapel in Thornton any Sunday unannounced and make your own judgement'.

The summer of 1819 was a period of discontent in Thornton given the recent spate of bad harvests and industrial depression and so Patrick devoted himself to the pastoral care of his parishioners – a wise move given what would ensue. The following month's services at Haworth were covered by several local clergy. Later the Archbishop of York wrote to Patrick on 8 October requesting he take the service at Haworth the following Sunday. Patrick felt the need to inform the trustees via a letter to Stephen Taylor of the situation so as not to exacerbate the resistance he had previously encountered. The service must have been problematic as Patrick's resignation from the living of Haworth was finally accepted by Henry Heap on 21 October.

The series of events that were to transpire at Haworth after Patrick's withdrawal are so bizarre and hilarious that they are worth recounting. The Vicar of Bradford, Henry Heap, was defiant in refusing to be undermined by the trustees and decided to once again choose his own man and nominated Revd Samuel Redhead to the living at Haworth. On 31 October, Redhead arrived in Haworth where he proceeded to walk up Main Street accompanied by lay churchman Mr Rand. En route they were jointly jostled and jeered at by the crowd all the way to the church, and the service was nothing short of a chaotic disaster. Just as Revd Redhead rose to speak in the pulpit the whole congregation stomped their clogs and exited the building, leaving the minister and Mr Rand alone to conclude the service. A week later the locals upped their game; the abusive behaviour continued as they made their way up to the church, and shockingly when the service commenced a man rode backwards on a donkey with hats stacked on its head down the aisle to the laughter and amusement of the congregation, drowning out the voice of Revd Redhead! On attempting to read the second lesson the clog-stamping congregation took their leave from the church.

The last occasion that Revd Redhead tried to win over Haworth ended very badly. The now familiar scene of abusive entrance and disorder was made worse by a drunken chimney sweep dancing down the aisle at the church trying to hug Revd Redhead in the pulpit. The service was once again abandoned and the church doors locked. The crowds, still hungry for more games, were gathered in the churchyard and Mr Rand and Redhead had to take emergency refuge at the Black Bull Inn until safe passage out of Haworth could be ensured. It was clear by now that Revd Redhead was fighting a losing battle at Haworth and after a meeting with the archbishop he resigned.

Once again on 17 November, Patrick was assigned duties at Haworth officiating over two funerals and later a baptism and a wedding.

A resolution was finally reached with Patrick Brontë becoming the nominated next incumbent of Haworth, and so on 25 February 1820, he was officially licensed by the Vicar of Bradford with the support of the trustees on the provision that he resign his living at Thornton.

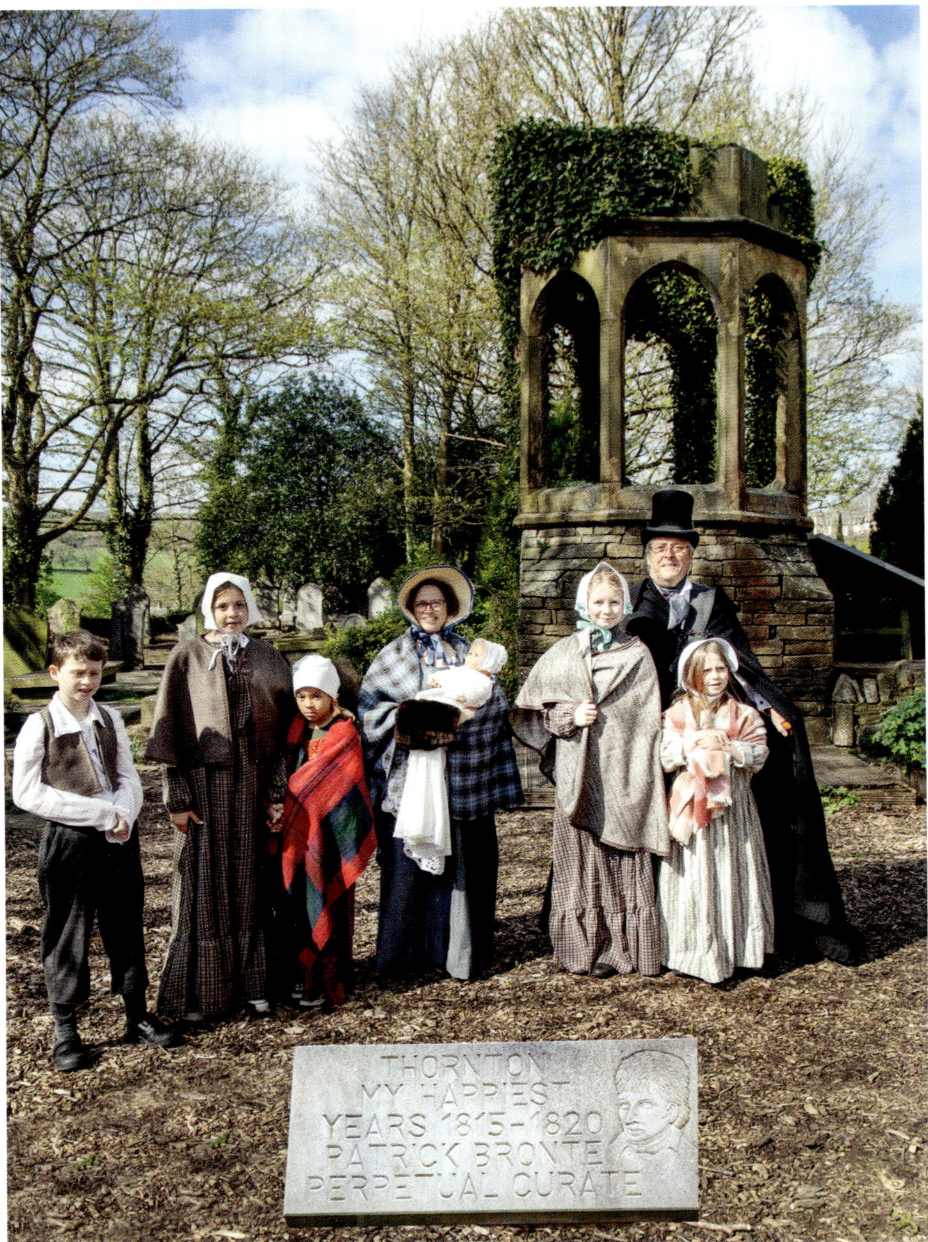

On 20 April 2025, the family's poignant journey to Haworth was re-enacted 205 years after their departure from Thornton.

Patrick continued his ministry at Thornton until well into April 1820. It is highly likely that during that time he visited Haworth to take some services, both as required and probably if only to be confident in himself that finally the parishioners at the village were accepting him as their new incumbent.

On 10 April, Patrick took his last funeral service at the old Bell Chapel. Although a precise day cannot be placed, we do know that between the 10th and 20th of the same month all the family possessions were packed and loaded onto a number of flat wagons, two of which were sent over by his now friend Stephen Taylor, the Haworth Church Trustee from Stanbury.

Revd Patrick Brontë, his wife Maria and their children, accompanied by two maids and all their worldly goods, then took the 6-mile journey over moorland roads to their new and forever home at Haworth. Just in time to celebrate Charlotte's fourth birthday on the 21st.

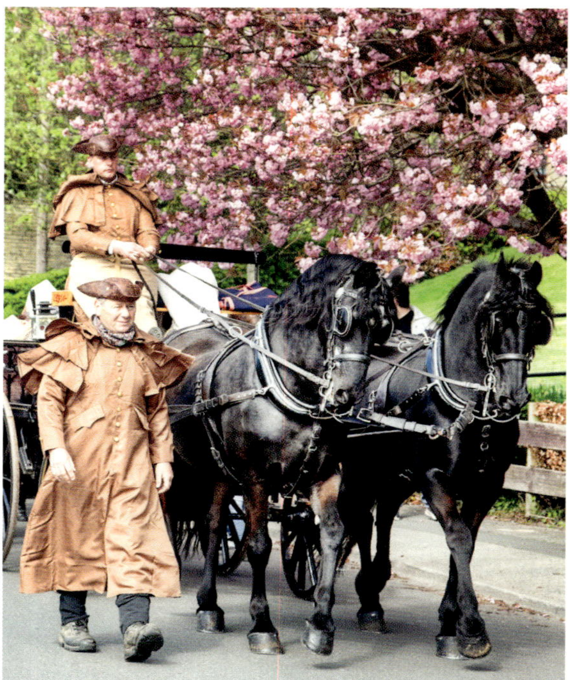

Left and below: In the re-enactment, Patrick is portrayed by Steven Stanworth, and Maria by Kate Hames. The Brontë children were played by excited locals who thoroughly enjoyed the historic event.

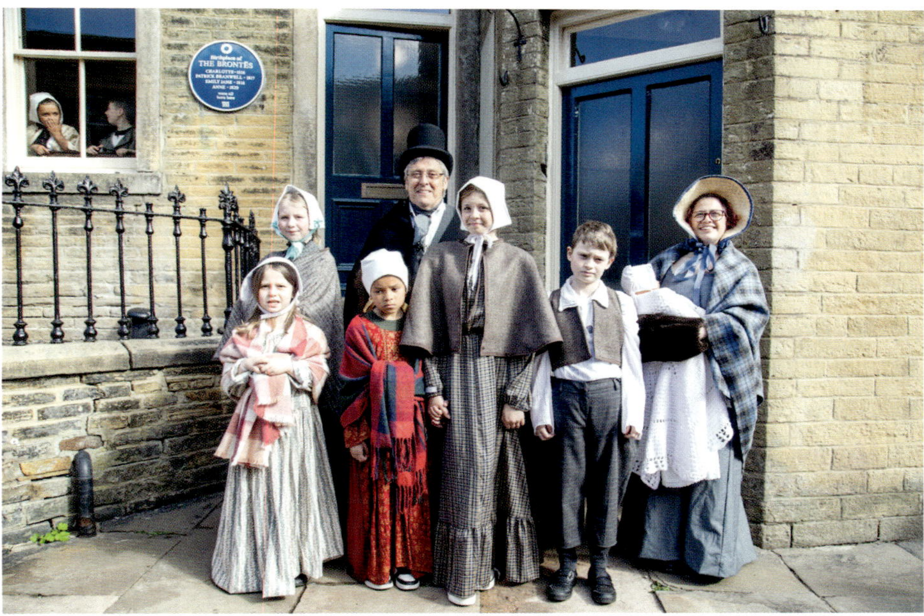

The 'Birthplace of Dreams' that had given those young children their first fertile seeds of literary genius would go on to flourish, garnering a worldwide adoration of their work. The happy home with six children and with all the hustle and bustle that goes with it sadly lacked the space required for a growing family. The reader must, as I the writer, can't help but feel a real sense of sadness knowing what tragedies would soon fall upon the family.

Things would never be the same after Thornton. Is it any wonder that Patrick, in old age with his family decimated, recounted his time there as: 'Thornton, my happiest years.'

Right: The entrance hall at the Birthplace.

Below: Local children at the Birthplace on the day of the re-enactment.

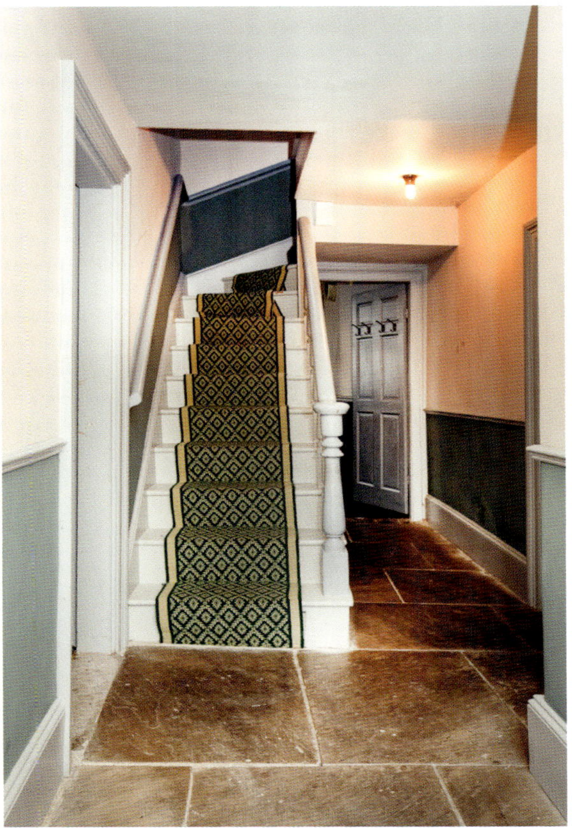

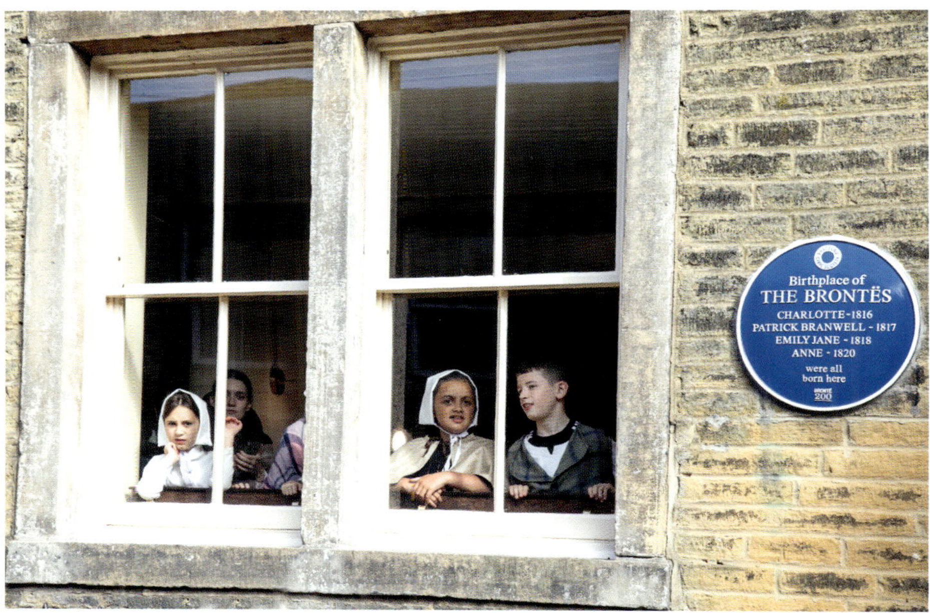

Elizabeth Firth, knowing she would be away from the village visiting Malton and Scarborough with her father when the Brontë family planned to move, said her goodbyes at the parsonage on Market Street on 5 April.

As recorded in Elizabeth's diary, Patrick would stay overnight at Kipping House several times over the following months as a breaking point for the journey when walking to attend meetings in Bradford. On 8 September Elizabeth and her father, John, were invited to dinner at the new home at the parsonage in Haworth.

Sadly, at the beginning of December John Scholefield Firth's health deteriorated to the point that Patrick attended Kipping House on 13 and 21 December as he declined further, both in the hand of friendship and to offer pastoral care. Elizabeth noted at the time that by God's blessing and Mr Brontë's words her father became happier.

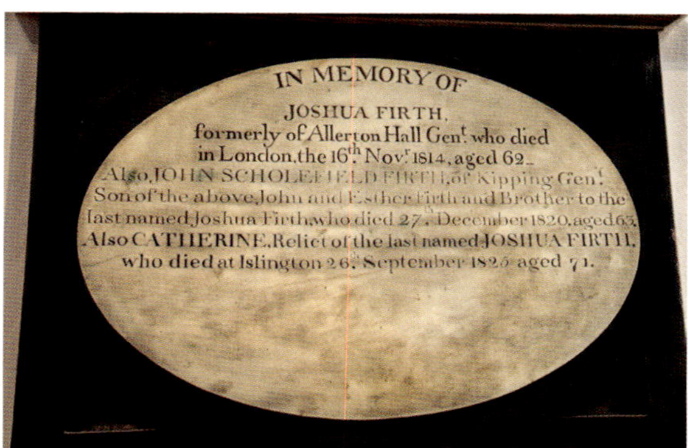

There, however, was to be no miracle recovery, as John passed away two days after Christmas day. Patrick officiated over his friend's funeral on 2 January 1821, at the old Bell Chapel.

Left: The Firth memorial can be found at St James' Church, opposite the Bell Chapel ruins where it was originally mounted.

Below: An artistic impression of the Birthplace painted by Bradford artist John Ellis.

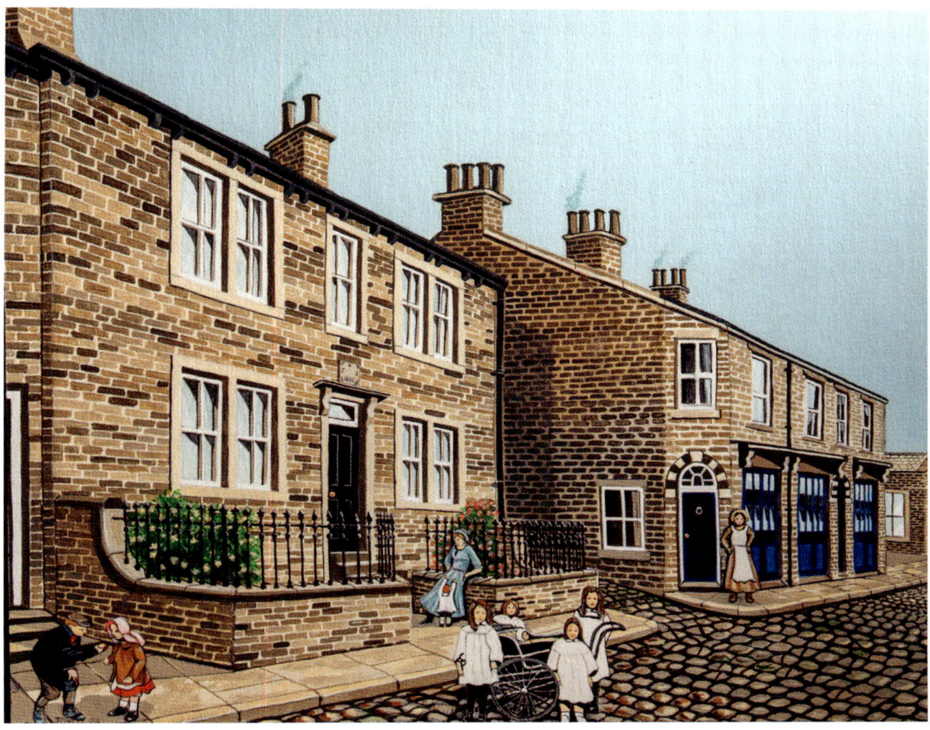

4

Haworth – Our Forever Home

So it came to be that the Brontë family arrived in Haworth, the village in which Patrick accepted the perpetual curacy of St Michael and All Angels' Church where he would serve his parishioners for forty-one years until his death in 1861.

They now had a larger house, a forever home the family could breathe in. They had space, where in time those young, curious and developing minds would write some of the finest nineteenth-century literature ever published.

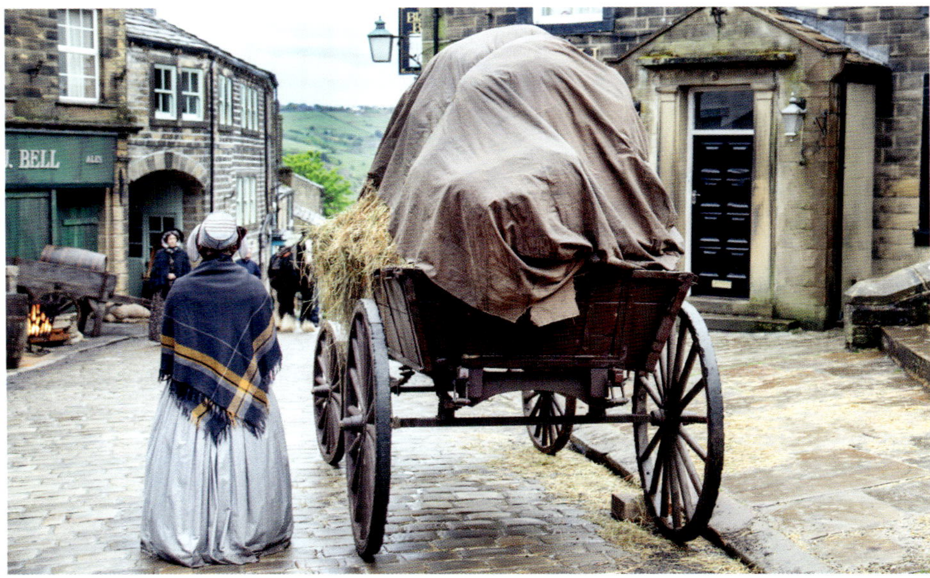

Here, the top of Haworth Main Street has been transformed to represent the village as the Brontë family knew it in the early 1840s, for the award-winning 2022 biographical drama film *Emily*. In the film Emily is played by Emma Mackey.

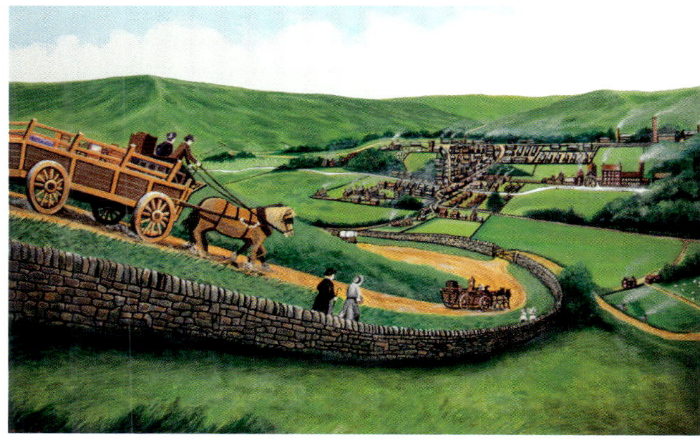

This painting is the work of Bradford artist John Ellis, a wonderful artistic interpretation of the family's first sight of Haworth, from the Brow, as they made their way from Thornton to their new home across the moors.

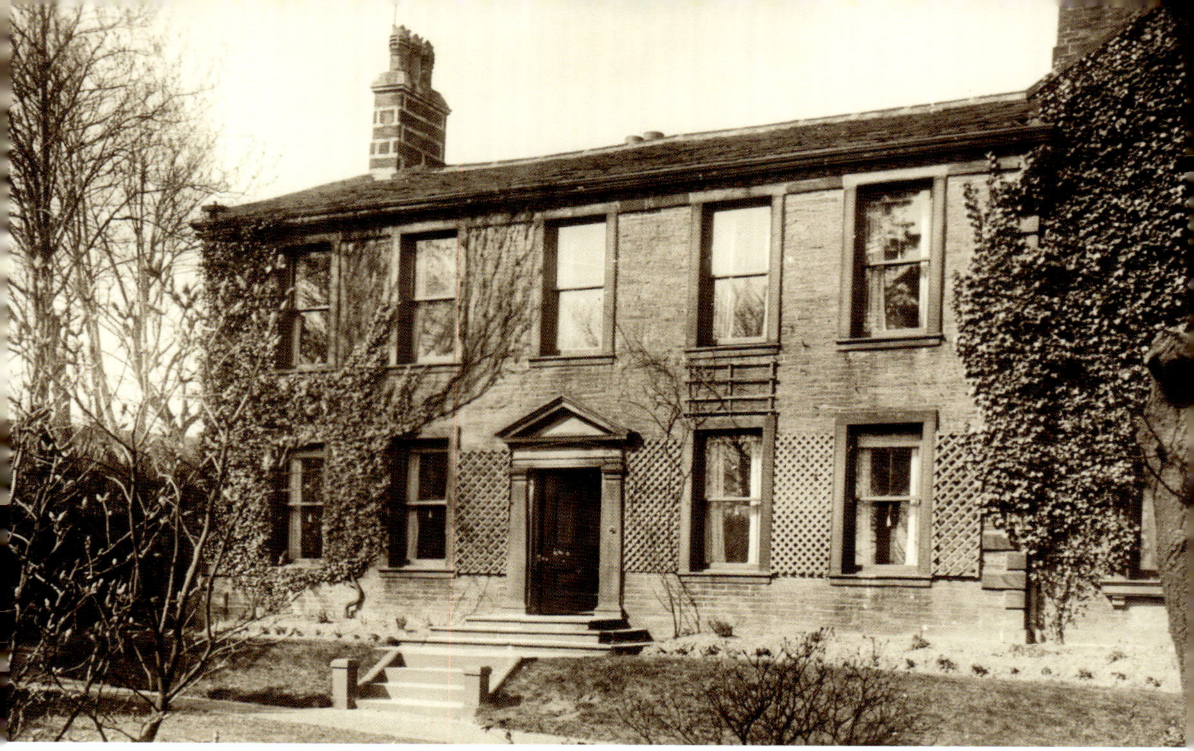

The parsonage was originally built for Revd John Richardson in 1778–79, who was the incumbent in Haworth from 1763 to 1791. The elegant, flat-fronted, late Georgian dignified house, built in local sandstone, was without doubt a suitable upgrade to the previous house at Thornton.

Boasting an impressive central entrance hall, it was flanked by two large accommodating front rooms with a kitchen and storeroom to the rear. Upstairs was equally as spacious; there were four bedrooms and a box room over the hall. In addition, there was a double-vaulted cellar and a small yard to the rear giving access to the all-important inspirational moor. To the front a high stone wall hugged the lawned front garden with flower beds at either side, a place where the children could play safely in comparison to the narrow alleyway at the side of their former home.

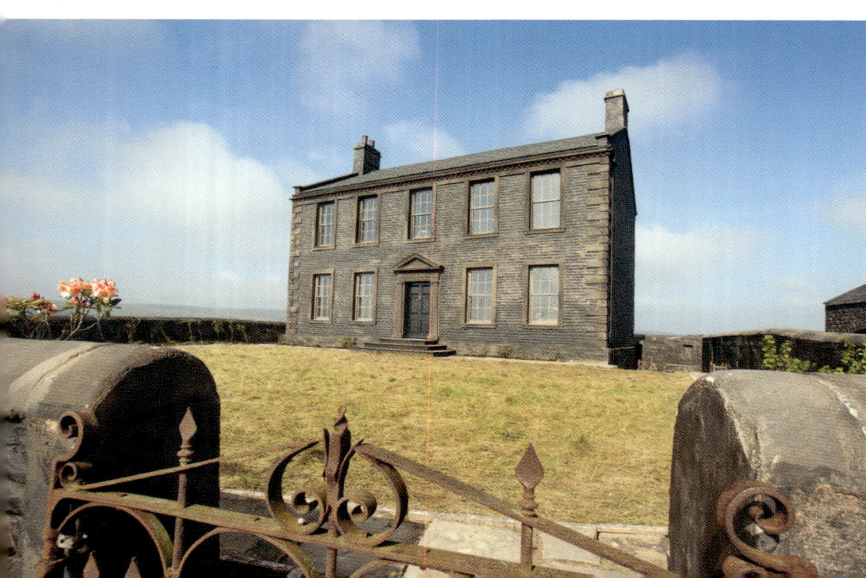

The temporary filmset in 2016 for Sally Wainright's *To Walk Invisible*, which depicts the parsonage as the Brontë family knew it in their period.

St Michael and All Angels' Church

The new incumbent wasted no time in getting to work with his ministerial duties; within days of arriving in April, he had performed three burials, four weddings and an equal number of baptisms.

The church footprint, although it is said dates to ancient times, had last been enlarged in 1755 to accommodate the large congregations that William Grimshaw attracted to the village. Grimshaw, who was firm friends with John Wesley, was the rector of Haworth from 1742 until his death from a fever in 1763. He was heavily involved in the Evangelical movement in that period and legend has it he was known as the 'flogging preacher', forcibly rounding up locals from the pubs and encouraging them to join his church services. He was known to preach up to thirty times a week. John Wesley wrote of him: 'A few such as him would make a nation tremble … he carries fire wherever he goes.' A stone font in the graveyard displays his name.

The church we know today was rebuilt by Patrick's successor Revd John Wade in 1879–81 and all that remains that the Brontë family would have known is the tower, although even that was raised to include a clock face. Wade also extended the parsonage, adding new north and west gabled wings.

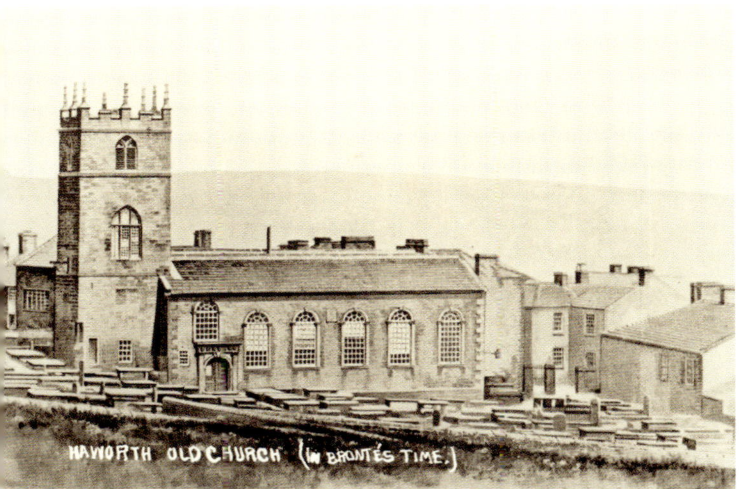

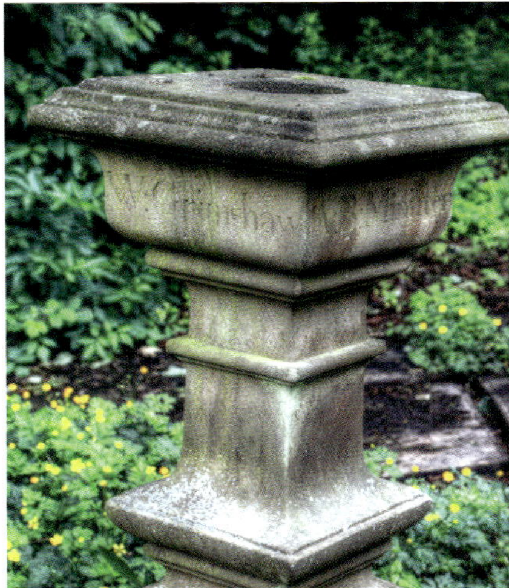

Above left: Haworth church as the Brontë family would have known it.

Above right: William Grimshaw's font in the graveyard.

Below left and below right: St Michael and All Angels' Church in more recent times.

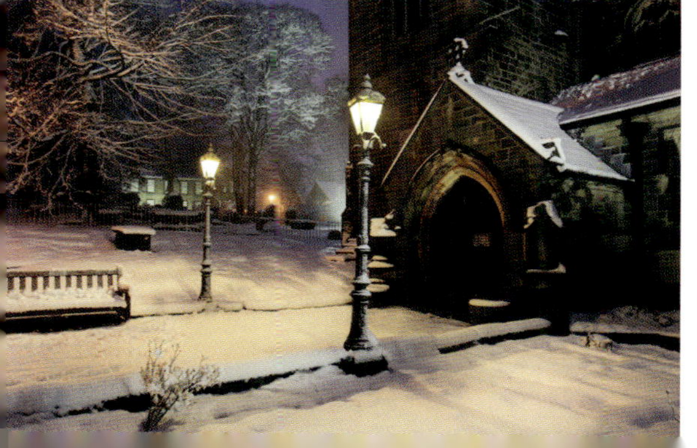

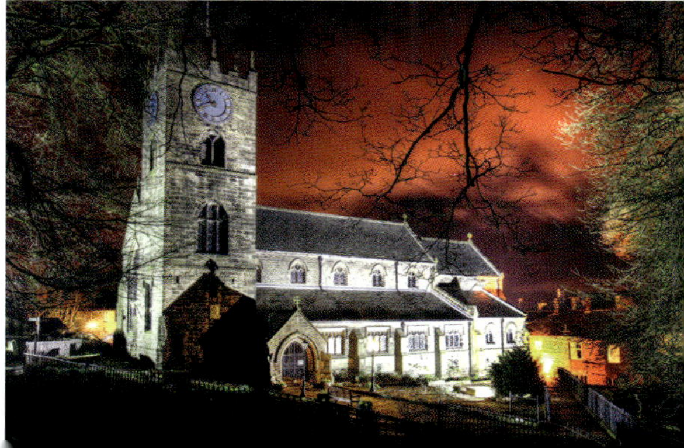

Haworth Village

In 1820, the village was expanding quite rapidly due to the ever-increasing rise in population as the Industrial Revolution gathered pace. With ten mills being placed locally by the River Worth, it's no surprise that more than a third of the inhabitants were gainfully employed in the textile industry. Many more worked from home, hand loom weaving or combing. There was also work in the quarries and in the agricultural sector. There were, in addition, a good number of tradesmen and professionals living in the area.

The parish of Haworth took in the surrounding villages of Stanbury, Oxenhope, Oakworth and Cullingworth, to which the conscientious Revd Brontë walked many miles back and forth tending his ever-growing flock. It is to his credit, as he was known to encourage baptisms, officiating over on average 290 of them per year.

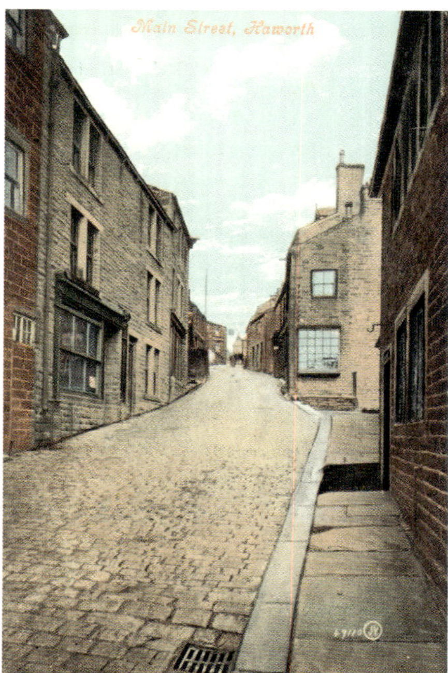

Left: Main Street, Haworth, in the early nineteenth century.

Below: This image shows the original Brontë Museum on the upper floor of the old Penny Bank (centre) where it was housed from 18 May 1895 until August 1928, after which it transferred to the old parsonage where it has remained to this day. The Brontë Society was first established in 1893.

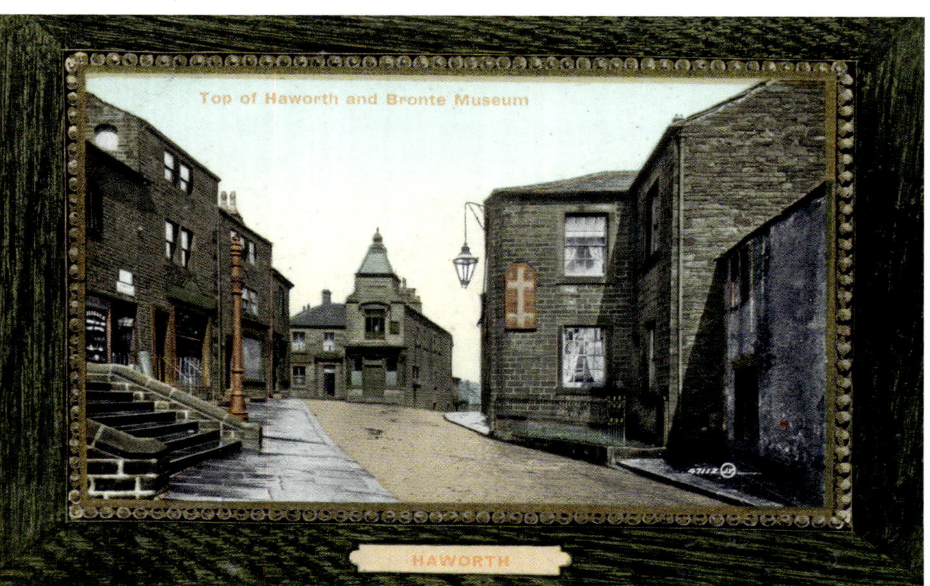

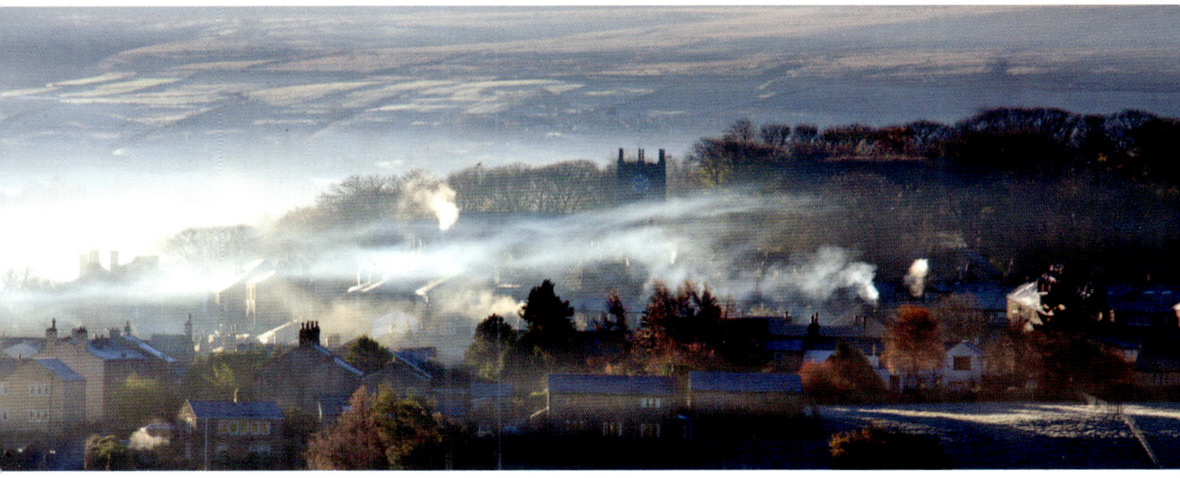

Haworth photographed on a cold, early winter's morning.

In early nineteenth-century Haworth there was a great deal of poverty, although saying that there was also evidence of prosperity. The very poorest working class often shared living space with other families in small back-to-back cottages or badly ventilated and damp basement dwellings. As you would imagine the general health of the population was abysmal, which was further exasperated by an inefficient water supply from the pumps or wells. Much of the water was contaminated by the overflow from the outhouse privies.

The mortality rate in the village was incredibly high and emulated the worst areas of the country in numbers. Families bringing ten children into the world could reasonably only expect five or six of them to live beyond infancy, which in turn brought the overall average age of death down to just twenty-five.

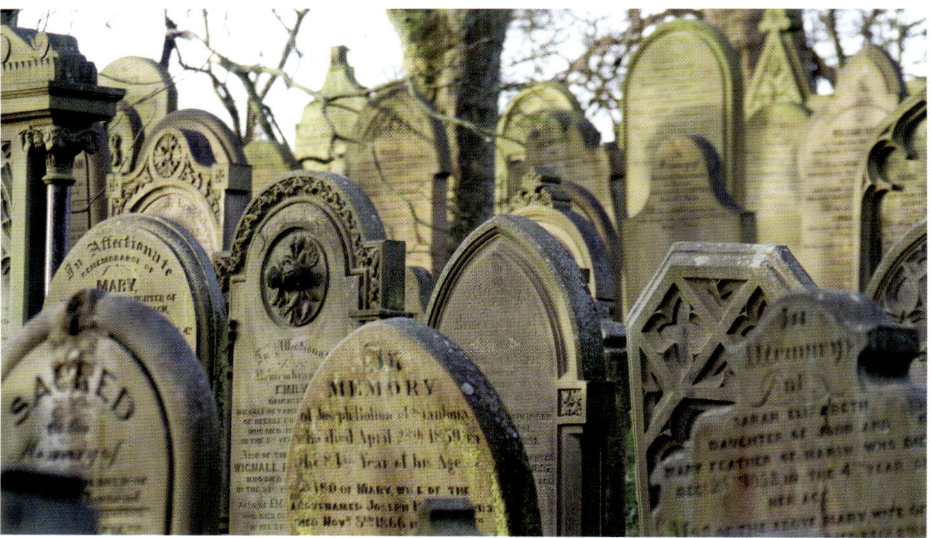

St Michael and All Angels' graveyard.

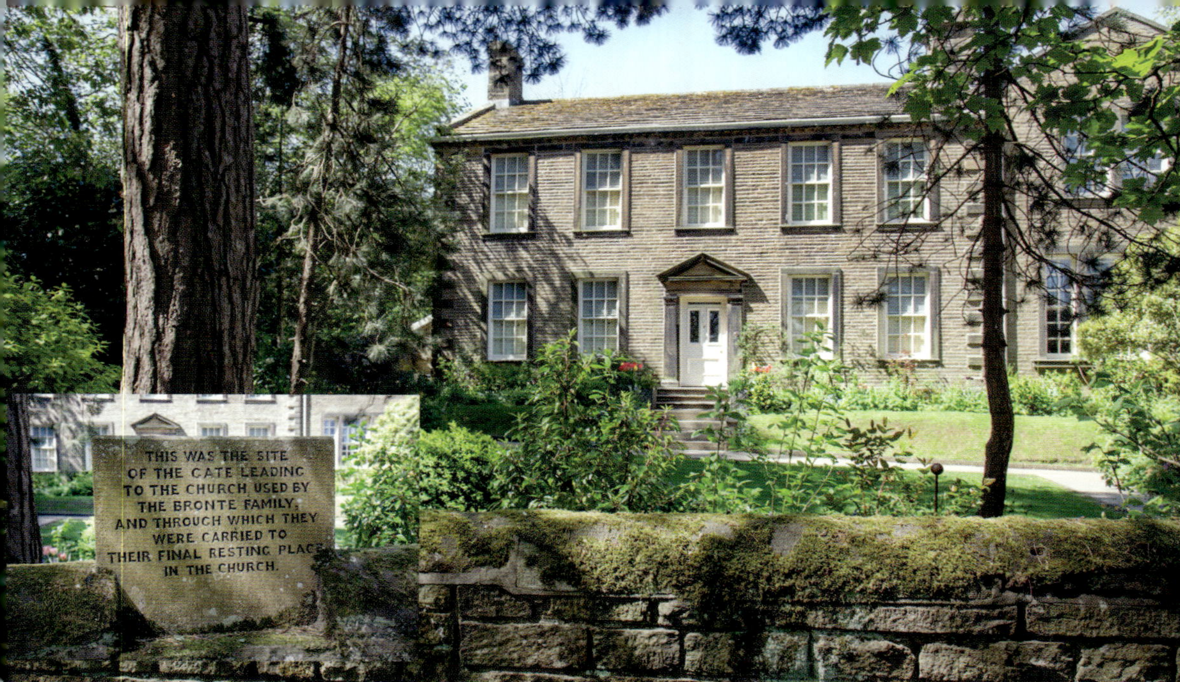

Haworth parsonage, spring 2025.

Despite the future looking bright for the family in their new home, it was sadly only a matter of months of their move to Haworth before tragic circumstances would befall them. On 29 January 1821, Maria senior collapsed with stomach pains at the parsonage. Patrick, sensing there was something seriously wrong, called in several doctors to examine her but alas not one of them offered any hope of recovery – all the opinions diagnosed cancer.

Maria had spent most of her married life producing six children in as many years. It must have been torturous for her as she clung onto life at the parsonage with the pain she was suffering. To be aware that she would not live to see her family grow must have been all-consuming, for the nurse had heard her cry out repeatedly 'Oh God my poor children – Oh God my poor children.' When she passed away on 15 September, less than eight months after her collapse, her youngest, Anne, was just twenty months old.

During her illness Patrick had taken on the night nursing himself but had employed a local woman to assist during the day so he could still carry out his duties. Through that dark, lonely period, he still performed 190 baptisms, sixty-two burials and twenty-one marriages. Upon Maria's sister, Elizabeth, returning from Penzance to help and supervise the nursing, the daily help was dismissed. Elizabeth Firth did much to assist; she visited Maria, twice in February, once in March, and later on 26 May, and she took the eldest children, Maria and Elizabeth, to stay with her at Kipping House for a month.

Maria's funeral took place on 22 September, with Patrick's old friend William Morgan of Christ Church performing the service, having married them only eight years previously. He too would have been locked in with the grief and terrible sadness the family felt. William Morgan would also suffer the loss of his wife, Jane, in 1827, but would remarry twice more in his lifetime.

Maria was laid to rest less than a hundred yards from her home under the old church flagstones, in a freshly opened vault that in time would house all but one of her children. None would exceed her thirty-eight years of age.

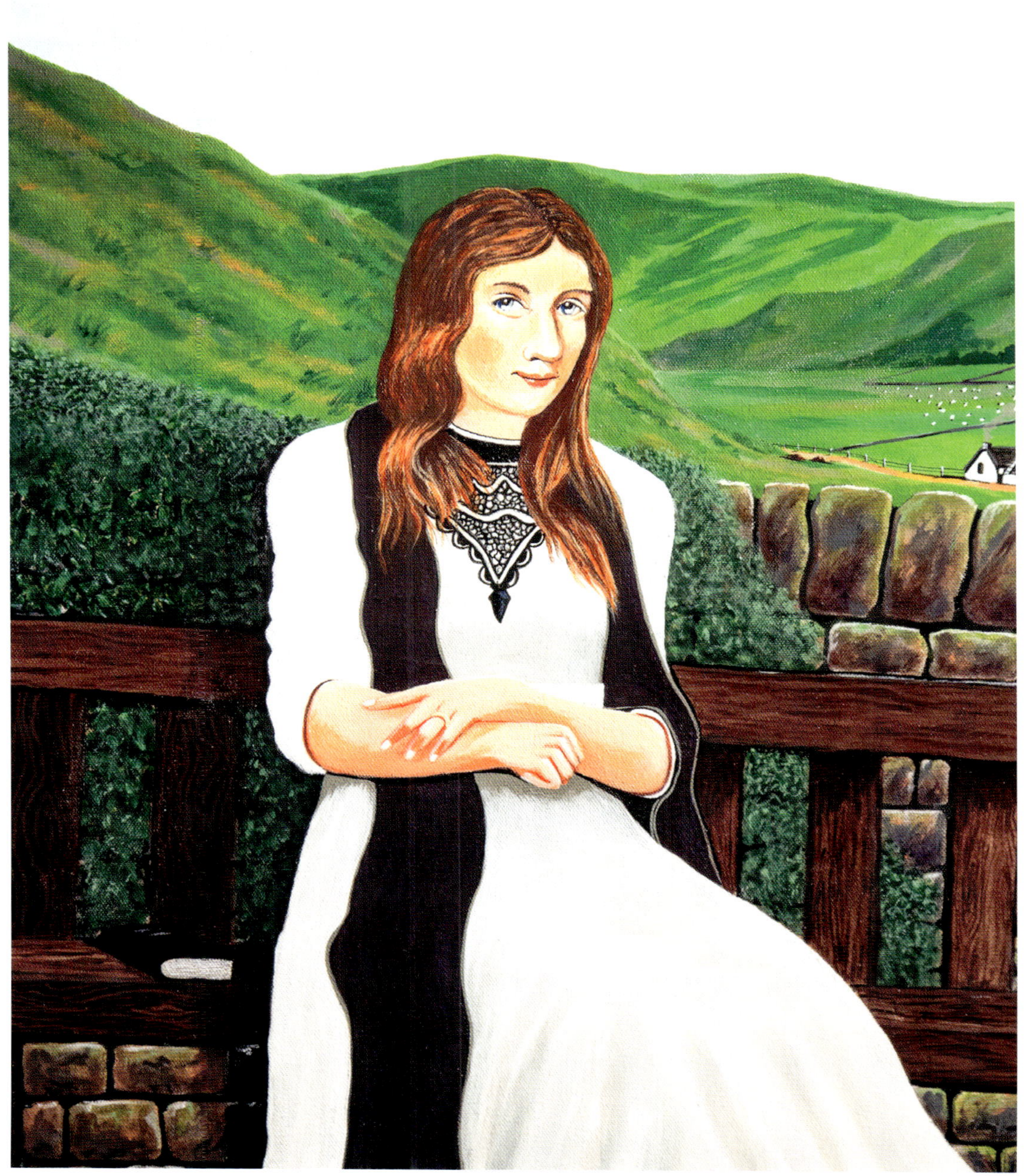

Maria Brontē (née Branwell) painted by Bradford artist John Ellis.

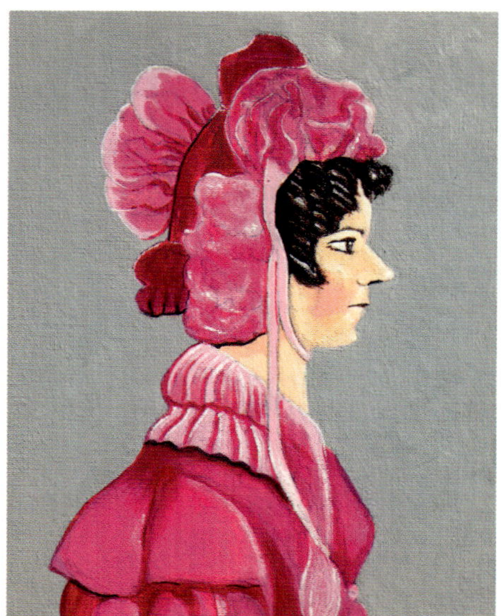

Elizabeth Firth, painted by Bradford artist John Ellis.

Patrick's previous salary at Thornton was £140. Add that to Maria's annuity of £50 per year and the family's joint income was £190. With Maria having passed away her allowance ended abruptly. Although Patrick's salary at Haworth then was £170 per annum, he was in effect £20 worse off than he was when in Thornton, and he had a larger house to manage. In addition, there had been unforeseen expenses incurred because of Maria's illness and he now found himself both grief-stricken and in significant debt. In the short term, he received financial assistance by way of one-off gifts and donations from friends and benefactors amounting to over £250, including two guineas from Elizabeth Firth, which would have been a very welcome lifeline at the time.

With not just financial worries to contend with there was furthermore the responsibility of how to provide care in the long term for his six young children, of which the eldest, Maria, was only seven years old when her mother died. Maria's sister Elizabeth Branwell had only arrived in Haworth as a temporary measure and was not expected to remain permanently.

That just left the young servants Nancy and Sarah, who were providing the motherly love and warmth the children would have been missing.

No longer the relatively young, handsome bachelor with the world at his feet, Patrick was now in his mid-forties and receiving a modest income in which to raise his motherless family. There was also little chance of imminent career advancement, added to which the village he lived in was quite literally a place to die for given its unenviable record of mortality. All in all, Patrick was not the greatest 'catch'.

Patrick was no quitter though. Unperturbed by his obvious position, he took matters into his own hands and went in search of a stepmother for the children, and if the surrogate mother had wealth, then so much the better.

On 8 December 1821, he visited Elizabeth Firth at Kipping House, who was to be his first choice. In fairness you can understand why; she was still single and at just twenty-four, was twenty years his junior, a good friend to the family, godmother to two of the children and now, following her father's death the previous year, a woman of considerable wealth. The additional benefit of her expertise to manage a house will not have escaped his thinking.

Having returned home to Haworth, Patrick wrote to her asking for her hand in marriage. She received the letter on the 12th and found the contents upsetting. No doubt the thought of devoting her life and financially supporting a poor clergyman and raising his six young children was an unacceptable proposition. After all Elizabeth, who was still relatively young, had prospects and she was not going to sacrifice them for Revd Brontë, for unbeknown to him she was being courted by the Vicar of Huddersfield, Revd James Franks, who was a much more eligible and attractive proposition. So much so that she married him on 21 September 1824.

In response to Patrick, she wrote him a letter on 14 December, the contents of which left Patrick in no doubt that he had been refused. Clearly the warm friendship that both parties had enjoyed so far had soured, for her entry in her diary that day simply said, 'I wrote my last letter to Mr Brontë.' She would have no further contact with the Brontë family for the next two years.

It would be a year or more before rumours surfaced in nearby Keighley that Patrick had proposed to one Isabella Dury, the sister of Revd Theodore Dury, the rector of that township. It would appear the gossip came about because of Partick's frequent visits there during the winter of 1822–23, where he preached at Revd Dury's church and also shared a common interest in the bible society with the vicar.

Idle gossip or not, it was certainly refuted by Isabella, on Valentine's Day in 1823 when writing to her friend Miss Mariner; she in no uncertain terms denied all knowledge of such a proposal, saying, 'I beg of you if you ever hear such a report you will contradict it as I can assure you it is perfectly unfounded, I think I never should be so very silly as to have the most distant idea of marrying anybody who had not some fortune, and six children into the bargain. It is too ridiculous to imagine any truth in it.'

Moving on, and some might say determinedly so, he turned his attention to a former love, Mary Burder, who was mentioned earlier in the book when Patrick was the curate at Wethersfield some fifteen years prior. He at first wrote to her mother on 21 April 1823, informing her of his current circumstances and enquiring of the same regarding her family and if her children were married. Within the letter, he also mentioned that he might pass through her neighbourhood in the coming summer when travelling south. It would be some months before she replied and it is evident from the content that she informed him that Mary remained unmarried. With the knowledge that Mary was single Patrick wrote to her directly, but rather foolishly, expressing his delight that she was still a spinster, saying, 'I experienced a very agreeable sensation in my heart on reflecting that you are still single.' He once again related his circumstances and further enquired if she or her mother would object to him visiting her at her home, and if she would consent to see him, he would travel down as soon as he could get cover for his ministerial services. Mary, in her response, rejected his request to visit and informed him that her single status was by choice and she was more than happy with her life and now benefitted from a handsome income. She did, however, offer sympathy as to his current situation and signed off as 'your well-wisher, Mary D Burder'. Patrick, with further obstinance, continued to pursue the request for a meeting but nothing was to come of his attempts to reacquaint their relationship.

Mary did not stay single for long as she married a clergyman the following year. You can see two striking similarities between Elizabeth Firth and Mary; they both had wealth and they also married a vicar, just not the Haworth-based one.

The fallout between Patrick and Elizabeth must have hurt him. She had been a loyal friend all through his time in Thornton, and to lose that friendship, as well as his wife, all in the same year would have been crushing to the best of us. I am pleased then to write that by early October 1823, normality was resumed and the friendship was restored.

When Elizabeth Firth wrote in her diary on 4 October 'Mr Brontë called – renewed acquaintance', two and a half years had passed since he had left the village of Thornton, yet he was still drawn back there and to Miss Firth. With the

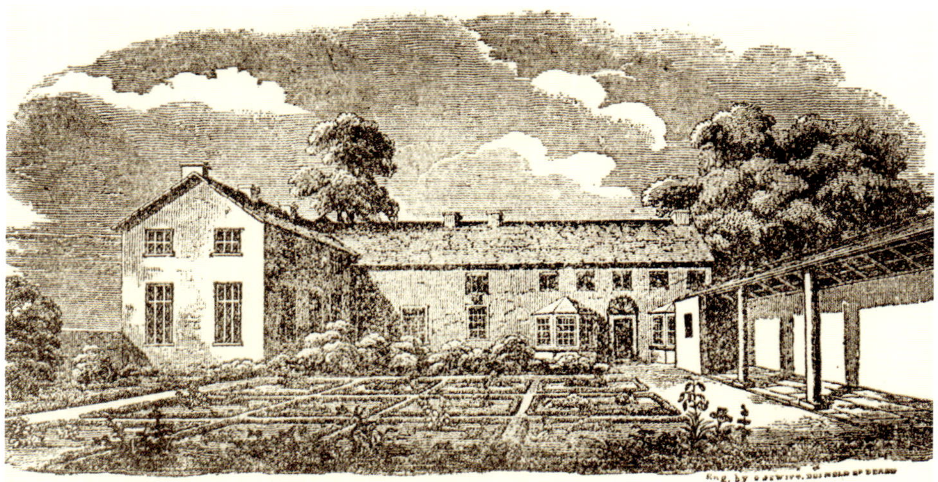

Cowan Bridge School, 1824.

children growing up fast and needing a formal education, it is understandable why he might seek the advice of Elizabeth – after all she was godmother to two of them.

Patrick's aunt, Elizabeth Branwell, had been at Haworth helping for over two years now and quite possibly would have been urging Patrick to come up with a long-term plan so she could return to Cornwall. The servant girls Nancy and Sarah, although devoted to the children and by now young women themselves, Nancy now being twenty years old, were not educated to a level where they could adequately school the children.

Patrick would not have failed to realise that if anything were to happen to him, the family would have been left destitute with no savings to support them. Having said that, he would have had a certain confidence that Aunt Branwell or Elizabeth Firth would not have seen the children enter the workhouse.

As it happens Elizabeth Firth recommended her old boarding school at Crofton Hall, near Wakefield, for the eldest girls, Maria and Elizabeth. Elizabeth could well have assisted with the fees as they were £28 per year, a not inconsiderable sum back then. As it happens the girls did attend the school not long after Patrick had visited Thornton. However, their stay was only for a short period with the fees being unsustainable.

Just when the situation seemed almost impossible, there appeared a notice in the *Leeds Intelligencer* advertising the opening of a new boarding school for the daughters of clergymen at Cowan Bridge, near Kirby Longsdale, 40 miles from Haworth. The fees at £14 were infinitely more achievable than the ones at Crofton Hall and the girls would still receive a recognised education. The vicar of Keighley, Patrick's friend Revd Theodore Dury, may have also recommended the school as he was an appointed trustee in the early years.

Although the school opened in January 1824, it would be 21 July before Patrick took Maria, by now aged ten, and the nine-year-old Elizabeth on the coach from Keighley to Cowan Bridge. With a mind to the future and recognising Maria's powerful intellect, he arranged for an education befitting the role of a future governess. He paid an additional £3 for her to study French and drawing. Elizabeth, however, was given a basic education more suited for her to gain future employment as a housekeeper.

On 10 August, Charlotte, who was now eight, joined her older sisters at the school, closely followed by six-year-old Emily on 25 November the same year.

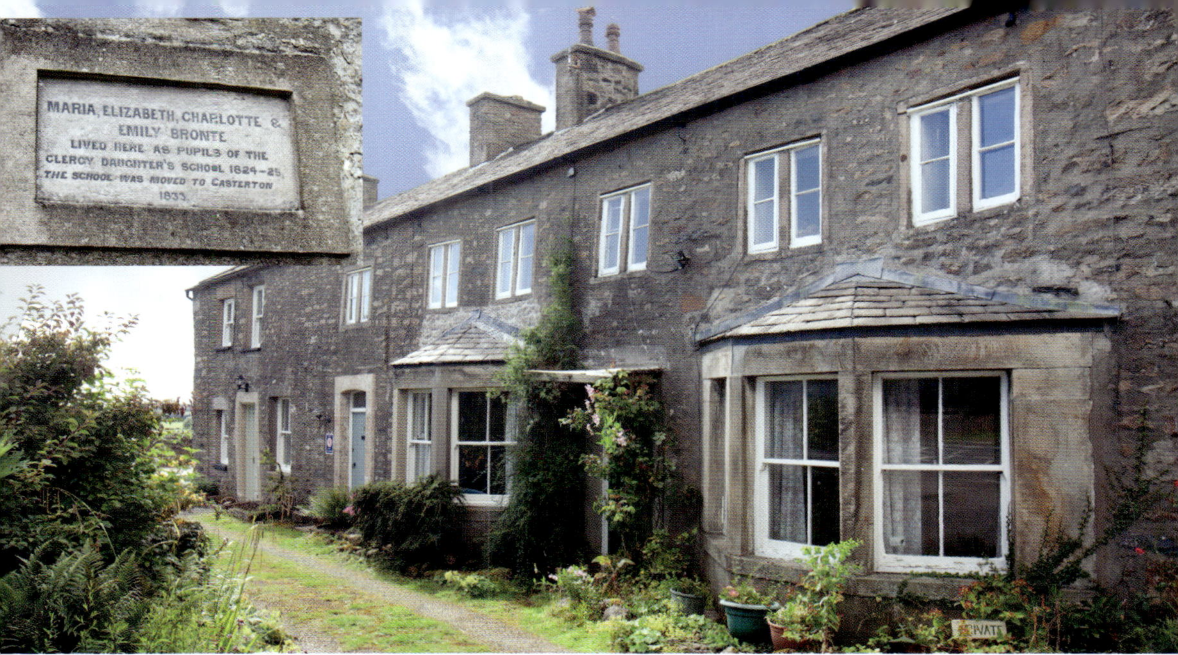

The former Cowan Bridge School, now converted to housing, shown here in spring 2025.

Inset: A plaque at the former school memorialises the Brontë girls' time as pupils there.

Conditions at the school were austere and discipline was strict – the pupils were required to wear a distinctive uniform, but this was not unusual to other contemporary schools of that era. The education facility was to have a lasting impression on Charlotte, as she immortalised it as 'Lowood' in *Jane Eyre*.

Interestingly, when Charlotte was first assessed upon entering the school it was noted: 'Reads tolerably – writes indifferently – ciphers a little and works neatly. Knows nothing of Grammar, Geography, History or Accomplishments'. In terms of grammar the same comments were made in relation to both Maria and Elizabeth. Emily was spared of any reference to her grammar; her notes were short and sweet: 'Reads very Prettily & Works a little'.

With four children at boarding school and the family at home reduced to just Anne (aged four) and Branwell, who was by then seven, the necessity of keeping the Garrs girls employed there was much removed. As much as the sisters had lovingly cared for the children, it is clear from the school's assessments of them that their educational abilities were poor and so it would seem the timing of getting the older girls a formal education was critically correct. Elizabeth Firth, now Mrs James Clark Franks, was to visit the girls at the school in September whilst on her honeymoon touring the lakes. She gave each of the girls two and a half shillings before leaving. It would seem she approved of the establishment because she raised no concerns.

Nancy Garrs by this time was engaged and in fact ready to leave service to get married. Patrick, mindful of the sterling service the sisters had given the family, assisted Sarah to find alternative employment by way of a recommendation. She, however, did not take up the position he found her and instead was apprenticed to a dressmaker in her hometown of Bradford. Later in 1829, Sarah also got married and emigrated to America. The Garrs girls were replaced by Tabitha Aykroyd who, at fifty-three years old and a Haworth resident, was employed at the parsonage as the housekeeper.

After all the turmoil and tragedy that had so far ensued after leaving Thornton, it now appeared that sustainable order and provision was now firmly in place.

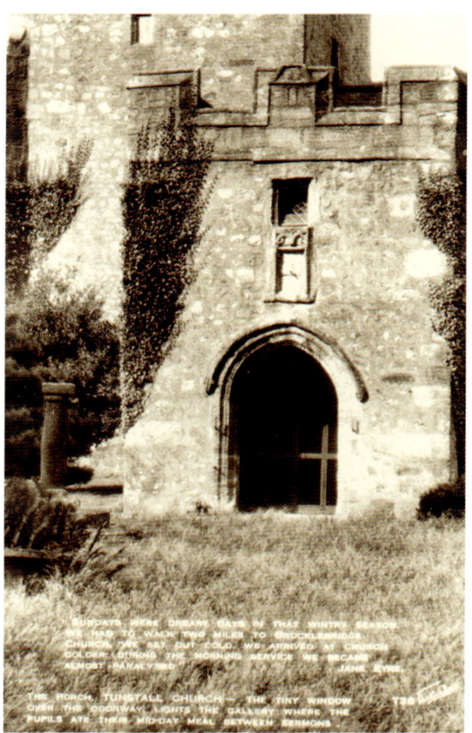

St John's, Tunstall.

As part of the normal routine at the Cowan Bridge School pupils would attend the morning and afternoon services every Sunday at St John's, Tunstall. The church, unfortunately, was situated 2 miles away and required the girls to make the journey by foot, trekking across the fields and, with winter arriving, it was not the easiest of walks.

Given the distance, it was deemed unrealistic for the pupils to go back to school for midday meals and then return to St John's to attend the afternoon service. A practical solution came by providing packed lunches, thus enabling them to remain at the church. Although fed, it would mean the girls unfortunately would often be sat in damp and wet clothes for several hours in the cold church between sermons.

By December 1824, the eldest Brontë girl, Maria, was beginning to show symptoms of consumption. Within weeks her condition was serious enough to warrant Patrick, in February 1825, travelling to the school to bring her back to the parsonage to be cared for.

Despite Aunt Branwell and her father nursing her at the parsonage, sadly Maria passed away on 6 May. Revd William Morgan, the man who had baptised her just eleven years previously, performed the burial service and she was laid to rest next to her mother in the family vault. It is said that Charlotte recreated Maria as Helen Burns in *Jane Eyre*.

If Maria dying was not enough to endure, Elizabeth, who had remained with her sisters at Cowan Bridge, was reported also to be suffering from the effects of consumption. At the same time there was an outbreak of low fever that was running through the school. The fever, which was a type of typhus, caused enough concern for the doctor to recommend that all pupils be sent away from the source.

The school's founder, Revd William Carus Wilson, moved the children to his holiday home at Silverdale, near Morecambe, except for Elizabeth, who was by now too ill and was sent back home to Haworth on 31 May. With his eldest child lying in her grave and the second eldest daughter suffering from the same ailment that had put her there, it is no wonder that Patrick, fearing for Charlotte and Emily's health, travelled to Silverdale and brought them home the day after on 1 June.

Elizabeth passed away at the parsonage just two weeks later, on 15 June at the age of just ten.

On her tombstone is inscribed the following message taken from Matthew 18:3:

Verily I say unto you, Except ye be converted, and become as little children, ye shall not enter the kingdom of heaven.

5

New Beginnings

Taking a moment to reflect on the family's journey, ten years and one month had passed since Patrick, along with his wife Maria and their two young children, had arrived at the parsonage in Thornton, full of natural hopes and expectations as they embarked on their new lives.

And yet here, a decade on, of the original family unit there was only Patrick left as the sole survivor, his wife and two eldest daughters all buried under the flagstones of St Michael and All Angels' Church in Haworth. Now with four motherless young children left to bring up, it is no wonder that his old life back in Thornton where his family was complete was his happiest time.

Who knows what Maria and Elizabeth could have achieved if they had lived. Certainly it would appear that Maria, described as 'a girl of fine imagination and extra-ordinary talents' by Ms Andrews, who was a teacher at Cowan Bridge School, was destined for great things. She might have in the fullness

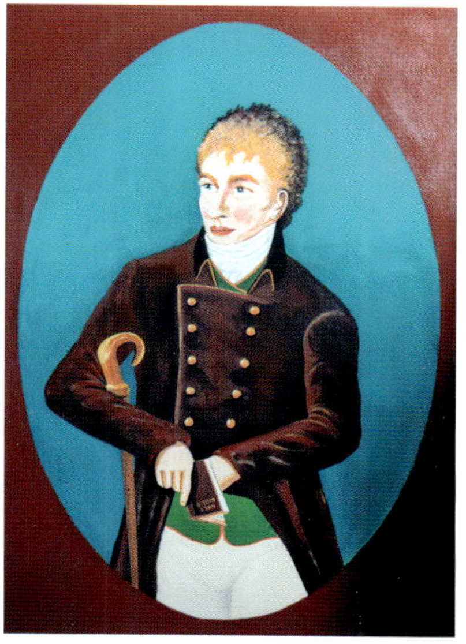

Patrick, depicted in his younger years, painted by Bradford artist John Ellis.

of time been equally as famous as her younger sisters, writing on a similar level. Unfortunately, we will never know.

Twenty-four years later in 1849, when Charlotte, writing to her publisher's reader (a publisher's reader or first reader is a person paid by a publisher to read manuscripts from the slush pile, and to advise their employers as to quality and marketability of the work), said that Maria had left an indelible impression upon her, remarking on her early developed intellect, wisdom and fortitude of character. Sadly, with both Maria and Elizabeth, we only know of them today because of their famous literary sisters and be it not for their published works their names would be lost to history amongst the many thousands of people whose names are written and etched on the tombstones in Haworth churchyard.

Now in the middle of 1825, with the family dynamics drastically altered in many ways, Thornton, and the life that had overlapped to Haworth, was over.

The servant girls Nancy and Sarah were gone, his wife and two eldest children dead. Elizabeth Firth, who had welcomed them to the village and was a good friend to the family and an important part of their social circle, was now married and living in Huddersfield, a five-hour walk away. In any event, Elizabeth had a husband and in time children to keep her busy as the new Mrs James Clark Franks.

This left Patrick, his four children and faithful Elizabeth Branwell (Aunt Branwell) attended by Tabitha Aykroyd at the parsonage in Haworth. With all his various unsuccessful marriage proposals firmly in the past he was to remain single for the rest of his life.

The Twelve

Patrick Brontë believed in education for girls as well as boys, and it is thanks to him that all his children were taught to read and write, and in turn given the freedom to embrace their creativity. He provided them with as much poetry, novels, plays and periodicals of the day to read as possible and did not restrict the girls to material felt suitable for young ladies, allowing them instead to read controversial poets like Byron. This was quite unusual for nineteenth-century parents. The children responded by devouring the books and text, feeding their inquisitive minds. Patrick knew it was vital for the girls to be well read and informed, so they could go out into the world and make their own way, earning their own livings. This was in effect the start of their literary apprenticeship. In 1826, Patrick presented nine-year-old Branwell with the gift of twelve toy soldiers, which led to a series of games based on 'the twelve' and evolved into stories detailing an intricate imaginary world. They created tiny books about them, so small we need a looking glass to read them today. It was the first step to the great Brontë novels we know and love. Given the fact the Napoleonic Wars were relatively recent history and the Duke of Wellington was still very much a hero, it is no wonder one of the soldiers was named after him.

This is how Charlotte Brontë described the event that inspired their early stories, written by her on 12 March 1829:

Papa bought Branwell some wooden soldiers at Leeds. When Papa came home it was night, and we were in bed, so next morning Branwell came to our door with a box of soldiers. Emily and I jumped out of bed, and I snatched up one and exclaimed: 'This is the Duke of Wellington! This shall be the Duke!' when I had said this Emily likewise took one up and said it should be hers; when Anne came down, she said one should be hers. Mine was the prettiest of the whole, and the tallest, and the most perfect in every part. Emily's was a grave-looking fellow, and we called him 'Gravey'. Anne's was a queer little thing, much like herself, and we called him 'Waiting-boy'. Branwell, chose his and called him Buonaparte.

Twelve Wooden Soldiers, lovingly created by Bradford artist John Ellis's expert hand.

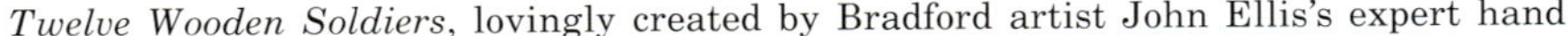

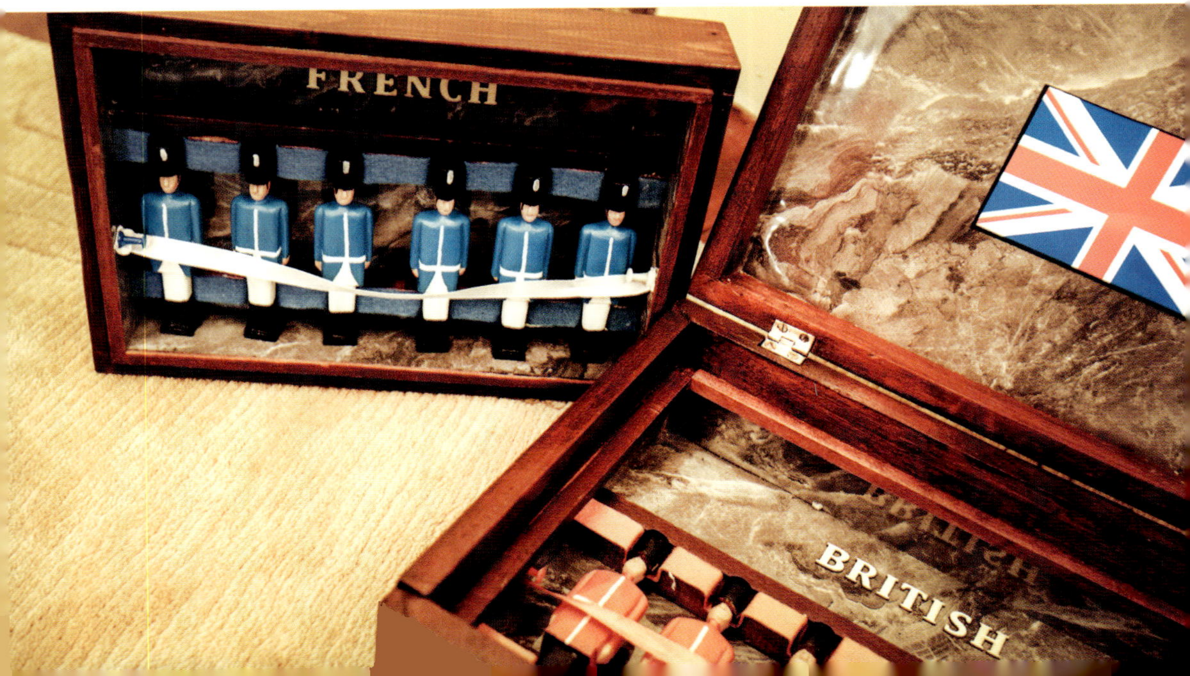

Elizabeth Branwell (Aunt Branwell)

Aunt Branwell was forty-five years old at the time she arrived in Haworth to temporarily assist in caring for Maria. Unbeknown to her then, she was never to return to her native Cornwall, not even for a holiday. Her life now was devoted to caring for her deceased sister's family, a huge sacrifice by any standard. Just when she decided to move her life permanently from the seaside in Cornwall for the cold seclusion of Haworth is unclear. It may have been because of witnessing Patrick struggling, with no potential new wife on the horizon, or that in the four years since Maria had died, the affection she had for the children had evolved from the love of an aunt into much stronger maternal feelings, or a combination of the two. Whatever the reason, it is hard to imagine how Patrick would have coped without her unwavering support and presence.

Aunt Branwell thought her task was to give the girls the basics of an education to assist them in the future. The home schooling included English, a little French, maths and some history, as well as household management and needlework. Although it is said she ran a strict regime, she also shared stories of her childhood adventures in Penzance regularly. The stark contrast between the port's comings and goings and the wild coastline of Cornwall against the brooding moorlands of Haworth captivated the children.

Having settled into her role, she was remembered for clicking round the parsonage in patten's (wooden overshoes) to protect her feet from the cold, damp stone floors. She was known to hardly venture from the house other than to attend church and felt the cold keenly, keeping her bedroom fire grate burning constantly. The encouragement given to the girls' education and Bible readings sat well with Patrick's ideology. The education she received at Chapel Street in Penzance afforded her the experience for the position she now found herself in.

Like Maria, Aunt Branwell had the luxury of a yearly annuity, which made her financially independent and allowed her to both contribute to the household expenses and fund various day trips and adventures to broaden the minds of her young charges. Her life had purpose and meaning, and she shared her wealth of knowledge with the Brontë children. Branwell was particularly close to Aunt Branwell, despite Patrick overseeing his education. In later life when Patrick's eyesight was poor, she would read aloud for him. Elizabeth was to spend twenty-one years at Haworth as a surrogate mother and companion, before passing away in October 1842. She was laid to rest alongside her sister and two nieces in the family vault beneath the church flagstones.

But for Aunt Branwell leaving the girls equal shares in the York & North Midland Railway, which were worth just under £300 each as financial inheritance, they might never have published in 1846/47. The girls used Aunt Branwell's bequeathed money to finance their publications. Branwell received only a 'Japanese-dressing-case' in her bequests as she had confidence that he would make his own way in the world. George Taylor, Stephen Taylor's son, was one of her executors. George was Patrick's churchwarden for twenty-one years in succession.

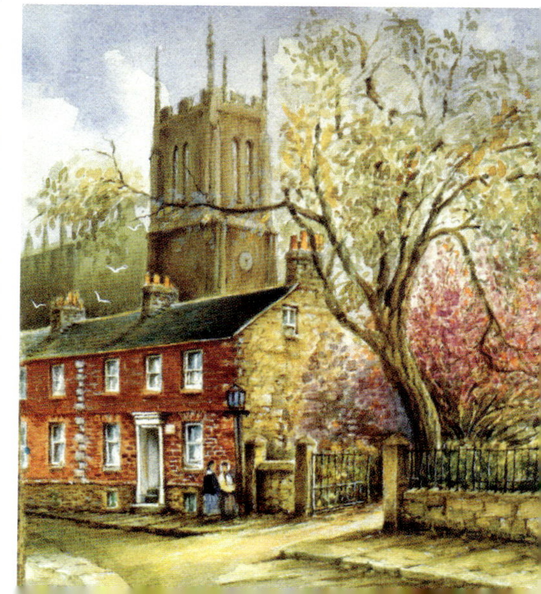

Elizabeth Branwell's former home, Chapel Street, Penzance.

Tabitha Aykroyd

Just like Aunt Branwell, Tabitha Aykroyd, who never married and was affectionately known as Tabby, was an important figure in the children's upbringing, contributing much to their creative development. When she entered the parsonage in 1824, as the cook/housekeeper, she was already in her early fifties. Patrick and Aunt Branwell had decided that an elderly woman was better than two young ones in reference to the Garrs girls she replaced.

Tabitha was an excellent choice, and in a way took on a warm grandmother role. She would inspire the children with interesting tales of days gone by, as they sat huddled round the kitchen fire on cold winter nights. It is clear she was a firm favourite with the young Brontës, who regarded her as like one of their own family.

When she slipped on the icy cobbles on the steep Main Street in December 1836, dislocating and shattering her leg, it was the children who protested to the point of refusing to eat when Patrick and Aunt Branwell thought she should be let go in the interim. The girls, aware of how Tabby had looked after them all for so many years, took on all her household chores between them while nursing the faithful servant back to health. Her leg was never to heal properly and she walked with a limp thereafter. Emily, who spent more time in the kitchen with Tabby than her sisters, was particularly fond of her, and more likely because of the walks on the moors she took the children on, the very moors that are the landscape for *Wuthering Heights*.

As Tabitha progressed into old age her leg injury would sometimes flare up, and on one occasion in 1839 went to live with her sister Susanna Wood, at nearby Lodge Street. However, she had returned to the parsonage by 1842. In the meantime, in 1839, Martha Brown, who was just eleven at the time, was employed at the parsonage in a junior capacity that would evolve as she took on more of Tabitha's chores with her health diminishing. Martha remained in service with the family until Patrick's death when she was thirty-three.

Tabby, who died on 17 February 1855, would see all the Brontë children die before her; that is apart from Charlotte, who survived her by just over a month. She is forever immortalised as the model for Nelly Dean in *Wuthering Heights*, and as Martha the housekeeper in Charlotte's novel *Shirley*.

As another mark of respect, she was laid to rest at the head of the churchyard, close to the parsonage's garden wall. The memorial stone reads: 'Sacred to the memory of George Aykroyd of Haworth Hall, who died Jan 6th, 1839, aged 76 years. Also of Susanna Wood, who died April 19th, 1845, aged 90 years. Also, of Tabitha Aykroyd who died Feb 17th, 1855, in the 85th year of her age. Faithful servant of the Brontë Family for over thirty years.'

Tabitha's grave (centre, to the front of the iron railings).

Charlotte, painted by Bradford artist John Ellis.

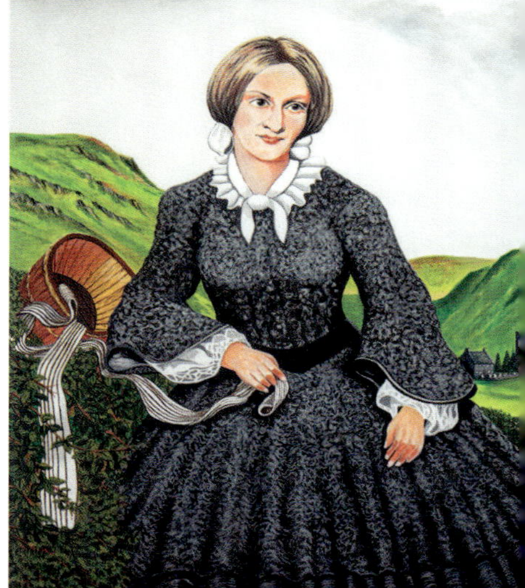

Charlotte had to grow up fast; with the deaths of her elder sisters in 1825, the responsibilities of being elevated to the eldest child fell upon her nine-year-old shoulders. Over the next few years all the children remained at the parsonage being educated by their father and aunt. At this time they began to read insatiably. The four of them made very little attempt to integrate with other children outside of the parsonage and relied solely on each other for company.

Charlotte was intelligent enough to realise from an early age that her father lacked a private income and she, along with her sisters, would have to eventually earn their own livings. Options were limited due to social restraints and accepted behaviour for women of that era. The respectable careers for impoverished middle-class females were usually in the teaching profession, either in a school or employed by a private family as a governess.

With a view to achieving the education required, on 17 January 1831, at the age of fourteen, she enrolled at Roe Head Boarding School, Mirfield. The school was in direct contrast to Cowan Bridge, being a haven of respect and learning and was run by the inspirational headmistress Miss Margaret Wooler. Roe Head was an incredibly important learning centre for Charlotte, both in terms of the education she experienced and the lifelong friendships with Ellen Nussey, Mary Taylor and Margaret Wooler she made there. Margaret Wooler, seventeen years later when Patrick was too ill to attend her wedding, gave Charlotte away, in the father of the bride role. An early written description of Charlotte by her well-dressed attractive friend Mary Taylor reads very poor:

I first saw her coming out of a covered cart, in very old-fashioned clothes, and looking very cold and miserable. She was coming to school at Miss Wooler's. When she appeared in the schoolroom, her dress was changed, but just as old. She looked a little old woman, so short-sighted that she always appeared to be seeking something and moving her head from side to side to catch a sight of it. She was very shy and nervous and spoke with a strong Irish accent.

Although lacking in social graces and a formal education, she more than made up for it with her intellectual abilities – her knowledge of art and literature was extensive, not to mention knowing the Bible virtually inside out. Surprisingly she was well versed with the works of Lord Byron, which was frowned upon for young women. As an avid reader, she devoured books, including her father's classical texts and the popular books of the period. While at the school she wrote a novella, *The Green Dwarf*. She also applied herself working hard and rose to the top of the first class, for which she was awarded a silver medal for her achievement three terms in succession. Not bad at all for a girl who on first impressions resembled a country bumpkin.

After eighteen months at the school, sixteen-year-old Charlotte returned home to Haworth in early June 1832, having made dramatic improvements to her life both in her education and social circle. Back at the parsonage she passed on her education to Emily and Anne, who were by now fourteen and twelve years old, respectively.

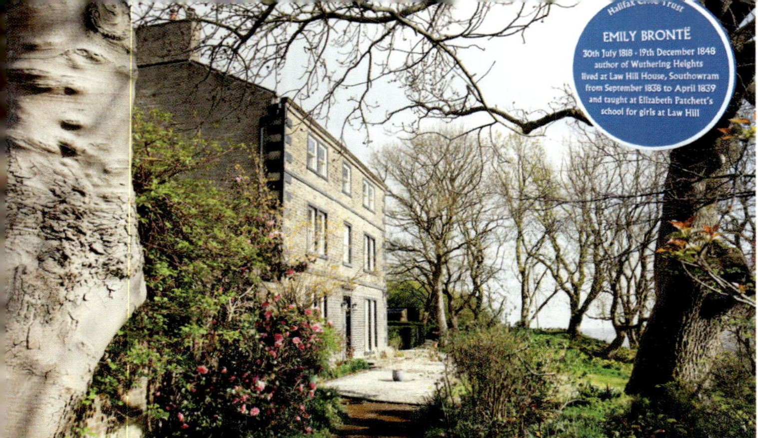

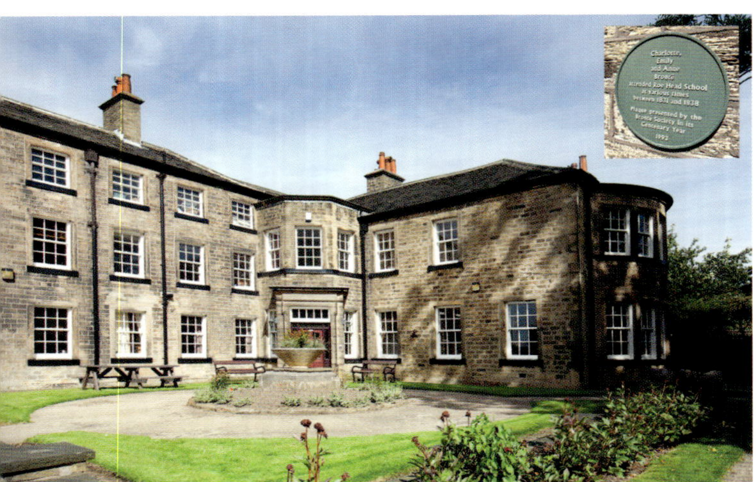

Law Hill School, Southowram, near Halifax, photographed in 2025.

Roe Head School in the present day is now known as Hollybank, providing residential care, plus a range of therapies and enrichment activities for children, young people and adults with profound and multiple disabilities.

Charlotte was to return to Roe Head, but this time as a teacher in 1835. She was joined by Emily, as a scholar. At seventeen years old Emily would have been one of the oldest pupils there. Except for the six months at Cowan Bridge School ten years previously, she had never been away from home for any length of time since. She was to find the transition being away from her beloved moorland home difficult. After just three months she was allowed to return to Haworth. Anne, who was more adaptable, was then sent in her place, where she remained until 1837. Quiet and diligent, she was to leave no lasting impression upon the school. Charlotte left the employment of the school in 1838.

Elizabeth Clark Franks (née Firth) lived close to Roe Head School with her husband. In 1836, Charlotte and Anne spent the summer with them at the Clark Franks' invite. The visit was under duress as the girls would have preferred to be at Haworth. Sadly, Elizabeth passed away just a year later, on 11 September 1837.

Despite having no formal education Emily, in September 1838, obtained a position as a teacher at Law Hill School, Southowram, near Halifax. This was to be her one and only attempt ever to earn an independent living. She replaced Maria Patchett, who had left to get married a year earlier. The school for young ladies had over forty pupils between the ages of eleven and fifteen, of which half of them were boarders. Charlotte, when writing about Emily's duties in October 1838, said: 'Hard labour from 6 in the morning until near 11 at night, with only one half-hour of exercise in between – this is slavery. I fear she will never stand it.'

Under such slavery Emily, who had become devoted to the house dog, found her health suffering under the strict, disciplined, demanding routine of the school and she left her £20 a year position in March 1839, returning to Haworth just six months after arriving. She is remembered for reputedly on one occasion telling her class that she preferred the dog to any of them.

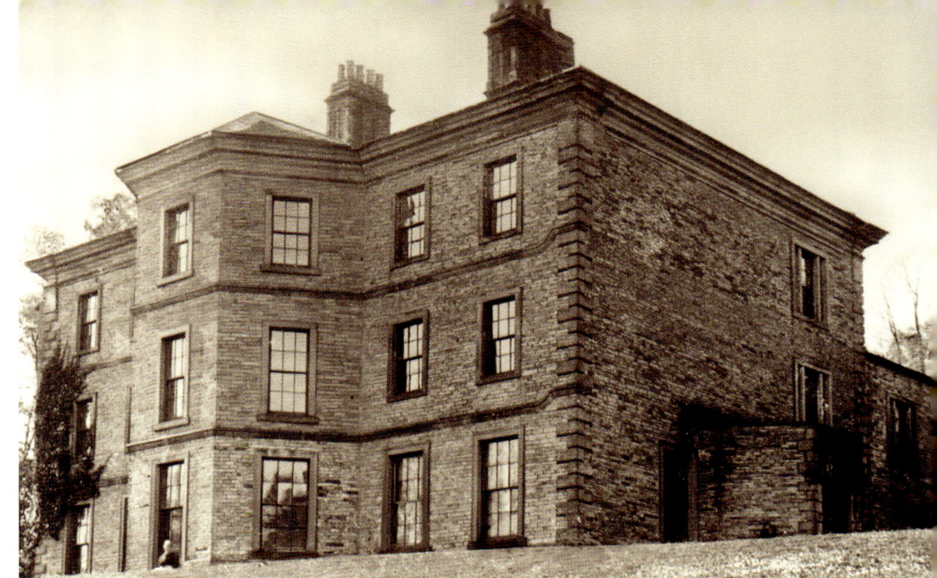

Stonegappe, Lothersdale. The house is claimed to be the model for Gateshead, home of the Reed family in Charlotte's *Jane Eyre*. In 2025, the house remains a private residence.

Although Emily was back at the parsonage in Haworth having given up on any aspirations of a career as a governess, Charlotte and Anne, aware that without income and connections it would be unlikely they would attract a husband, continued in their pursuit of making good. That said, Charlotte received her first proposal of marriage in February 1839. The offer of holy matrimony, which she turned down, came from her friend Ellen's brother, Henry Nussey.

From April 1839, Anne was employed as a governess to the two eldest children of the wealthy Ingham family at the imposing eighteenth-century Blake Hall in Mirfield. Anne found her charges, six-year-old Cunliffe and his five-year-old sister Mary, difficult to discipline and over-indulged. On one occasion after the children refused to take lessons Anne, reduced to tears, confessed to their mother that they were beyond her control. In another event witnessed by Mrs Ingham when entering the schoolroom, she found Anne had tied the children to a table leg, ensuring they could not escape lessons. It is said that the horrific Bloomsfields in *Agnes Grey* are based on the Ingham family.

Charlotte, in May of the same year, had too obtained a post as governess, only 12 miles away from Haworth, to the Sidgwick family at Stonegappe, Lothersdale, near Skipton. Although she found the house and surroundings favourable, she did not get on with Mrs Sidgwick and like Anne found the children, Mathilda, aged seven, and four-year-old Benson, beyond her control. By the middle of July, Charlotte was back home with Emily. A month later William Weightman was appointed curate at Haworth church. In September, Charlotte took her first holiday with her old school friend Ellen Nussey, to Bridlington or 'Burlington' as it was known then, on the East Yorkshire coast. They lodged at Easton House and spent four enjoyable weeks there.

Meanwhile Branwell's career, which had begun and ended in Bradford, as a portrait painter that he had established in June 1838 had failed. Rather than compete with the well-established artists in the area, he had mostly retired to the George Hotel, drinking with other aspiring young artists and writers. He returned home to Haworth in debt.

Christmas saw the whole family reunited and all four children unemployed when Anne returned home having been dismissed from her position. The Inghams had determined there had been no improvement in their children's education and held her responsible.

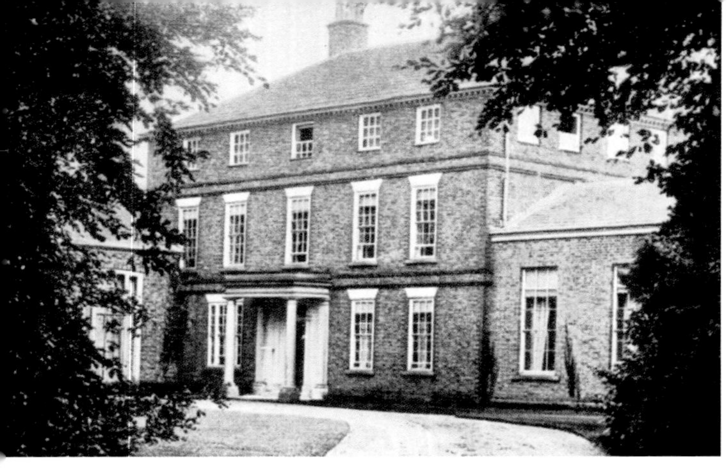

Thorp Green Hall, the large three-storey house seen to the left, is believed to have been destroyed by fire in 1895, although some believe it was demolished in the early twentieth century. In 1912, a new hall was constructed close to where the original had existed. In 2025, Thorp Underwood Hall is occupied by Queen Ethelberga's private college, which celebrates its links to the Brontës to this day.

Anne, like Branwell, was usually seen as living in the shadow of her older sisters Charlotte and Emily. However, Anne and Branwell are distinguished by two things. Branwell, who had always hoped to carve out a career in literature, achieved a small measure of success when he became the first of the Brontë siblings to publish a poem, 'Heaven and Earth', in the *Halifax Guardian* on 5 June 1841. Anne had greater success than her sisters in terms of making her own way in the world of work. When Anne took her second and last governess position for the Robinson family at Thorp Green Hall, Little Ouseburn, in May 1840, she would remain in their employment until June 1845, longer than Charlotte and Emily had achieved collectively. Anne was much happier working for Revd Edmund Robinson and his wife, Lydia, educating four of their five children, than she had been for the awful Ingham family. The Robinson family are represented in *Agnes Grey* as the Murrays. Charlotte, meanwhile, between March and December 1841, worked as a governess for a Mrs White, at Rawdon.

During her time with the family, Anne would accompany the Robinsons on their annual summer holidays to Scarborough, where the family would stay at the superior Wood's Lodgings. The Grand Hotel, in the popular seaside town, now occupies the site of the former lodgings known then as No. 2 The Cliff.

It would appear that on her trips home to Haworth, a mutual fondness had arisen between Anne and William Weightman, her father's curate, so it was a great sadness when the popular young man died of cholera on 6 September 1842, aged just twenty-six. A plaque in Haworth church exists to his memory.

In 1843, Branwell joined Anne at Thorp Green, to tutor the Robinson's only son, Edmund, named after both his father and grandfather. Branwell had in the last few years been employed in various roles including tutoring in Broughton in Furness, for Mr Postlethwaite in the first six months of 1840, of which he was dismissed from for allegedly drinking. He was then employed by the Leeds–Manchester railway at Sowerby Bridge in October 1840, before being promoted to clerk-in-charge at Luddenden Foot in Halifax. He was dismissed from that job in April 1842 for negligence in keeping accounts.

On 29 October 1842, Aunt Branwell passed away and Charlotte and Emily, who were in Brussels at the time, duly returned home to Haworth on hearing the sad news.

Unfortunately, Branwell was linked to scandal at Thorp Green Hall, for it is widely believed he had betrayed Revd Robinson by having an affair with his wife, Lydia. He was dismissed in disgrace and returned to Haworth, a month after Anne, who had left the Robinson's employment in June 1845. Patrick's new curate and Charlotte's future husband, Arthur Bell Nicholls, had arrived in Haworth just ahead of Anne that May.

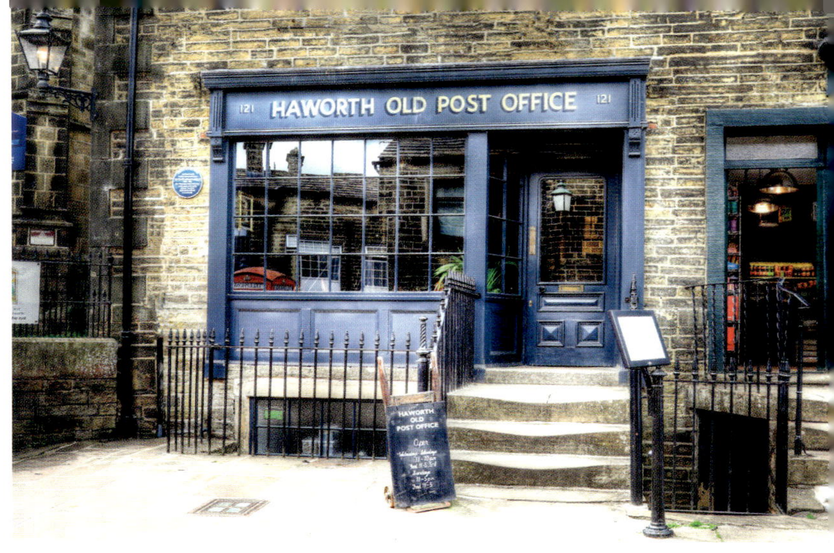

As the village post office at the time of the Brontës in Haworth, this is the very location from which the sisters posted the manuscripts of their acclaimed works. In 2025, you can experience a taste of history, served over the original early Victorian Brontë post office counter, where they offer a superior experience serving a range of cuisine and drink.

Charlotte and Emily's visit to Brussels, which was supported by Aunt Branwell's money, was because of the sisters' decision to open their own school in Haworth, having become increasingly unhappy in their work as governesses. They had told their aunt that by studying abroad at the Pensionnat Heger, the well-respected school for girls, they would gain a competitive advantage by improving their languages at their own school at the parsonage. Eventually the scheme was abandoned when the 'Misses Brontë's Establishment for the Board and Education of a Limited Number of Young Ladies' failed to secure the patronage of one single pupil.

Upon his disgraced return to Haworth, Branwell, self-indulgent in his torment, fuelled the rumour mill in the village by declaring his passion for Mrs Robinson to anyone who would listen. Charlotte, who herself had fallen in love with the married Monsieur Constantin Heger, who was initially her teacher and later her colleague in Brussels, hypocritically had no sympathy for Branwell. She proved to be a harsh critic of his behaviour. Charlotte's love interest, however, was a closely regarded secret for decades, either known or guessed by very few.

Branwell, wallowing in self-pity, sought oblivion in drink. Claiming he was too ill to find employment, he declared his intention to write a novel, which was a dream all the siblings had shared – to become authors. Unsurprisingly, Branwell's novel was never completed.

After Branwell's declaration to write, Charlotte became the driving force for the sisters to publish. This was further fuelled by her discovery of Emily's poems in the autumn of 1845. Charlotte found them wild, melancholy and elevating and worthy of publication. Emily was outraged that Charlotte had delved into her secret world uninvited. Charlotte eventually won her round and collectively the sisters pooled their work.

They used pseudonyms. The decision to do that was forced on Charlotte by Emily and Anne. They did this to avoid the contemporary prejudice against female writers. All three women retained the first letter of their Christian names: Charlotte became Currer Bell, Emily took Ellis Bell, and Anne was Acton Bell. Although *Poems by Currer, Ellis & Acton Bell*, printed in 1846 by Aylott and Jones of London, only sold two copies, the sisters were unperturbed. With their appetites whetted and a determination to follow a literary career established, they began in earnest to work on their famous novels, the very novels we all know and love to this day.

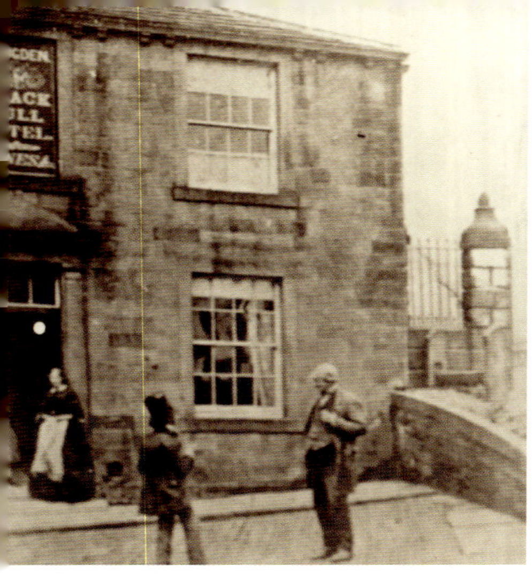

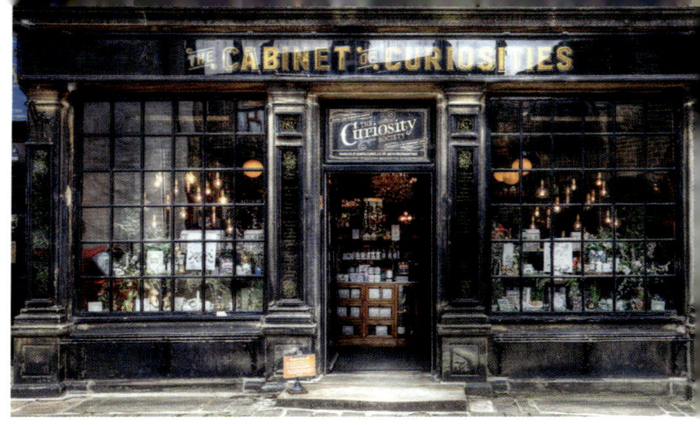

Above: The Apothecary, now known as 'The Cabinet of Curiosities'.

Left: The Black Bull as Branwell would have known it.

Branwell, as the only son of the family, was expected to be the one who would go on to achieve greatness, to be able to provide and support his sisters in the event they were unable to carve out their own wealth or find husbands. Sadly, his was a life of promise unfulfilled.

After his disgraceful dismissal from Thorp Green in 1845, Branwell spiralled back in Haworth, drinking in the Black Bull public house and purchasing laudanum at the Apothecary across the road.

Whether or not an affair took place is a matter of long debate; certainly Lydia strongly denied any such infidelity took place, whereas Branwell maintained the opposite.

On 26 May 1846, when Lydia Robinson's forty-six-year-old husband Edmund passed away, Branwell briefly had a fancy that he would return to the woman he professed to love. He was clearly oblivious to how the class distinctions of that period made such an idea fanciful at best. Lydia had no intention of marrying the penniless, lovesick Branwell, thus making him lord of the manor. She cleverly put paid to that notion by informing him that there was a stipulation in her husband's will that if she resumed her relationship with him, she would forfeit the estate and her children. It will come as no surprise that this was in fact a lie and no such clause existed. It was in effect the slamming of the door in his face. She did, however, send him £20, which he immediately invested in obtaining alcohol at the inns of Halifax and Haworth.

Branwell, resenting the fact that in all his life he had 'done nothing either great or good', passed away on 24 September 1848, at the age of thirty-one. Charlotte shortly after his death wrote:

Branwell was his Father's and his sisters' pride and hope in boyhood, but since Manhood, the case has been otherwise … I do not weep from a sense of bereavement – there is no prop withdrawn, no consolation torn away, no dear companion lost – but for the wreck of talent, the ruin of promise, the untimely dreary extinction of what might have been a burning and a shining light. My brother was my junior; I had aspirations and ambitions for him once – long ago – they have perished mournfully – nothing remains of him but a memory of errors and sufferings – There is such a bitterness of pity for his life and death – such a yearning for the emptiness of his whole existence as I cannot describe …

Mrs Robinson, in the same year Branwell died, married the seventy-five-year-old wealthy widow Baronet Sir Edward Dolman Scott, and at the age of forty-eight became Lady Scott.

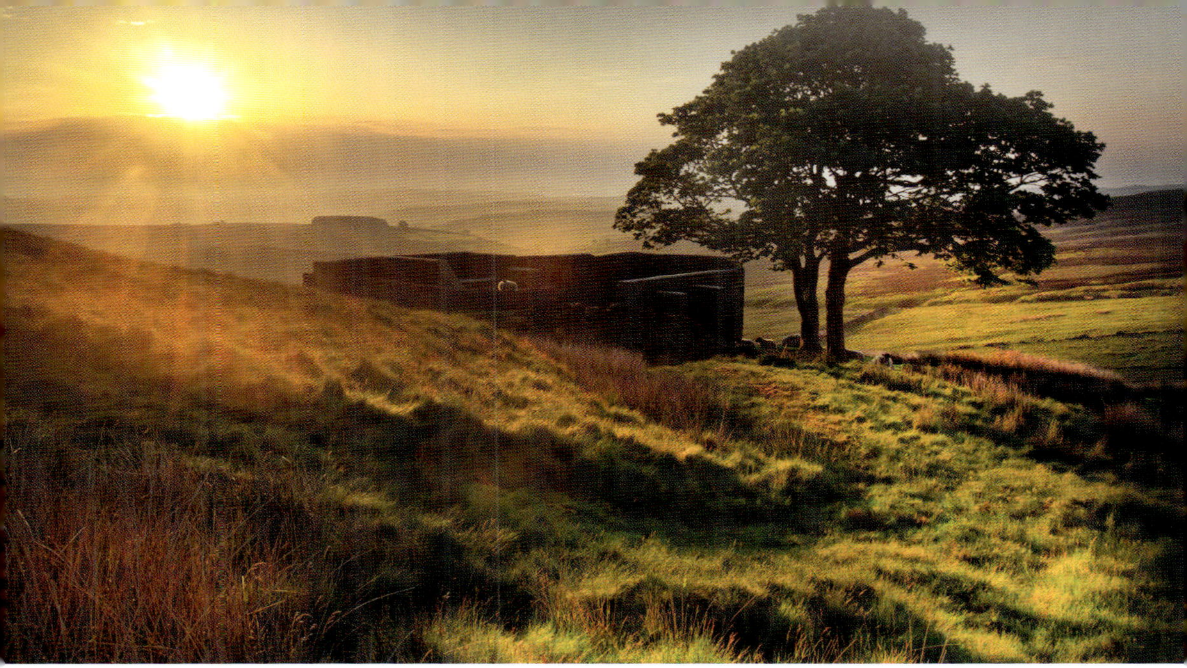

Withens (also known as Top Withins), the ruined farmhouse high on the moor near Haworth, is said to be the model for Emily's *Wuthering Heights*. A plaque on the wall says, 'This farmhouse has been associated with "Wuthering Heights", the Earnshaw home in Emily Brontë's novel. The buildings, even when complete, bore no resemblance to the house she described, but the situation may have been in her mind when she wrote of the moorland setting of the Heights.'

When Emily Brontë's masterpiece of literary genius *Wuthering Heights* was published on 24 November 1847, she had just over a year left to live. Sadly, she was never to realise the worldwide success of her work, with her real name on the cover of her classic Gothic novel.

It is said that when attending Branwell's funeral she contracted a terrible cold and never left the confines of the parsonage again. Throughout her illness she was steadfast in her resolve to be self-sufficient and refused all medical assistance until just two hours before she expired. She passed away at 2 p.m. on Tuesday 19 December, with her dog Keeper lying beside her deathbed. Emily wasn't for accepting death like Branwell, and even though Dr Wheelhouse, who had finally been called, realised it was too late for any medical miracles, she fought her imminent demise to the very end. She died from tuberculosis.

The year 1848 was a harsh year for the Brontë family, for just two days short of three months after Branwell, Emily joined him in the family vault along with her mother, two elder sisters and aunt, beneath the church flagstones. The funeral service was officiated over by Arthur Bell-Nichols. Emily's faithful dog Keeper followed her coffin all the way to the vault. The carpenter who made her coffin said he had never constructed one as narrow before; it measured just forty centimetres in width, a clear indication as to just how thin she had become in her last months.

For days after the funeral Keeper wailed pitifully for his mistress outside her bedroom door. Her closest friend had been her sister Anne. Jointly they had shared their own fantasy world, Gondal. Ellen Nussey had described the sisters as 'like twins' in childhood.

Having only published her one novel, it is claimed that she had started to write a second. However, the manuscript, if one ever existed, has never been located.

1849 would not prove to be any less tragic for the Brontë family. Anne, the baby of the family, was to face her own mortality. She had been complaining of abdominal pains for some weeks before Emily's death, which were further exacerbated by her grief, putting her health into decline. Over the Christmas period it was obvious to all that she wasn't improving after contracting influenza. Patrick, only recently having lost two children, decided to bypass Dr Wheelhouse and called in Dr Teale, a specialist from Leeds, well experienced in cases of consumption. In the first week of the New Year, on 5 January, Dr Teale examined Anne at the parsonage and the family's fears were confirmed: Anne, like Branwell and Emily, had the consumption.

There was nothing to be done, other than attempt to slow down the degenerative progress of the terminal disease. The specialist recommended quiet and rest, and for her to take cod-liver oil and carbonate of iron. Charlotte, desperate to save her one remaining sibling, sought out a second opinion in the form of Dr John Forbes, a leading authority in England on consumptive cases. He, knowing Dr Teale, confirmed the original diagnosis and treatment plan. He also warned that any hope of a recovery was folly. Anne, resigned to what lay ahead, faced her situation with courage when writing to Ellen Nussey, discussing her hope to travel to the seaside where the sea air might restore her health.

I have no horror of death; if I thought it inevitable I think I could quietly resign myself to the prospect, in the hope that you, dear Miss Nussey, would give as much of your company as you possibly could to Charlotte and be a sister to her in my stead. But I wish it would please God to spare me not only for Papa's and Charlotte's sakes, but because I long to do some good in the world before I leave it. I have many schemes in my head for future practice – humble and limited indeed – but I should not like them all to come to nothing, and myself to have lived to so little purpose. But God's will be done.

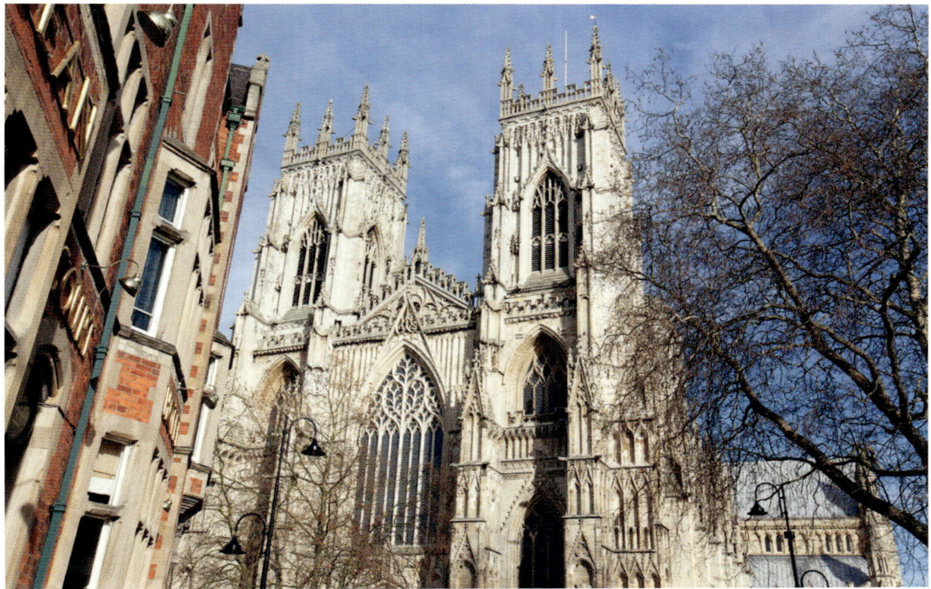

The magnificent historic York Minster.

With the hands of time ticking, arrangements were made to fulfil Anne's desire to visit the coast. And so it came to pass that on the evening of 23 May, Charlotte's lifelong friend Ellen Nussey arrived to stay overnight at Haworth Parsonage, so collectively with Charlotte, the small party could embark on the pilgrimage to Anne's beloved Scarborough together. First taking the train to Leeds, they then made their way to York, staying at the George Coaching Inn on Coney Street (the footprint of which now stands the Next retail store – a memorial plaque on the exterior wall marks the occasion). The following day, Anne wished to take one last look at the magnificent York Minster. She was so moved by the Gothic-style cathedral that she said 'if finite power can co this what is the …' – emotion took over and the quote ended.

The girls arrived in Scarborough on the 25th, staying at Wood's Lodgings, No. 2 The Cliff, the location of the Grand Hotel today. Anne, feeling revived, spent her last days surrounded by love, courage and faith. She enjoyed the beautiful views across the bay and even took a cart ride led by a donkey. Selfless Anne wished her faithful companions to explore the resort she had come to love through her visits with the Robinson family, to which Charlotte and Ellen reluctantly agreed to. On the morning of 28 May Anne had her usual breakfast of boiled milk and late morning felt particularly unwell. Charlotte called a doctor, who confirmed the inevitable – the end was near. Anne, who Ellen Nussey described as 'dear, gentle Anne', asked Ellen to be a sister in her stead. To Charlotte, who was quite unable to contain her grief, Anne whispered, 'Take courage Charlotte, take courage.' She was lucid to the very end and left this mortal world at around 2 p.m. that afternoon.

Anne's death was afterwards described in a letter to a friend by Charlotte:

She died without severe struggle, resigned, trusting in God – thankful for release from a suffering life – deeply assured that a better existence lay before her. She believed, she hoped – and declared her belief and hope with her last breath.

To spare her father the mental anguish of witnessing yet another funeral of one of his children, Charlotte took the decision to lay her sister to rest in the churchyard of St Mary's. The grave is in close proximity to the castle, with picturesque views over the town and sea below. Anne is the only member of the Brontë family not to have been buried within the confines of Haworth church.

Charlotte, after revisiting the grave on 4 June 1852, soon after wrote: 'On Friday I went to Scarboro', visited the churchyard – and stone – it must be refaced and re-lettered – there are 5 errors. One error still remains on the stone: Anne's age is given as twenty-eight instead of twenty-nine.'

Today, the lettering on the grave is much eroded, as is often the case with coastal cemeteries.

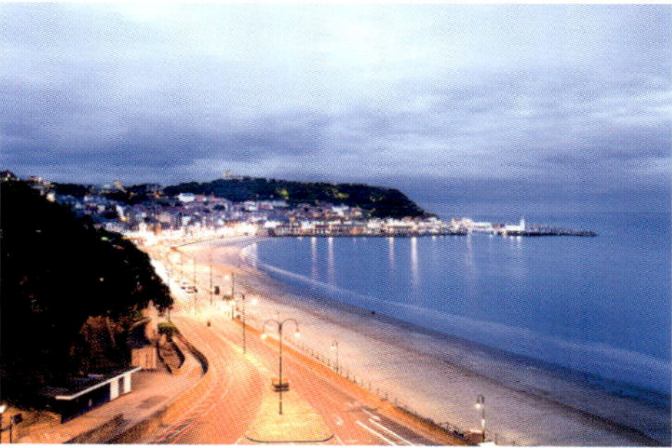

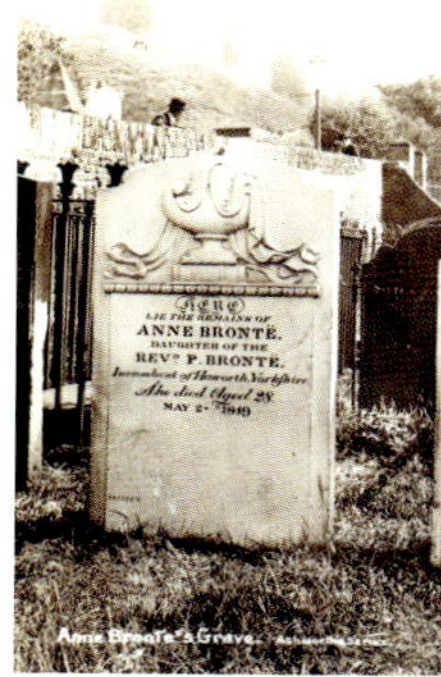

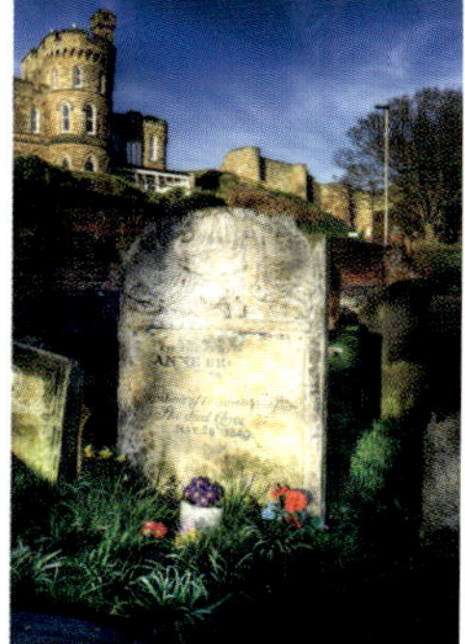

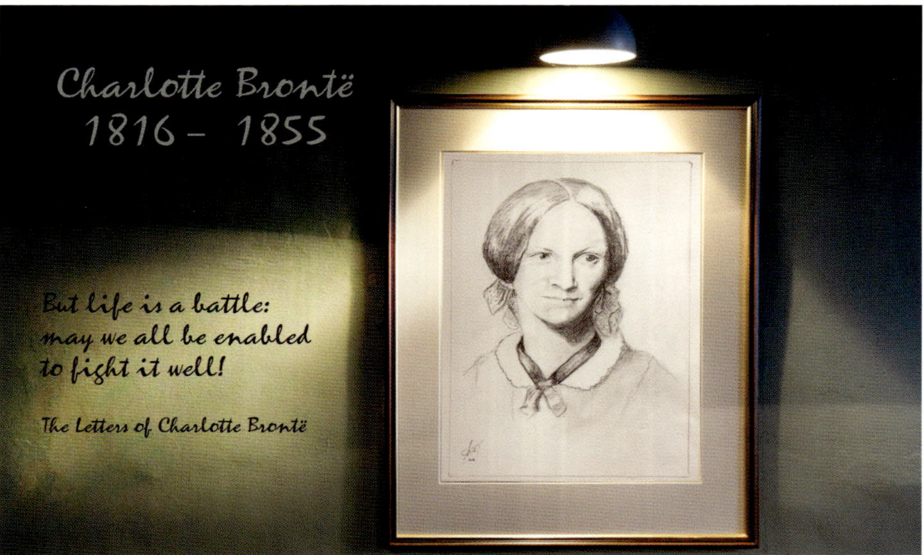

Charlotte, drawn by the late Sue Holt.

When Charlotte Brontë passed away in 1855, she was fully aware the novel that she had first started when she accompanied her father to Manchester, for the removal of his cataract, was a success. They had taken lodgings in August 1846 at No. 83 Mount Pleasant, and it is there, while Patrick convalesced in a quiet darkened room, that Charlotte first set quill to parchment, weaving her inimitable style with words, bringing to life her immortal *Jane Eyre*.

Following Anne's death, having unwillingly found herself the sole surviving sibling, she understandably suffered from increasing periods of depression. She found no inner peace walking the moors, as she felt both Anne and Emily's spirits permeating the very landscape they had all loved and enjoyed so much. A little over a year after Anne's death, Charlotte briefly found comfort when she met her childhood hero, the Duke of Wellington, at London's Chapel Royal on 9 June 1850.

In the last year of her life, the now famous author found happiness when she married her thirty-five-year-old father's curate, Arthur Bell Nicholls, at eight o'clock in the morning on Thursday June 1854. The wedding ceremony was performed by Revd Sutcliffe Sowden. Patrick gave word that he was too ill to attend, and Charlotte's old teacher from Roe Head, Margaret Wooler, stepped into the breach to give the bride away. George Taylor, Stephen Taylor's son from Stanbury, was one of the invited guests. The happy couple honeymooned in Arthur's native Ireland.

Wedded bliss was to last but a short period as thirty-eight-year-old Charlotte Brontë was to pass away at the beginning of holy week on the morning of 31 March 1855. Her last whispered words to her relatively new husband, as she lay on her deathbed, were 'I am not going to die, am I? He will not separate us; we have been so happy.' At the time of her death, she was believed to be in the early stages of pregnancy. Revd Sutcliffe Sowden, who had married her just nine months previously, was now called upon to conduct the sad task of performing her funeral service. Charlotte was reunited with her mother, aunt and four of her siblings in the family vault beneath the well-worn flagstones of her father's church. Like her mother, Maria, she had died in her thirty-ninth year.

The End of an Era

After Charlotte's death, Patrick lived on at the parsonage attended to by his son-in-law, Arthur Bell Nicholls. On 30 October 1859, he preached his last ever sermon from the pulpit of Haworth church. His health was clearly in a continual decline, and by early August 1860 he was confined to his bed, and rumours began to spread that he was on the verge of dying. He did, however, recover enough to walk round the garden, assisted by Arthur. It was a short blip, as by 25 October he was again confined to his bed chamber. On 4 April 1861, Arthur confirmed that Patrick was continuing pretty well, and while still confined to bed, his mental faculties remained quite unimpaired. The end was imminent though, and at around 6 a.m. on 7 June in the same year, he was seized with convulsions that rendered him unconscious, although he lingered, attended by Martha Brown and Arthur. Revd Patrick Brontë went to meet his maker at between two and three o'clock that afternoon, aged eighty-four. With no official grandchildren, he was the last of his line. It has been said that Branwell fathered an illegitimate child when in Broughton in Furness, though there is no factual evidence.

On the day of Patrick's funeral, 12 June, hundreds came to pay their last respects, and all the shops in the village closed voluntarily. The church was packed and every pew and available place filled – several hundred mourners had to remain outside in the graveyard – such was the feeling of loss by all. Arthur Bell Nicholls, visibly moved and wracked with grief, had to be physically supported. He was laid to rest at the side of Charlotte, in the family vault, the last time it would be opened, and the last burial within the church ever.

Patrick held Martha in high regard, for he left her £30, which was the equivalent of three times her annual wages, for her long and faithful services to both him and his children.

He had lived a full life and achieved enormous success by anyone's standards. Having risen from very humble beginnings in Ireland to studying at Cambridge University and then given fifty-five years of service to the church, he had also published a novel and poetry collections. Sadly, he suffered the grief and sorrow that came with witnessing the deaths of his wife and all six of his children.

But more, much more than this, he had fathered children with exceptional literary talents.

Right: The family memorial plaque in Haworth church, detailing their lives.

Far right: Patrick Brontë late in life. Painted by Bradford artist John Ellis.

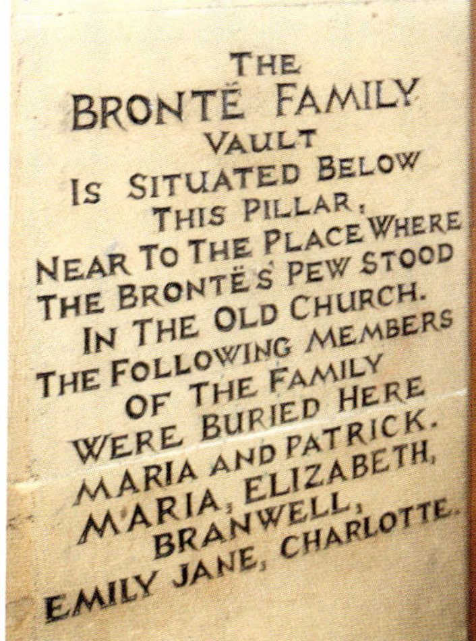

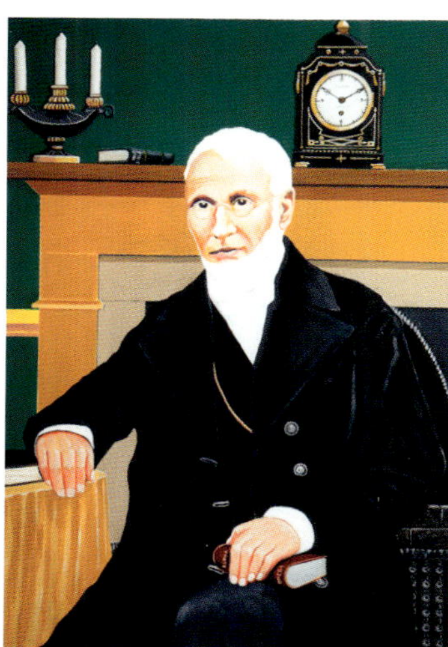

The Thornton Legacy

When John and Sarah Ashworth built the house in 1802, it was never intended to be a parsonage. However, the Church had different ideas when they bought the property in 1807. The first minister to benefit from living there was Revd Thomas Atkinson, who, being single, found it more than adequate for his bachelor requirements. As we know, Patrick Brontë and his wife, Maria, arrived in 1815, and despite living there for five years Patrick described it as ill designed and unfit for purpose.

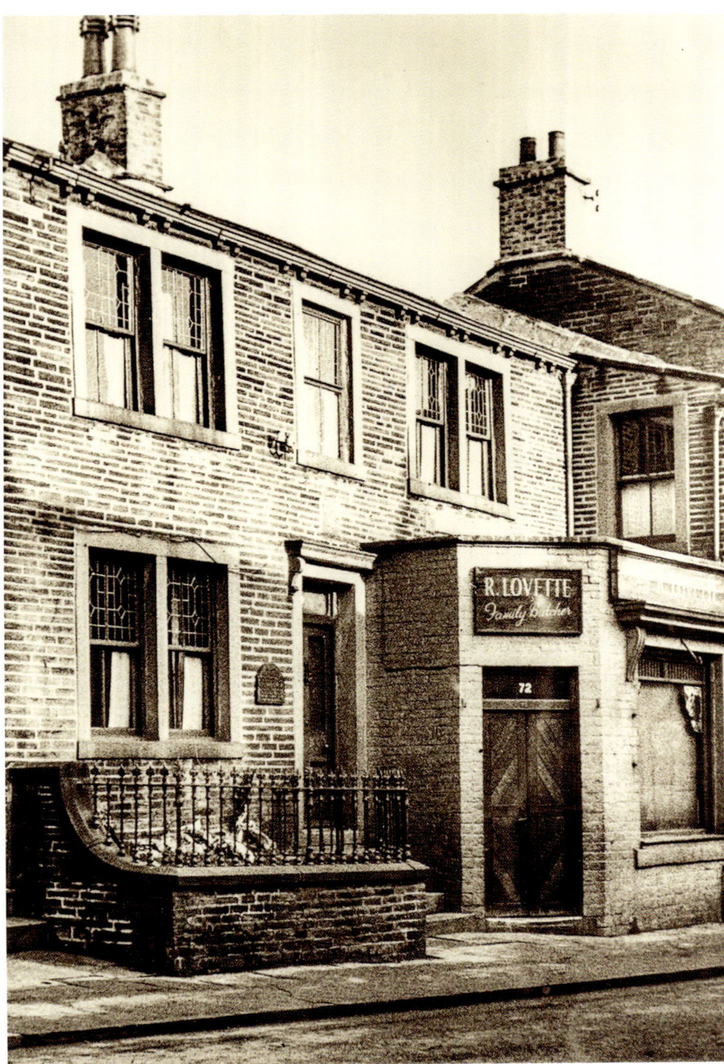

The Lovette family successfully ran a butcher's shop at the Birthplace for many years.

When the Brontës left Thornton in 1820, the parsonage served Patrick's successor, Revd William Bishop, until the church built a new parsonage at School Green. Now no longer required by the church, the property was sold in 1837.

Little is known of the years leading up to 1890 when the Jowett family purchased the property. However, an extension was added to the front, making the once symmetrical façade look odd in comparison. The two brothers Priestley and Charles Jowett ran a butcher's shop there and used the recently added barn to the rear as a slaughterhouse.

The Jowetts continued as owners of the house and butcher's shop until the spring of 1932 when Harold Ambler bought the house whilst maintaining his own butcher's business at No. 449 Thornton Road. Harold, his wife Alice, and their children George, Kathleen, Barbara and Jeffrey all lived in the property. Harold's mother was to move in, and she remained there until her death in 1935, which occurred at the house.

While the Amblers occupied the residential part of the house, Reggie Lovette rented the shop and slaughterhouse from 1935. The Lovettes successfully ran the butcher's shop there until 1979. During the Second World War years, 1939–45, Mrs Lovette ran the butcher's.

In 1944, Harold Ambler and the family moved to Denholme House Farm, and interestingly the house was then let to wartime evacuees for a number of years.

The Ambler family continued to own the house and Barbara Nield (née Ambler) and her husband Stanley Nield moved in from Alderscholes Farm in 1955. Stanley and Barbara raised their two children, Andrew and Jayne (now Dibb), there.

After the Lovettes retired in 1980, the butcher's ceased to be and became an extra living room. Jayne has happy memories of living there and even opened a tea and gift shop with her mum, where they sold refreshments and Brontë memorabilia from the former butcher's shop. The Amblers sold off the barn in 1986, and finally their connection to the 'Birthplace of Dreams' ended when the house was sold in 1987.

The author Barbara Whitehead, who wrote *Charlotte Brontë and Her 'Dearest Nell'* amongst many other books about the house, went on to restore the property to a period piece. Interestingly she encouraged tourists and students to visit by appointment. Marjorie Wilson, the author of the *Brontë Way*, operated guided walks around Thornton for guests of Barbara including showing people around the 'Birthplace'.

Marje recalls there were many Japanese students who came to stay and were told of the little bed in the corner where the Brontë children, Charlotte, Emily, Branwell and Anne, were born. Sadly, with her health failing, Barbara sold the house and moved to York in 1999.

During the following dozen or so years the house has had a chequered history. At one point it was converted into rental apartments and numerous residents came and went. One of the former residents, retired dentist Nikki Prescott, remembers her time living there with some affection. Nikki was the best friend of the late Lisa Singleton, who was a founder member of the original 2012 committee. Nikki herself has been fully supportive of the project, bringing the house into public ownership for many years.

In 2012, due to the bankruptcy of the current owners the former parsonage was placed on the market. A public meeting was held to broach the subject of the

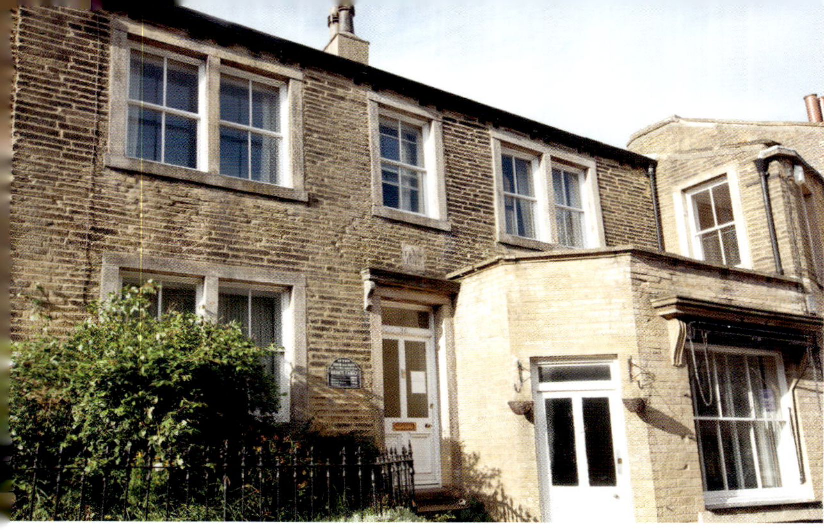

Left: The Birthplace with an uncertain future, prior to being sold in 2012.

Below: The Birthplace in 2014 and called Emily's.

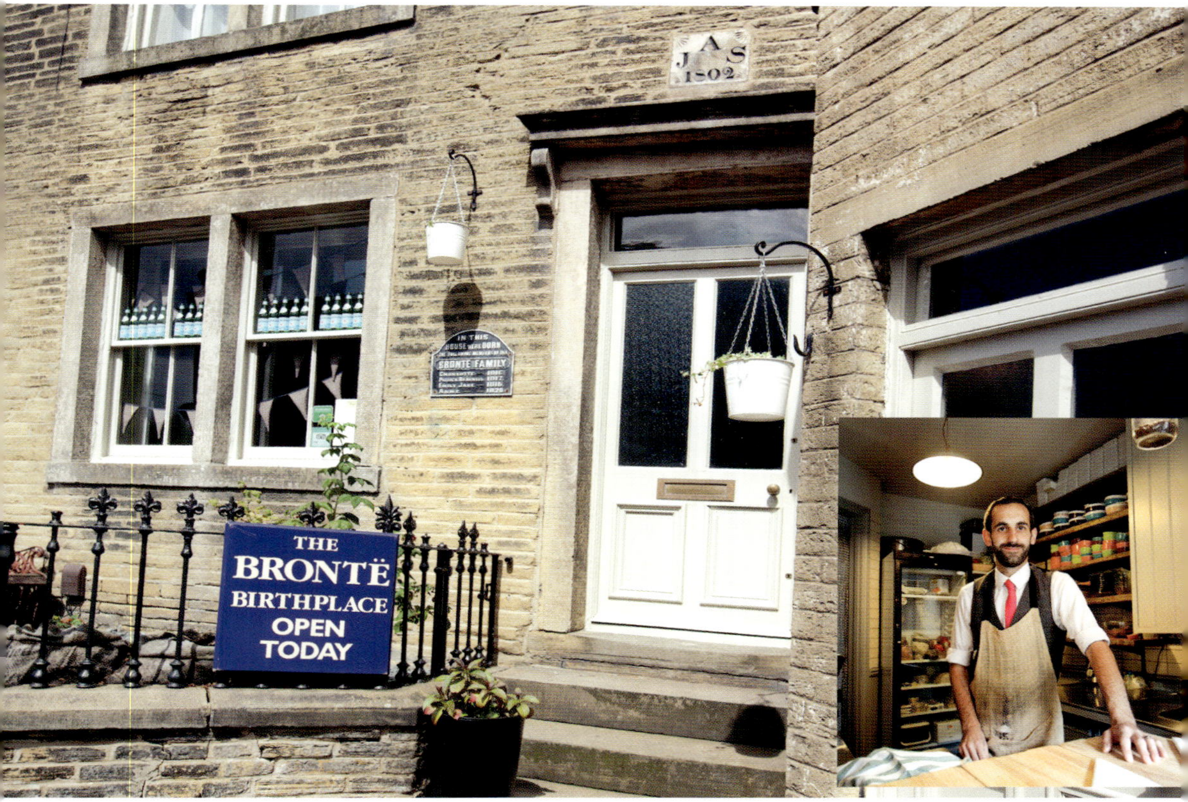

possibility of the house being bought for the community. Lisa Singleton, the former Lord Mayor Val Binney, Steve Stanworth and Sue Hayton formed the Brontë Birthplace Trust 2012 as a direct result of the meeting. Unfortunately, the sale was placed under time constraints and the trust failed in their attempt to secure a purchase. The house was then sent to auction at Elland Road, Leeds, where it failed to meet its reserve price. However, a private buyer made a bid that proved acceptable to the sellers and once again the house was in private ownership.

The private buyer was local business owner Mark De Luca; his vision was to live in the house and create a café. The café duly opened in 2013 and with a nod to the former residents it was named Emily's.

He had created an Italian-style coffee house bistro, which successfully served the community and afforded visitors a chance to see the fireplace in the parlour where Charlotte, Emily, Branwell and Anne were born whilst enjoying coffee and cake. Because the family occupied the upstairs rooms Brontë fans were only able to access the front two downstairs rooms. There was a lovely and warm atmosphere in the café area that was further enhanced by images, books and general memorabilia, especially relating to *Wuthering Heights*.

Sir Tony Robinson, aka Baldrick, of *Time Team* and *Blackadder* fame, visited Emily's on 4 June 2014 when filming the programme *Walking Through History* for Channel 4. He is seen below with joint author Mark Davis later that same day at the Midland Hotel in Bradford. Tony is holding a copy of Ann Dinsdale's and his recently published book *In the Footsteps of the Brontës* that Mark presented him with. Tony tapped his nose with the book and promised to read it that very night.

Customers arrived at Emily's in healthy numbers, and Mark De Luca even expanded his culinary delights to a horse box situated to the front of the house, complete with a pizza oven. Business was good; however, he, like all of us, could not have foreseen the events in 2020, and the disruption to both lives and businesses Covid-19 was to cause, not to mention the thousands of people who died as a result.

Sadly, after the pandemic had passed the business stayed closed until it was eventually put on the open market for sale.

A well-attended meeting was held at South Square in Thornton to once again formulate a plan with a view to purchase the property. There was overwhelming enthusiasm; all agreed that finally after 200 years of the family leaving it was only right to try and put the last piece of the jigsaw in place and bring the Brontës home.

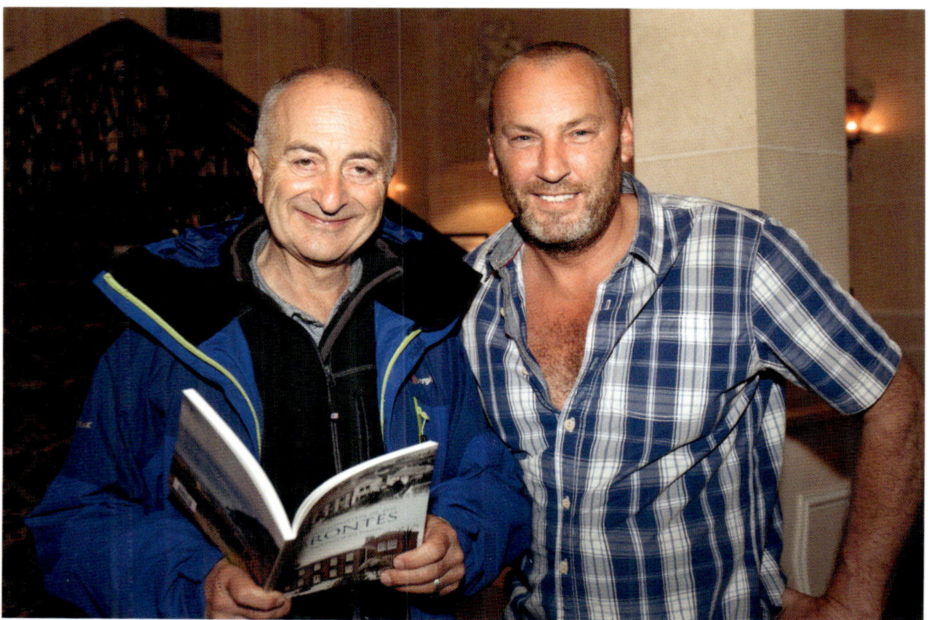

Sir Tony Robinson with Mark Davis at the Midland Hotel, Bradford, June 2014.

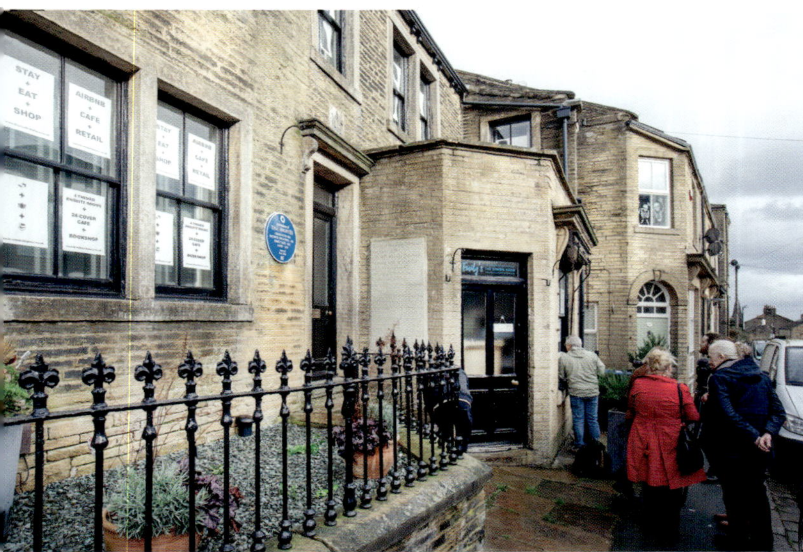

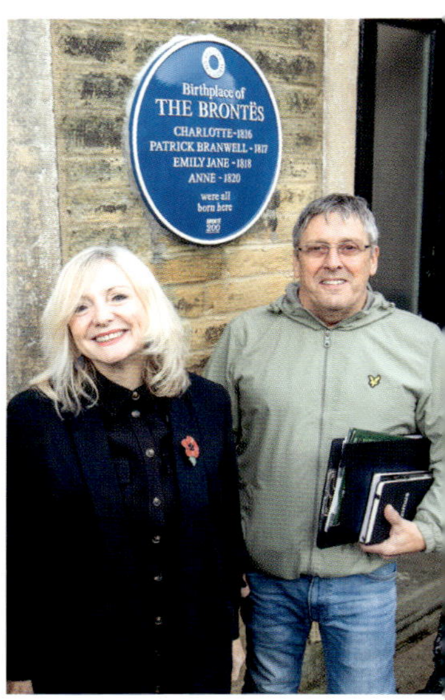

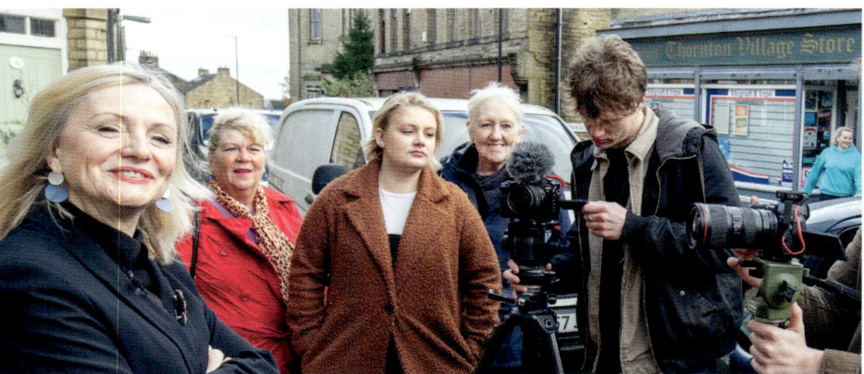

Above and left: The house is seen here in November 2023, when Tracy Brabin, the Mayor of West Yorkshire, visited prior to the purchase. She said: 'This will be a brilliant place to stay and study, which will draw people in from far and wide!'

As anyone that has been involved with a similar project will testify, these things are not always plain sailing. The journey to bring the house into public ownership was hampered by many challenges and obstacles.

Once a committee was created, the decision was made to be become a CBS or community benefit society. Steven Stanworth was elected as vice-chair of the committee, with Sarah Dixon as chairman. As the earlier group Brontë Birthplace Trust 2012 had found, time is not always your friend. It was fortunate that Mark De Luca had noted the community interest and generously gave the group six months' grace with a first option to buy.

With the clock ticking, a huge campaign was mounted where we, the committee, decided hell or bust. There might never be another chance like this and collectively the group recognised that, and with this in mind we launched a publicity campaign that was not just local or nationwide, it was worldwide. Interest came in from the four corners of the earth – Australia, Canada and the USA, as well as Japan, Italy and the Netherlands. And those countries are but a few in terms of the overwhelming support from Brontë fans far and wide.

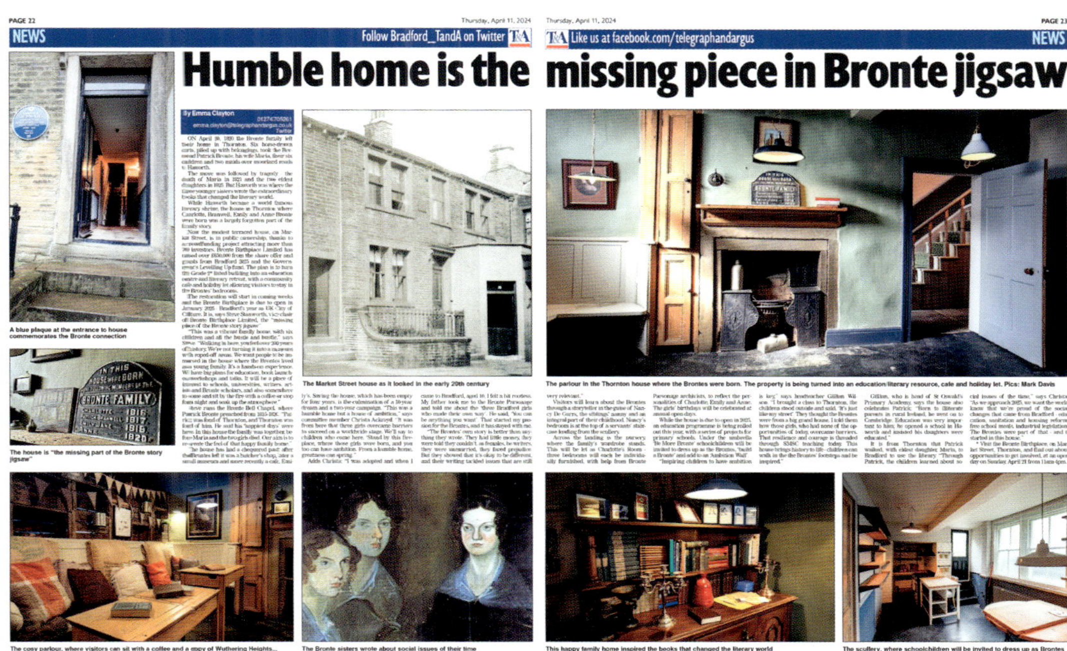

NEWS Follow Bradford_TandA on Twitter **T&A** · **T&A** Like us at facebook.com/telegraphandargus **NEWS**

Thursday, April 11, 2024

Humble home is the missing piece in Bronte jigsaw

By Emma Clayton
01274705261
emma.clayton@telegraphandargus.co.uk
Twitter

ON April 30, 1820 the Bronte family left their home in Thornton. Six horse-drawn carts, piled up with belongings, took the Reverend Patrick Bronte, his wife Maria, their six children and two maids over moorland roads to Haworth.

The move was followed by tragedy – the death of Maria in 1821 and the two eldest daughters in 1825. But Haworth was where the three younger sisters wrote the extraordinary books that changed the literary world.

While Haworth became a world famous literary shrine, the house in Thornton where Charlotte, Branwell, Emily and Anne Bronte were born was a largely forgotten part of the family story.

Now the modest terraced house, on Market Street, is in public ownership, thanks to a crowdfunding project attracting more than 700 investors. Bronte Birthplace Limited has raised over £600,000 from the share offer and grants from Bradford 2025 and the Government's Levelling Up fund. The plan is to turn the Grade 2* listed building into an education centre and literary retreat, with a community cafe and holiday let allowing visitors to stay in the Brontes' bedrooms.

The restoration will start in coming weeks and the Bronte Birthplace is due to open in January 2025 – Bradford's year as UK City of Culture. It is, says Steve Stanworth, vice-chair of Bronte Birthplace Limited, the "missing piece of the Bronte story jigsaw".

"This was a vibrant family home, with six children and all the bustle and bustle," says Steve. "Walking in here, you feel over 200 years of history. We're not turning it into a museum with roped-off areas. We want people to be immersed in the house where the Brontes lived as a young family. It's a hands-on experience. We have big plans for education, book launches, workshops and talks. It will be a place of interest to schools, universities, writers, artists and Bronte scholars, and also somewhere to come and sit by the fire with a coffee or stop from night and soak up the atmosphere."

Steve runs the Bronte Bell Chapel, where Patrick Bronte preached from 1815-1820. "Patrick was fond of Thornton, and Thornton was fond of him. He said his 'happiest days' were here. In this house the family was together, before Maria and the two girls died. Our aim is to re-create the feel of that happy family home."

The house has had a chequered past; after the Brontes left it was a butcher's shop, later a small museum and more recently a cafe. Emily's. Saving the house, which has been empty for four years, is the culmination of a 10-year dream and a two-year campaign. "This was a humble home but a house of ambition," says committee member Christa Ackroyd. "It was from here that three girls overcame barriers to succeed on a worldwide stage. We'll say to children who come here, 'Stand by this fireplace, where those girls were born, and you too can have ambition. From a humble home, greatness can spring.'"

Adds Christa: "I was adopted and when I came to Bradford, aged 10, I felt a bit rootless. My father took me to the Bronte Parsonage and told me about the three Bradford girls who made their own way. He said, 'You can be anything you want.' That started my passion for the Brontes, and it has stayed with me.

"The Brontes' own story is better than anything they wrote. They had little money, they were told they couldn't, as females, be writers, they were unmarried, they faced prejudice. But they showed that it's okay to be different, and their writing tackled issues that are still very relevant."

Visitors will learn about the Brontes through a storyteller in the guise of Nancy De Garrs, the siblings' nanny and an integral part of their childhood. Nancy's bedroom is at the top of a servants' staircase leading from the scullery.

Across the landing is the nursery, where the family's wardrobe stands. This will be let as Charlotte's Room – three bedrooms will each be individually furnished, with help from Bronte Parsonage archivists, to reflect the personalities of Charlotte, Emily and Anne. The girls' birthdays will be celebrated at annual open days.

While the house is due to open in 2025, an education programme is being rolled out this year, with a series of projects for primary schools. Under the umbrella 'Be More Bronte' schoolchildren will be invited to dress up as the Brontes, 'build a Bronte' and add to an Ambition Wall.

"Inspiring children to have ambition is key," says headteacher Gillian Wilson. "I brought a class to Thornton, the children stood outside and said, 'It's just like my street'. They thought the Brontes were from a big grand house. I told them how those girls, who had none of the opportunities of today, overcame barriers. That resilience and courage is threaded through SMSC teaching today. This house brings history to life – children can walk in the the Brontes' footsteps and be inspired."

Gillian, who is head of St Oswald's Primary Academy, says the house also celebrates Patrick. "Born to illiterate parents in rural Ireland, he went on to Cambridge. Education was very important to him; he opened a school in Haworth and insisted his daughters were educated."

It is from Thornton that Patrick walked, with eldest daughter Maria, to Bradford to use the library. "Through Patrick, the children learned about social issues of the time," says Christa. "As we approach 2025, we want the world to know that we're proud of the social changes that came from Bradford - education, sanitation and housing reform, free school meals, industrial legislation. The Brontes were part of that - and it started in this house."

* Visit the Bronte Birthplace, on Market Street, Thornton, and find out about opportunities to get involved, at an open day on Sunday April 21 from 11am-4pm.

The Market Street house as it looked in the early 20th century

The parlour in the Thornton house where the Brontes were born. The property is being turned into an education/literary resource, cafe and holiday let. Pics: Mark Davis

The house is "the missing part of the Bronte story jigsaw"

A blue plaque at the entrance to house commemorates the Bronte connection

The cosy parlour, where visitors can sit with a coffee and a copy of Wuthering Heights...

The Bronte sisters wrote about social issues of their time

This happy family home inspired the books that changed the literary world

The scullery, where schoolchildren will be invited to dress up as Brontes

A double-page spread in the *Telegraph & Argus* featuring Mark Davis's images promoting the project.

The decision to allow members of the public to buy into the project and become shareholders was reasonably successful, with 650 investors raising £117,000. The target for the whole project far exceeded the revenue from shares and so grants were to play a crucial part. The grant team, led by Sue Hayton, did sterling work in facilitating grants from the National Lottery Heritage Fund, BD25, the Rural England Fund and the Community Ownership Fund. With the grants successfully approved and in place, the committee were now able to make a formal offer.

The group will always be indebted for the positive press coverage and special thanks go to Emma Clayton for keeping the Brontës and their birthplace in the news locally, along with others for national coverage on various television news programmes – so greatly appreciated. Pictured above is just one of the many articles by Emma published in the Bradford *Telegraph & Argus* featuring Mark's (joint author) photography.

After much patience by all, the house was finally purchased and saved for the public. Brontë Birthplace Limited is now the official owner of The Brontë Birthplace, Nos 72/74 Market Street, Thornton.

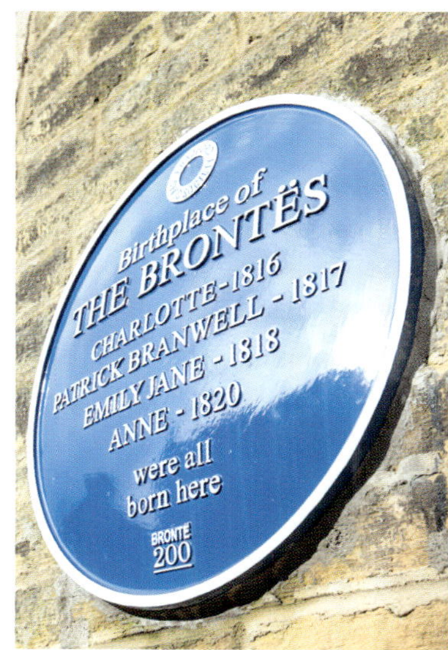

The blue plaque mounted to the side of the front door at the Birthplace, denoting the birth years.

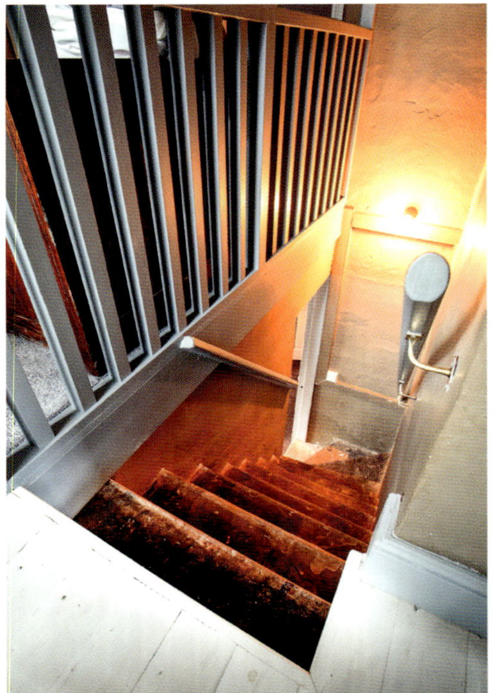

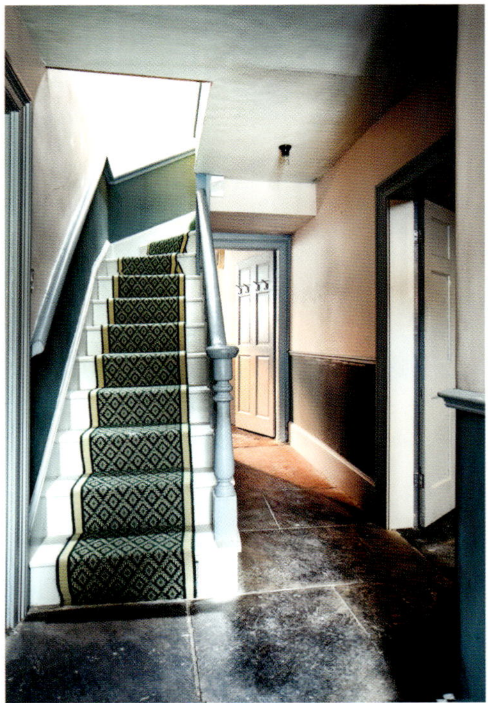

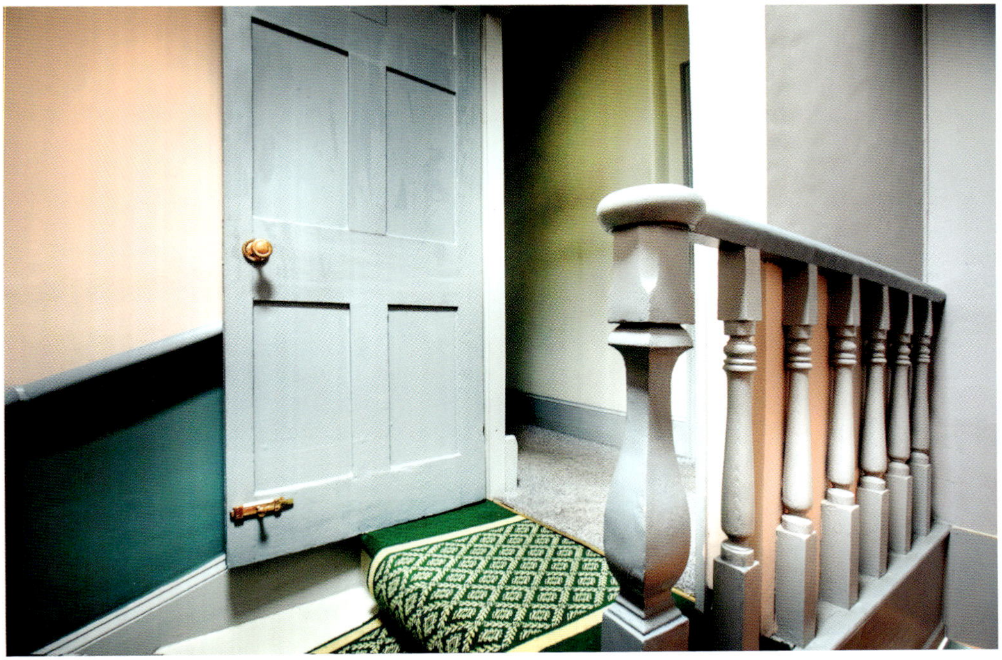

Above right: The main staircase. *Above left*: The secret back stairs. *Below*: The first-floor landing of the main staircase.

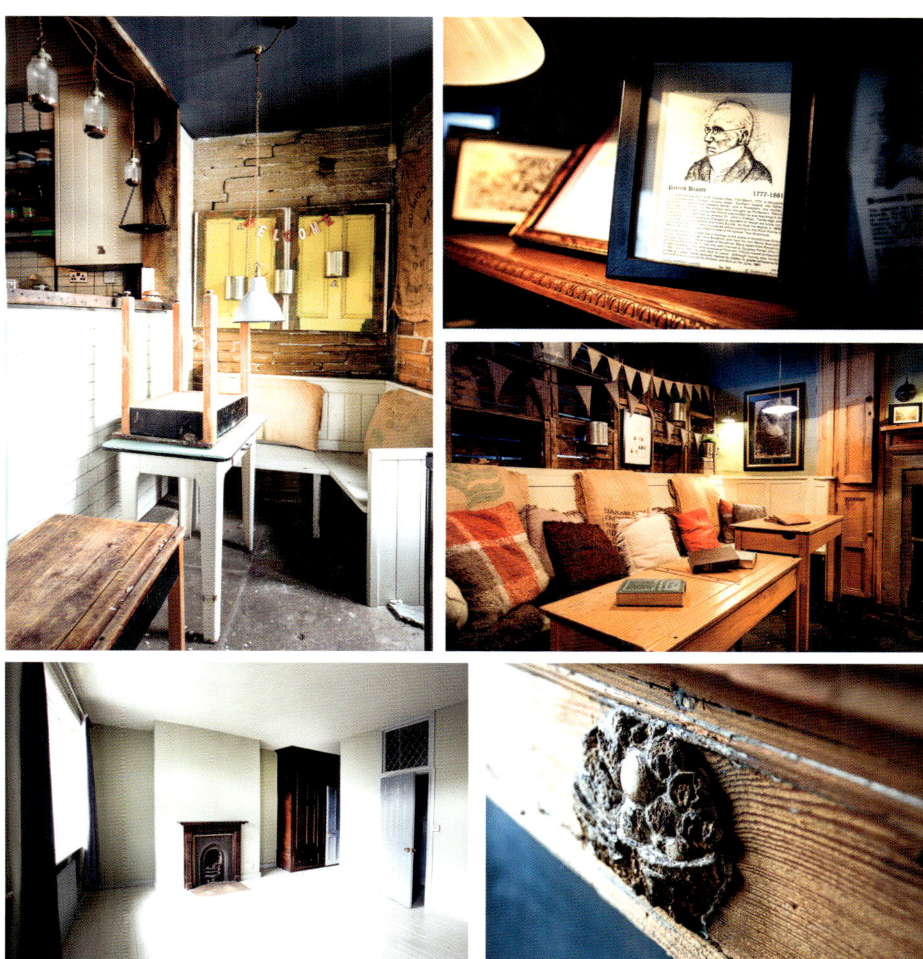

A series of images showing the Birthplace in late March 2024.

23 March 2024 marked an historic occasion; a large bunch of keys were freshly collected in eager hands, various members trying to work out which of the three locks we had keys to, struggling to find the right one, and (joint author) Mark Davis eventually finding the correct key and opening the front door wide. At last, after all the careful planning and patience we were in.

This was the first time we had been allowed inside after making the offer to purchase. Little had changed since the café had closed – in many ways it was in its own time warp. We were pleasantly surprised to find many items of memorabilia were left around the building, as seen in these pictures.

Top left: The cosy nook in the former café. *Top right:* The fireplace where the four youngest Brontë children were born. *Bottom left*: The main bedroom with its original fireplace and wardrobe from the Brontë's day. This room was originally occupied by Patrick and Maria Brontë but became the night nursery for all the children. Middle right is the café seating beside the famous fireplace.

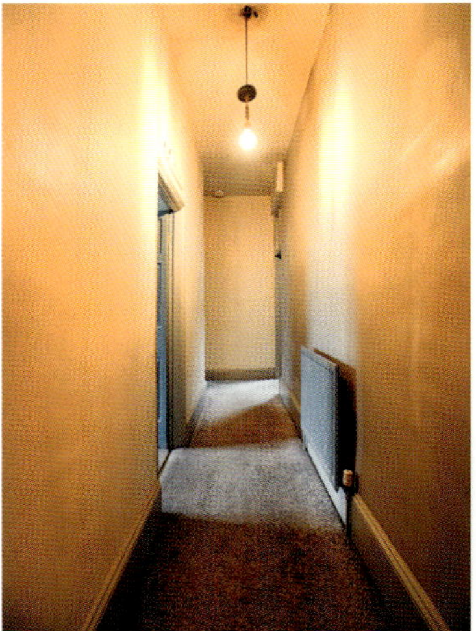

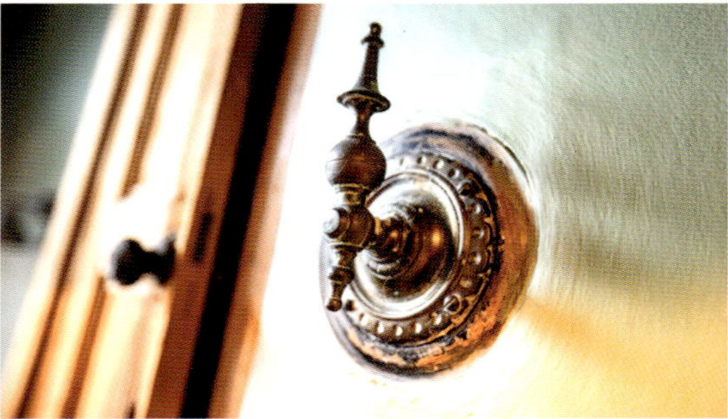

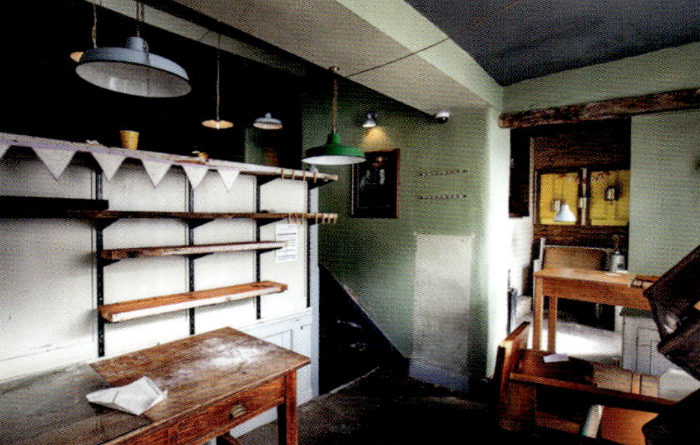

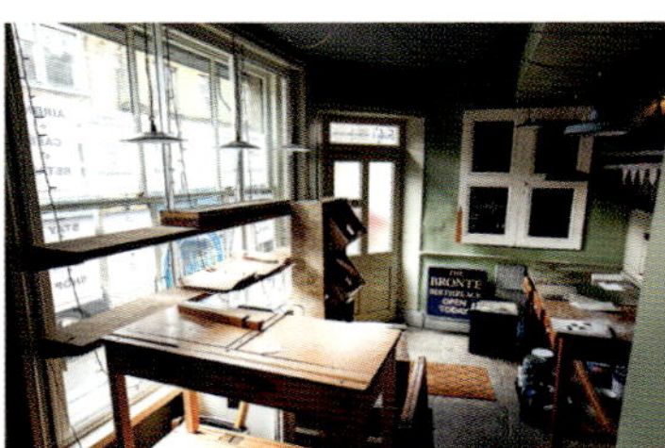

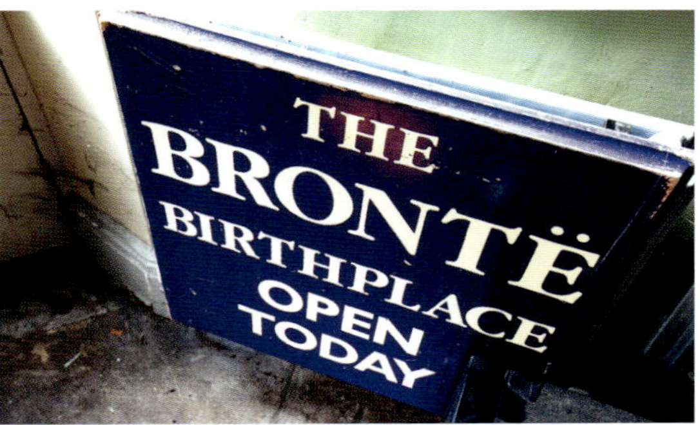

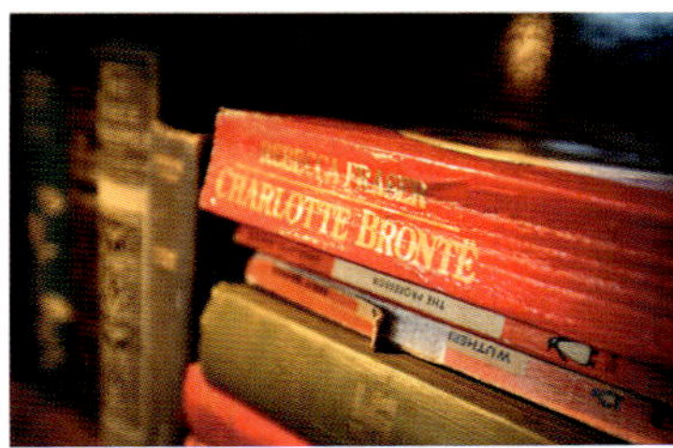

Further images showing the Birthplace in late March 2024.

Continuing our journey of discovery through unseen parts of the house, excitedly meandering in and out, we wandered along the narrow corridor joining the three bedrooms (top left picture), the parts we had never seen, and we were literally walking in the Brontës' footsteps. We were all beginning to realise the magnitude of our actions; the possibilities were endless as to what was achievable. Onwards we went down the main staircase to see the café area with some of its seating still in situ (middle left and middle right), and we look at the shop extension from the original building, casting an eye out onto Market Street still unable to comprehend what the group had achieved. We needed time to process this, time we probably didn't have. Laid in a corner finally we see the blue café sign (bottom right) which adorned the fence in the tiny front garden and now awaiting our renovations to once again announce 'Brontë Birthplace open'. We could only speculate how long it was going to take to breathe new life into this humble little house.

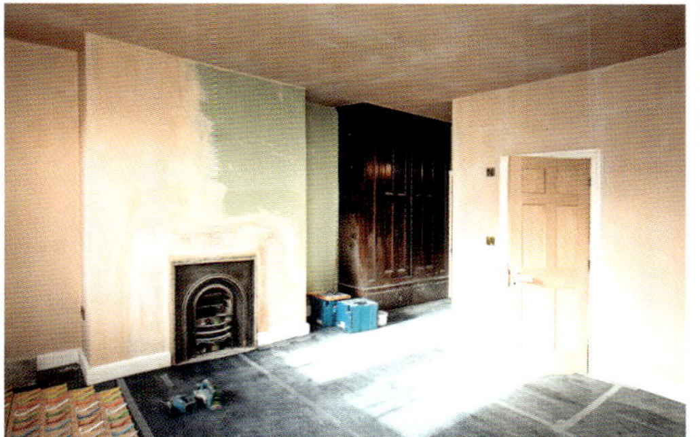

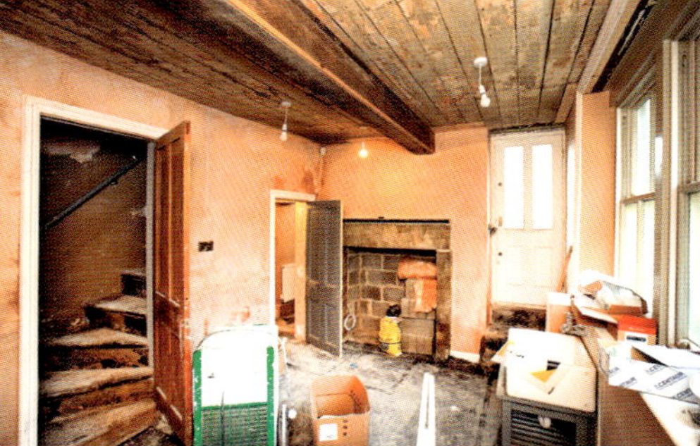

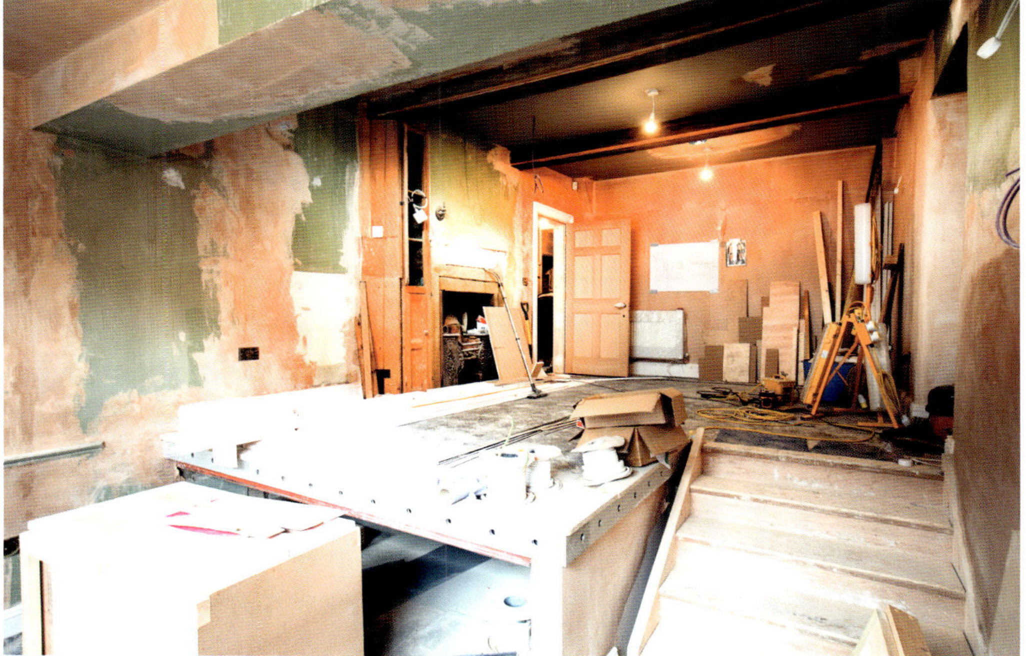

The house undergoing sympathetic restoration in early 2025.

After a lengthy tendering process the refurbishments began in earnest. There were to be many trials and tribulations along the way. The images above show the start of renovations with a look at the replastered main bedroom, which (top left) is starting to take shape but with much to do. Top right we get a tantalising glimpse of the recreated scullery fireplace and the exposed original ceiling boards. Also visible is a sneak peek at what we are starting to refer to as 'secret back stairs' previously unseen by the public, which were originally used by Nancy and Sarah Garrs, the Brontë housemaids who are mentioned earlier in this book. The girls would use the stairs so as not to disturb the rest of the household. We must at this time pay tribute to the architect Chris Eyres for his design of the new-look scullery and the buildings advisor Adrian Tingle for the wonderful fireplace. The lower image perfectly shows the parlour floor extended to its original length and features the famous fireplace. The refurbishments were set to take some three to four

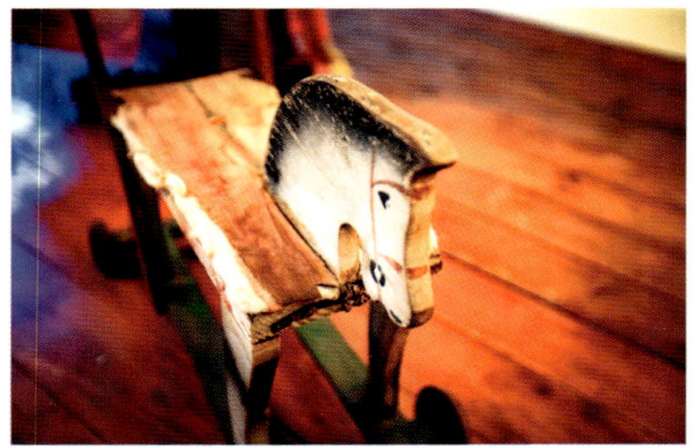

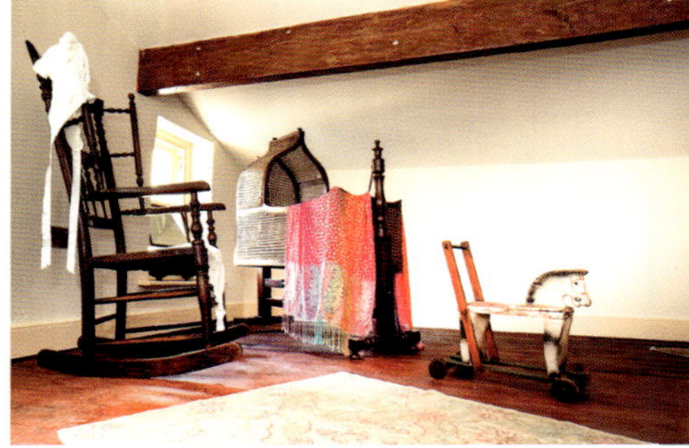

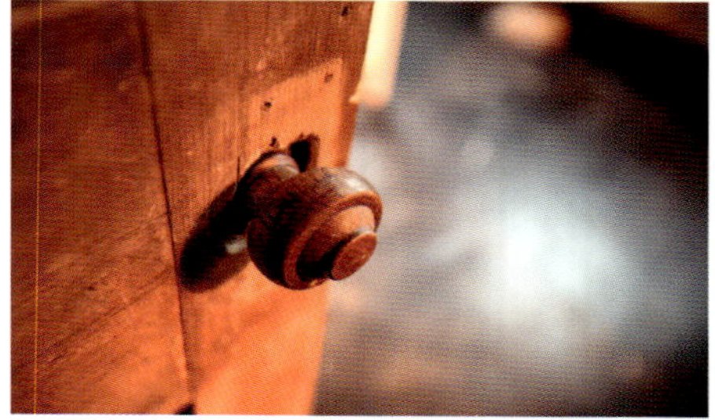

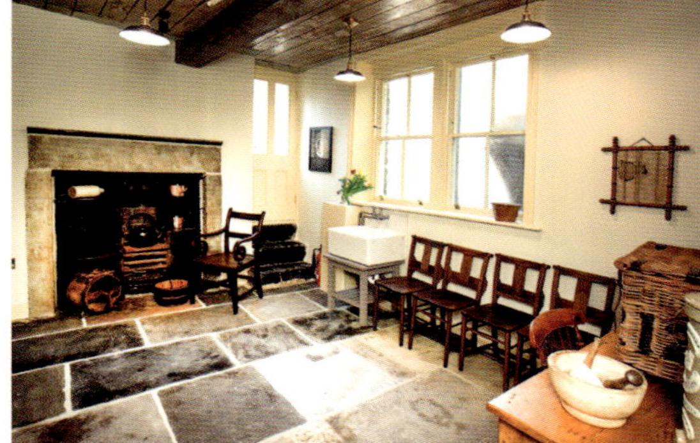

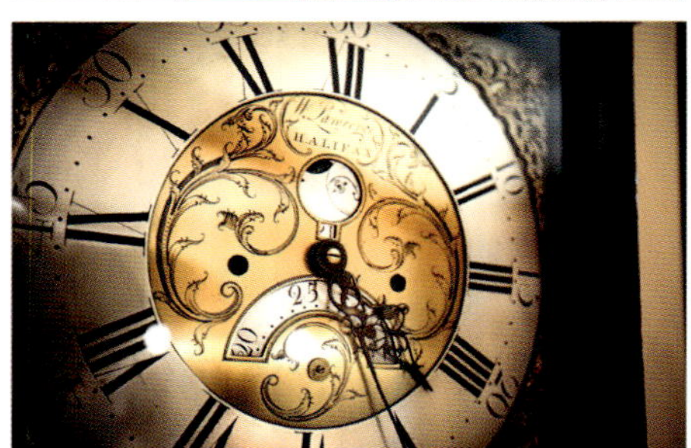

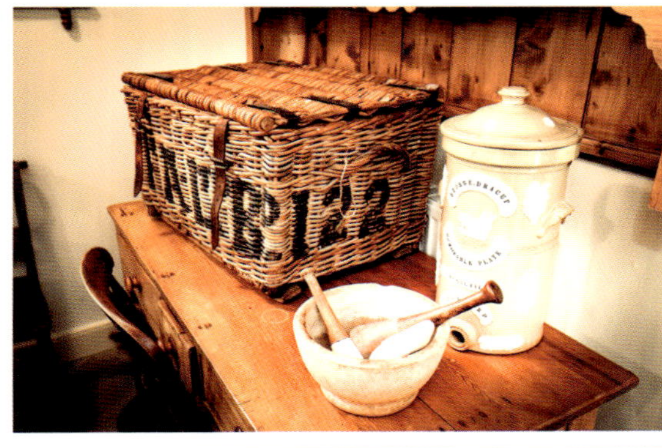

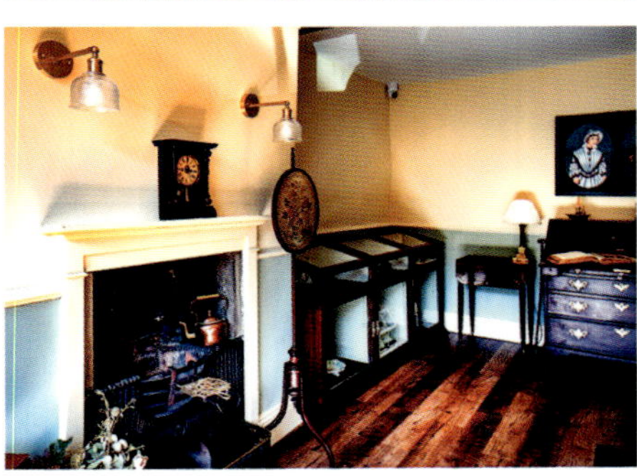

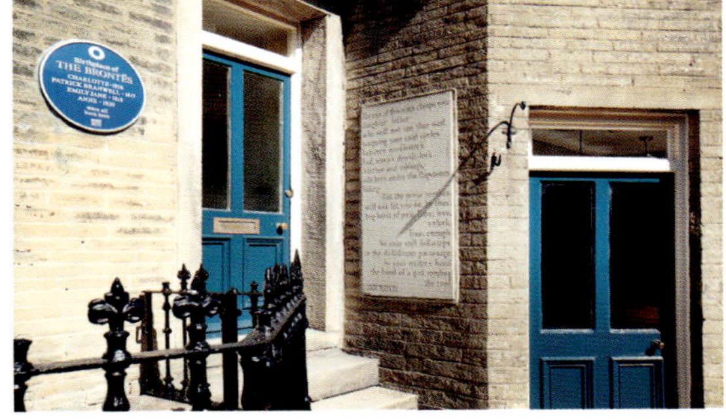

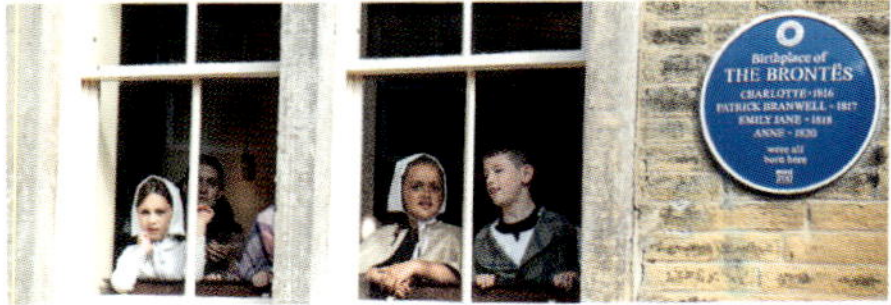

April 2025 and the Birthplace is ready to welcome visitors.

months to complete; however, there were, as with all of the best-laid plans, certain delays. There appeared to be a major problem with the front wall, which required extensive surgery, thus setting the project back. The team managed to overcome the issues and get it back on track. All things considered the refurbishments progressed well.

By April 2025, the regeneration was all but complete and ready to accept visitors. The extensive refurbishments along with the furnishings have transported the old parsonage back to represent the Regency period. The carefully selected early nineteenth-century colours and fittings were all chosen to enhance and complement the original features.

The images you see on both pages represent the scullery, cooking range and the maids' quarters at the top of the mysterious kitchen back stairway. Brontë fans can enjoy the immersive experience of stepping back in time to a bygone age. The maid's room is furnished with a period crib, sewing kit and child's toys, all enhanced by the natural light that floods in from the small window. The front left parlour with its bookcase and writing desk along with the rare Halifax grandfather clock is simply magnificent. The valuable clock was kindly donated by Ian Parry, a Welsh Brontë fan.

In addition to running tours, the house also serves as an educational centre for schoolchildren and adults alike, aimed at Brontë knowledge development.

The front parlour, where the four younger Brontë children were born, is where people will be able to enjoy refreshments and lunch, whilst soaking up, and reflecting on, the historical significance of the very room that is the 'Birthplace of Dreams'.

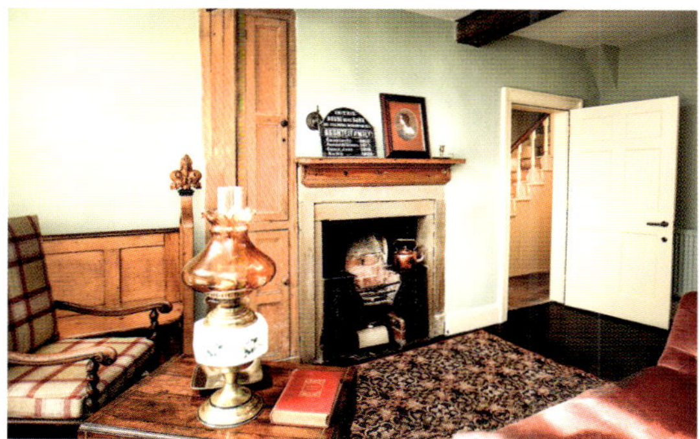
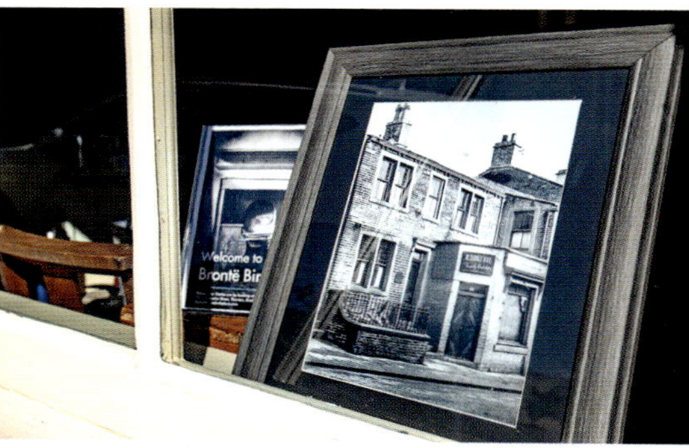
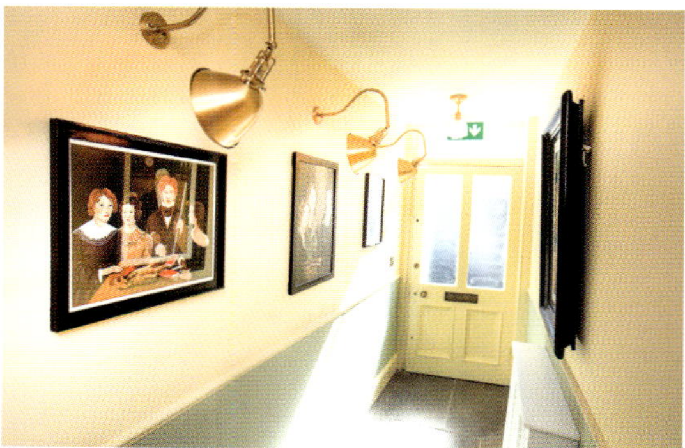
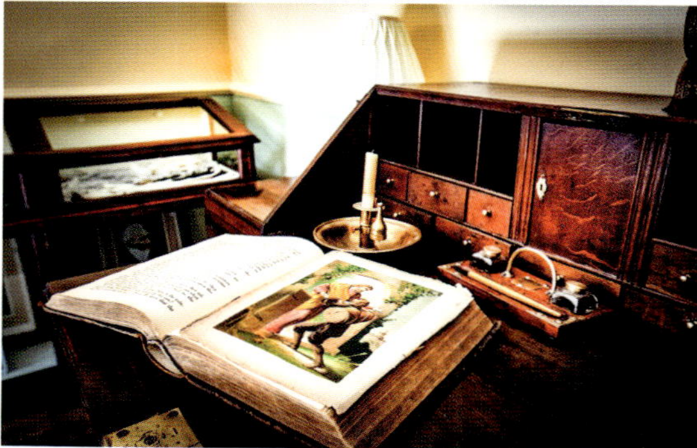

Now completed, the Birthplace firmly resembles a house of the Regency period.

Royal Approval

As Bradford's City of Culture 2025 celebrations and events gathered momentum the city was proud to be honoured with a visit by King Charles III and Queen Camilla on 15 May.

Initially arriving at Bradford Live (pictured below), the royal couple attended various events before Queen Camilla travelled without the king to Thornton, where she was welcomed by applauding, excited locals and visitors lining the street outside the Brontë Birthplace.

After all of the hard work that had been put into the regeneration of the house from conception to receiving the queen, this was indeed a momentous occasion. Once the tour of the house was completed, Her Majesty unveiled a prepared plaque that both marked the occasion and officially declared the historic Brontë house and educational centre open.

With official royal recognition and approval, the final piece of the Brontë jigsaw is now firmly in place.

In the truly inspirational, composed original and written words of Queen Camilla, 'Be More Brontë'.

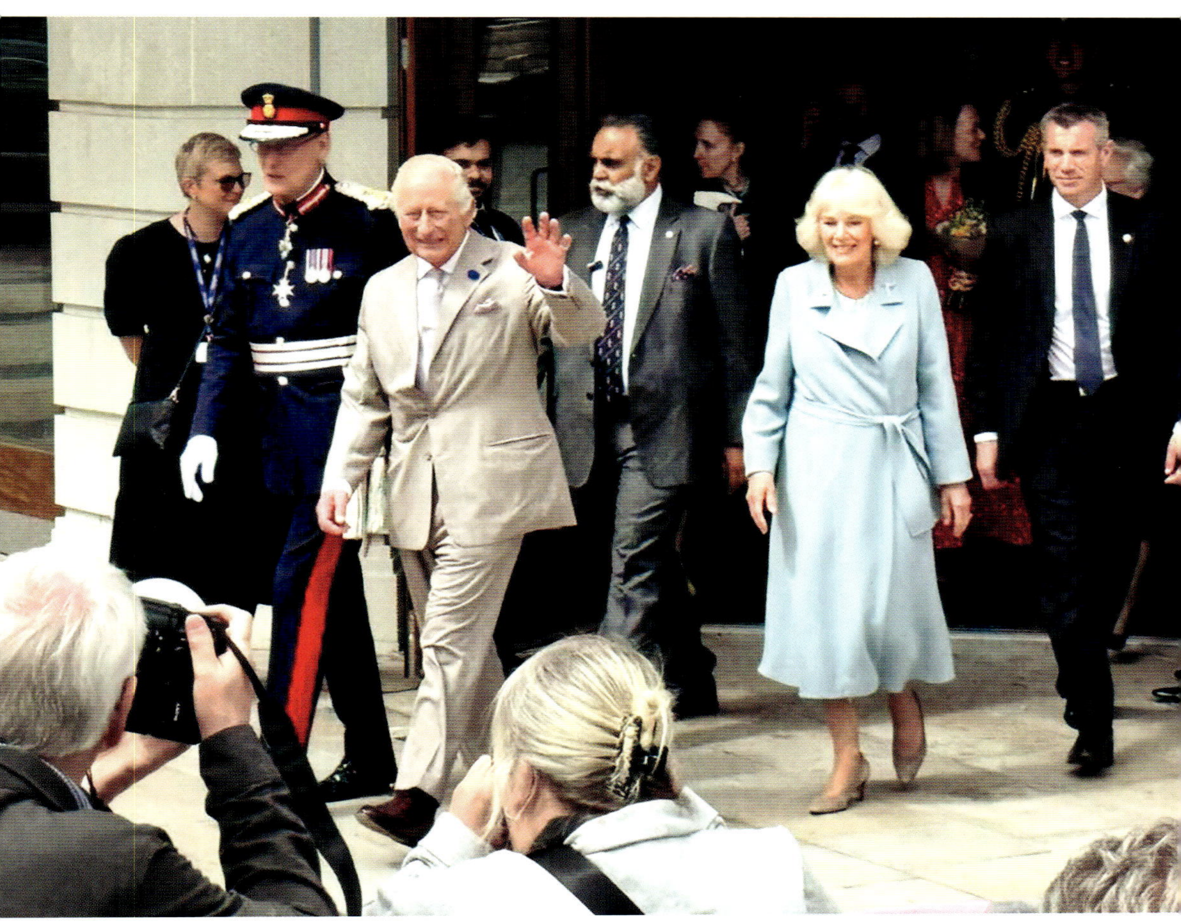

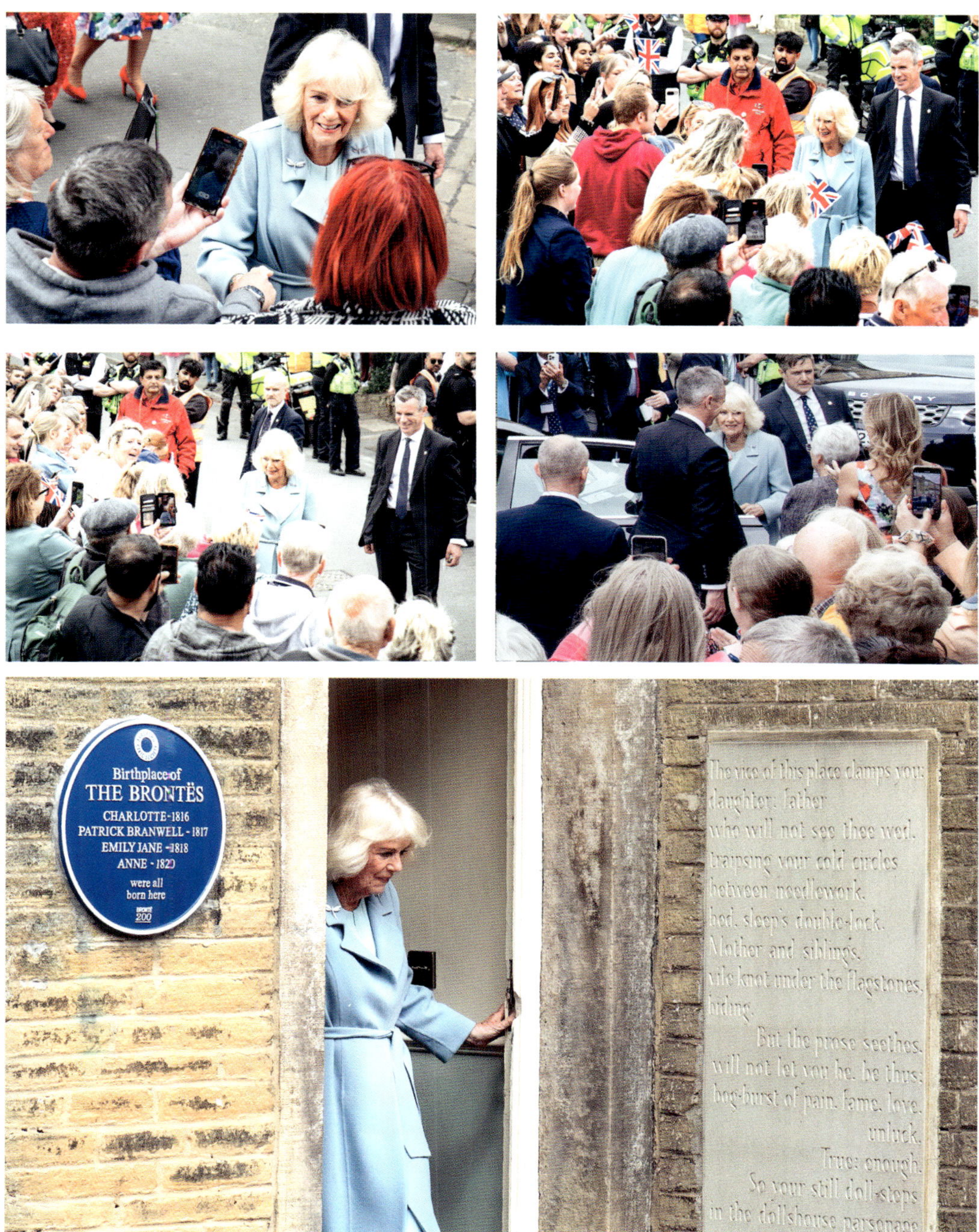

Above: The crowds that had waited patiently for hours at Thornton were thrilled when, before leaving, the queen, took the time to talk to as many people as possible, as can be seen in these photographs.

Opposite: King Charles III and Queen Camilla visiting Bradford Live, 15 May 2025.

Thornton Village

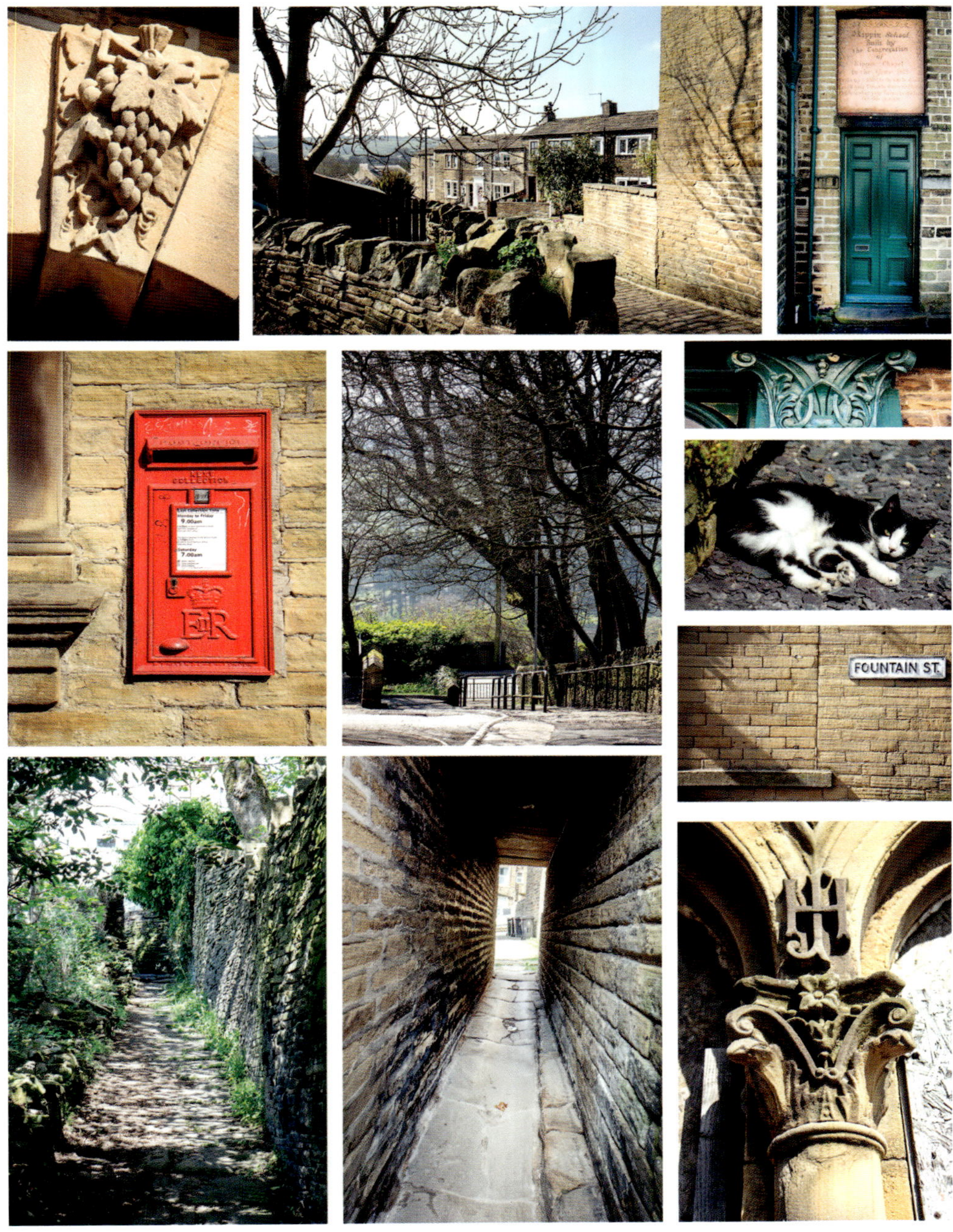

Above: A collection of images encapsulating the charm of Thornton village in 2025.

Opposite: St James' Church is a lovely, warm and welcoming sanctuary, with so much for the visitor to see relating to the Brontë family.

Stepping out of the Brontë Birthplace front door, the immediate area itself is more than worthy of exploring. You do not have to walk far in either direction to see quaint cobbled streets, snickets and passageways well worn by clog and hoof. Market Street itself has retained a quaint charm that in many other villages has been lost through modernisation and development. You can find some of the houses on the street that were standing during the Brontë family's time by the dates scribed into the stonework. Unique sculpted stonework that adorns many of the properties makes the village, which has a strong community, even more interesting. Just a short walk away to Lower Kipping Lane, where Elizabeth Firth lived, there are beautiful views across the valley, taking in the picturesque old 1870s railway viaduct. A short stroll down Thornton Road and you will find St James' Church, which was consecrated in 1872. The church is situated opposite the old Brontë Bell Chapel and has a lovely warm and welcoming atmosphere. There is a full-time small Brontë exhibition on show including artefacts and copies of the Brontë children's baptisms. The memorial tablets on the wall that used to be in the Bell Chapel are particularly interesting. Patrick's desk, also from the Bell Chapel, is on show along with the baptism font. In addition, there is a highly polished and much-loved brass plaque erected in honour of the Brontës.

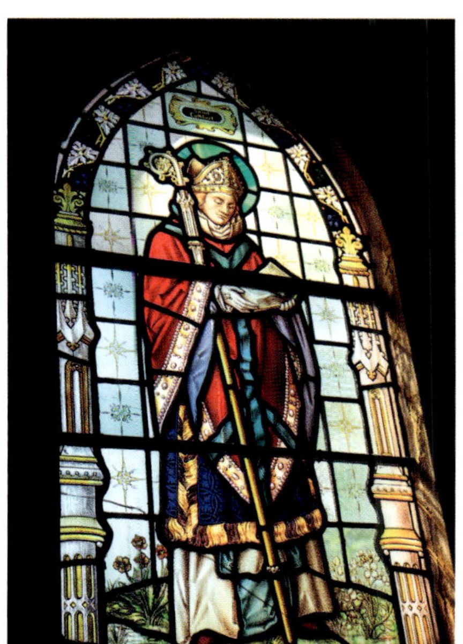

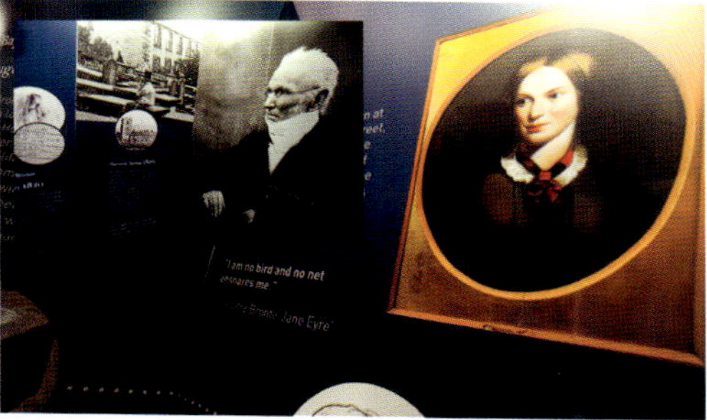

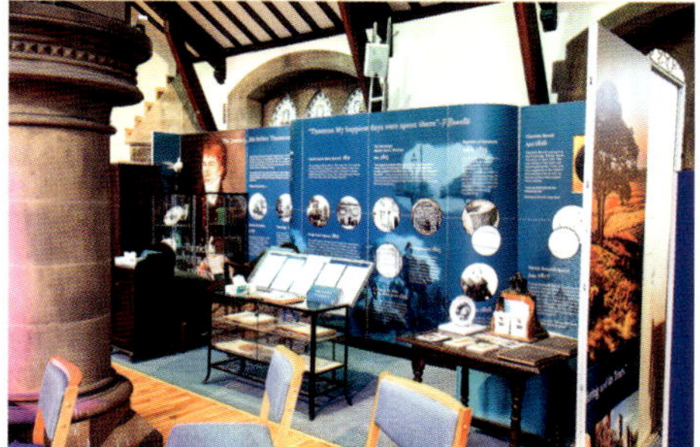

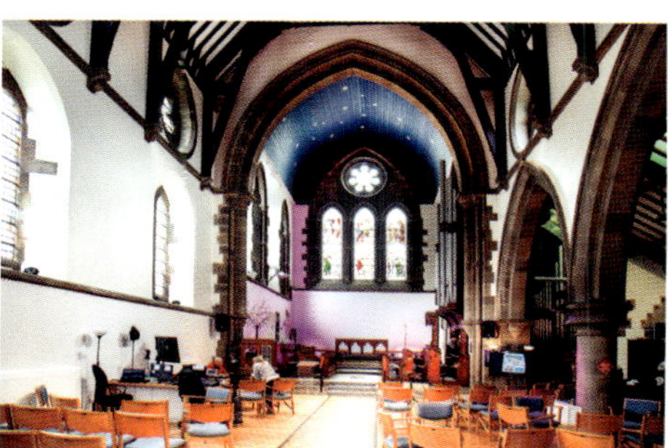

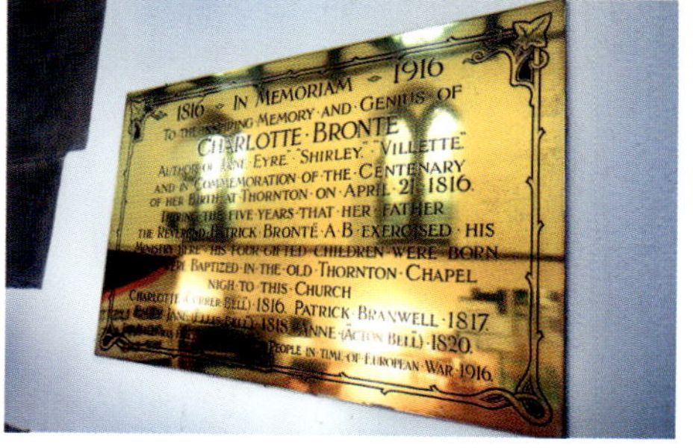

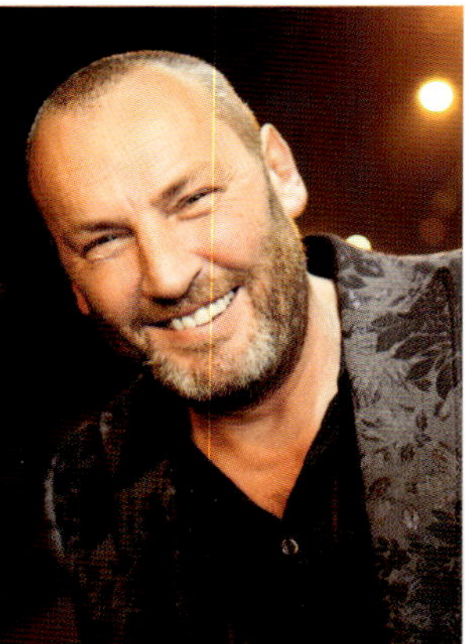

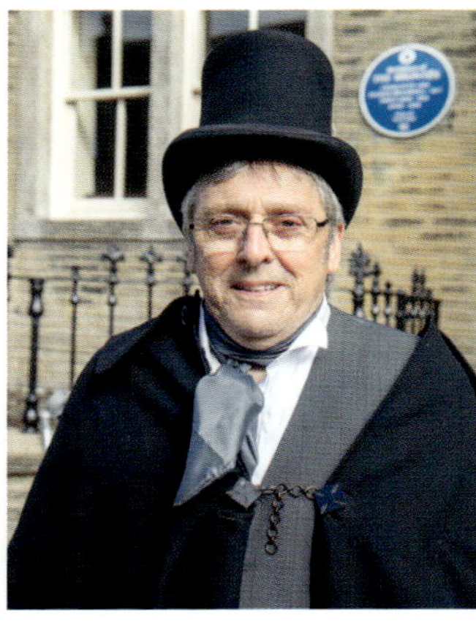

Above left: Mark Davis, author and professional photographer.

Above right: Steven Stanworth, the keeper of souls.

The Authors

Mark Davis, who is Bradford born and bred, is committed to delivering the perfect photographic image. A fearless, versatile, and passionate photographer whose photography is both admired and awarded, he is equally at home whether at great height or at ground level. As a keen social historian focusing on nineteenth-century social injustice and crime, he has sixteen published books under his belt, ranging from *Charles Dickens' London* to *Voices from the Asylum*. He has appeared in various documentaries focusing on former pauper lunatic asylums and Bradford's rich and illustrious history. Mark makes his home near Haworth amidst the rugged landscape that inspired the Brontës and which continues to inspire him to deliver world-class photographs.

Steven Stanworth, like his co-author, is also from good Bradford stock and grew up just a stone's throw from Mark at Horton Bank Top. Bradford's history is in Steven's veins, with a particular love for the Brontës; indeed, he has devoted over twenty-five years of his life to tending and caring for the ruined Brontë Bell Chapel and cemetery where Patrick Brontë was perpetual curate from 1815 to 1820. He is a founder member and vice-chairman (2023–25) of the Brontë Birthplace group that were to purchase and restore the property, breathing back the Brontë legacy to the house. Steven has worked incredibly hard with others to get the job done, including furnishing and decorating the house in the Regency style.

John Ellis

We are truly indebted to Bradford artist John Ellis, aka Jonny Moonshine (pictured right), for all his wonderful artwork featured in this little book. Though still mourning the relatively recent loss of his partner, he has nevertheless put his heart into his creativity and used this soulful time to be expressive in his work.

John is seen here with his painting of Charlotte Brontë, his favourite piece of artwork from the series.

Sue, your most loyal friend and partner, will be looking down on you Jonny, absolutely bursting with pride.

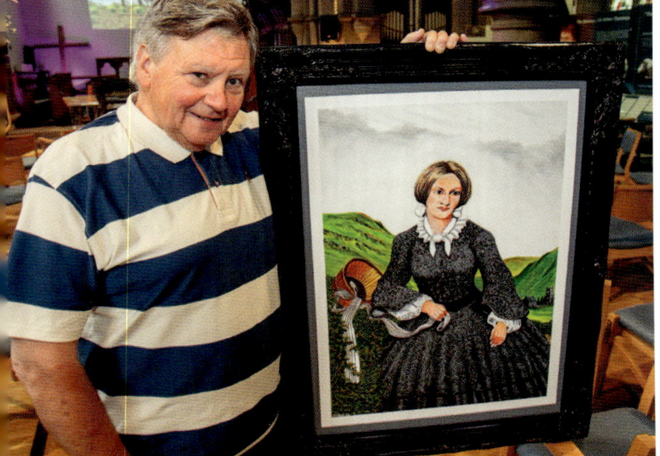

John Ellis, aka Jonny Moonshine.